EXPLAINING WARS OF CHOICE

EXPLAINING WARS OF CHOICE

ARMED HUMANITARIAN INTERVENTION AND FRAMING

JOHN M. CALLAHAN

ACADEMICA PRESS
LONDON-WASHINGTON

Library of Congress Cataloguing-in-Publication Data

Names: Callahan, John M. (John Marshall), author.
Title: Explaining wars of choice : armed humanitarian intervention and framing / John M. Callahan.
Description: Washington, DC : Academica Press, 2018. | Includes bibliographical references and index.
Identifiers: LCCN 2018004166 | ISBN 9781680530612
Subjects: LCSH: Humanitarian intervention--United States--Decision making. | Intervention (International law)--Government policy--United States. | United States--Military policy--Decision making. | United States--Foreign relations--1989---Decision making.
Classification: LCC JZ6369 .C35 2018 | DDC 341.5/84--dc23
LC record available at https://lccn.loc.gov/2018004166

Academica Press
1727 Massachusetts Avenue, NW, Suite 507
Washington, DC 20036
editorial@academicapress.com

For orders call
(978) 829-2577

DEDICATION

For Mom, who is with me in spirit, and for Dad. You're my best friend too.

TABLE OF CONTENTS

Chapter Page

LIST OF FIGURES

PREFACE

This book is an outgrowth of my dissertation work. At the time of writing, I was working as a public affairs planner for a now defunct deployable public affairs unit. As a result, I wanted to blend my interest in decision making with framing, particularly noting the rise of social media. As to the cases for the study, I was looking for "Wars of Choice" in which the U.S. interest was acting outside of its own direct interest, and it seemed to me that the best set for review, Post-Cold War, were the forced humanitarian operations which periodically dominated the history of the period.

With that in mind, the work ties framing into the decision making process, attempting to discover if framing efforts are part of the calculus when making plans. This is particularly important for "Wars of Choice" as there is often little public support for them. I found that individual movers and shakers, the "powerful actors" of the study, were critical to the decision making process. It is therefore my hope that policy makers and scholars alike can find guidance and sources for their own explorations in this work.

In terms of humanitarian intervention as a topic, the nature of the cases studies means that the book also provides analysis of how the topics of sovereignty, human security were impacted by the crises and interventions described.

In short, the work brings together several significant threads of research and presents them in a unified fashion. And, hopefully, it provides a useful set of case studies and conclusions.

ACKNOWLEDGMENTS

This book is dedicated to my sister Mary and nieces Aurora and Aurelia are always there for me, and make sure that I have enough Pellegrino on hand for proper analysis of the great issues.

I also want to thank Dan Conley, who helped keep me focused on what the book was supposed to be, while providing critical reviews. Jeffrey Bradford, a friend from undergraduate days with whom I reconnected, coincidentally in my first semester as a Ph.D. student, helped provide editorial advice and academic input. Paul Tyson provided articles and reports as well as wisdom and a calming voice. Allan and Lucy Harley have virtually adopted me as their American Son and encouraged me through this effort, along with their daughters Lizzie and Phoebe.

I am deeply grateful to my Ph.D. dissertation committee and for the patience and wisdom of the members of it. The mentorship of my committee chair, Dr. Simon Serfaty, was critical to my success. Dr. Regina Karp has both educated and mentored me for nearly two decades, and her efforts to push me outside of my theoretical box, have, I hoped, been reflected in this book.

CHAPTER I - INTRODUCTION

In March, 2011, the Obama administration made the decision to intervene militarily in the Libyan civil war. While the U.S. had undertaken such interventions before, what was unusual in this case was the reasoning set forth for U.S. action. Normally, U.S. national security is the chief framing tool for the justification of intervention abroad, however, in this case, security threats to the U.S. were not mentioned as fundamental causes for the intervention. Instead, the growing humanitarian crisis, and the threat that Muammar Al-Gaddafi posed to his own people was given as the reason. This was not first U.S. intervention to be couched in this terms, but it was rare for the language of human rights to be applied as the primary motivation to enter into an open militarized conflict, and not to a natural disaster or manmade disaster such as starvation, as had been the case in Somalia in 1992. The intervention which followed took place under NATO and United Nations auspices, and was sold as defending the people of Libya from the depredations of their leaders. A further facet to the intervention was the purposeful vilification of Gaddafi as an attempt to create a media frame and support for the intervention. While such vilification of enemies is nothing new in history, it is less common in the realm of humanitarian assistance in intervention, in which the enemy is customarily the symptom, such as famine, sickness, or homelessness, rather than the cause, or perceived cause.

How did such a change in U.S. policy making and political reasoning come about? What was the decision making process which led to the decision to intervene, and to explain that intervention in humanitarian, rather than U.S. security terms? Was it the result of a deliberative staff process, or that of the influence of a few key individuals? Furthermore, if the process recommended armed humanitarian intervention in Libya, does it always work? How does the decision making process used in the Libya intervention compare with earlier cases of armed humanitarian interventions, such as the Somalia intervention under Presidents George H.W. Bush, the 1998 Kosovo intervention under President Bill Clinton, and the decision of the U.S. not to intervene in the Rwanda crisis of 1994? How could some crises be shaped as U.S. national security problems, while others could not? Current theories on national security decision making and framing do not bridge the gap between the two, so this work attempts to do so. It is clear that senior leader engagement, and not a bureaucratic, interagency process per se, is at the root of these decisions, and that point is the hypothesis for the research which follows. This work will examine extant literature on the subject of U.S. foreign policy interagency decision making, problem framing, and development and implementation of framing strategies to determine the role of the individual leader in those processes. In each of the empirical case studies the research will seek to identify the decision making process which led firstly to the decision to intervene, and secondly to articulate that particular intervention in humanitarian, rather than other security terms.

The role of leadership in determining and framing humanitarian interventions is rising in importance as the United States has chosen to involve itself in an increasing number of such interventions in the decades since the end of the Cold War. While the notion of armed intervention seems to be out of favor (notwithstanding the unwilling intervention of the Obama team in Iraq and Syria to combat the Islamic State beginning in 2014, since it was not undertaken for primarily humanitarian reasons) at the present, this is does not obviate the need for research on the subject, since these sorts of interventions also fell out of favor twice before, after the perceived failure of the intervention in Somalia, and the success of intervention in Kosovo. The value in this research is in tying together the major armed humanitarian interventions and non-interventions to determine commonalities, both in how the intervention was planned and advocated in the government, but also how the issues were framed to broader audiences. The characteristics of successful interventions appear to include a small number of inspired, powerful, leaders who could not only influence the decision making process but also public opinion in favor of their desired outcomes. When no powerful leader or spokesperson emerged to carry a message forward, intervention either did not take place or else lost support or failed. The role of key individuals seems more important than ever given the preferred operating procedure of the current president, Donald Trump.

One part of the academic study of international relations tends to focus on the role of state actors and how they interact with each other. The idea that the unit of analysis for international relations research should be the state was reasserted by Kenneth Waltz in 1979 into what came to be known as the Neo-Realist school. Numerous schools of thought have risen to dispute parts of this approach, which basically posits that anarchy alone shapes state actions.[1] However, the processes by which the armed humanitarian interventions researched in the case studies points to a significant role for actors below the level of the state to influence international relations and communications, which is an interesting contrast to the Neo-Realist paradigm in which great powers are solely swayed by the need to balance against the strongest in an anarchical world. The nature of these interventions points to dynamics beyond the basic tenets of Neo-Realism to explain, since two of the three interventions, regardless of what was argued at the time, had little to do with threats to U.S. Security, and only one, Kosovo, threatened U.S. security arrangements, in the form of the NATO alliance, if not the U.S. itself.

Furthermore, this research attempts to tie framing together with decision making as processes, since they seem, on the surface to be linked together, and often involve the deciders as the chief framers of action. In other words, this study

---

[1] Waltz, Kenneth N. *Theory of International Politics*. Long Grove, IL: Colombia University Press, 1979. 88.

proposes to use armed humanitarian interventions not just to see how the decisions are made, but how they are sold, and how the process of synchronizing actions and word, or strategic communication, can develop into issue framing and have repercussions for the decision making process. These dynamics are of use across the gamut of foreign policy decision making practices, and need not be limited to military actions or the use of force.

This study utilizes a wide, cross disciplinary set of sources on the topics of U.S foreign policy decision making, armed humanitarian interventions and the issue framing processes utilizing the intellectual frameworks developed by Graham Allison, Robert Entman, and others to illuminate the reviewed literature and verify the gaps in research that the book will fill. Critical works reviewed include Allison's "Essence of Decision," Jonathan Bendor and Thomas Hammond's, "*Rethinking Allison's Models,*" Steve Yetiv's *Explaining Foreign Policy*, and others; as well as the Strategic Communication development process with Robert Entman's *Projections of Power* and Manuel Castells' *Communication Power* and moving into three case studies which will bring both the decision process and messaging cycle into focus. The case studies were developed using a combination of memoirs and first person accounts of events, selected studies of events by other researchers, most particularly when underpinned by previous policy involvement and subsequent interviews with the participants, and through other sources such as polling data and journalistic accounts.

Armed humanitarian interventions have come in and out of fashion in a cyclical fashion since the end of the Cold War, hand in hand with updated concepts of human security and the place of human security in a world which is still focused on the non-violability of state sovereignty. The first such intervention after the Cold War, in Somalia, is one of the case studies examined in this study. In that intervention, combat troops were deployed to secure food deliveries and to ensure supply routes in Somalia, which was at that time an ungoverned area. Following the success of the initial effort to feed Somalis, the mission was changed into a political one, of peacemaking and nation building, which ultimately led to its failure in 1993. That failure led to a rethinking of the concept and a temporary abeyance of militarized interventions.[2]

The next major armed humanitarian intervention, in 1999, took place in Kosovo and looked much more like traditional combat operations than had been the case in Somalia. The effort, undertaken exclusively by air forces, was designed to compel the Serbian government to stop atrocities in its province of Kosovo, and to simultaneously degrade its capability to do so. While Kosovo was generally seen as a success, it was not seen as a model to replicate in future armed humanitarian interventions. However, the lessons learned from it, combined with the lessons of a failure to intervene in another crisis, the Rwandan genocide of 1994, dovetailed into a serious international discussion on the meaning of state sovereignty and the rights owed to the citizens of a country by its political leadership. As after Somalia, there was a down time after Kosovo in which the appetite of the great powers for militarized interventions ebbed. Meanwhile the international community, considering Rwanda and Kosovo, developed the formal doctrine of Responsibility to Protect, which specifically exhorted the world community to consider national sovereignty to have been abrogated in countries which waged genocidal warfare on portions of their populace, or acted in other ways to violate the human rights of their citizens. Although the concept, which became known as R2P, was not fully adopted by the UN Security Council, especially in a lack of agreement on when force could be used, it survived challenge in the UN General Assembly in 2009,[3] and remains an implicit policy, becoming the measuring stick for future interventions.[4]

Whereas the gap between Somalia and Kosovo, approximately seven years, took place over the course of a single presidency, that of Bill Clinton, the next armed humanitarian endeavor would wait twelve years. This is primarily due to the fact that humanitarian interventions were replaced both by conventional and

---

[2] Weiss, Thomas. *Humanitarian Intervention.* Cambridge: Polity Press, 2012. 8.
[3] Bellamy, Alex J. *Global Politics and the Responsibility to Protect.* New York: Routledge, 2011. 42.
[4] Ibid. 162.

unconventional traditional warfare following the September 11 attacks on the U.S. While the U.S. flexed its hyper power, R2P was working its way through the UN, and influencing key thinkers and former foreign policy practitioners from the Clinton era as they considered how they might act differently if given the opportunity.

That opportunity came in the form of a new President, Barack Obama, who brought the aforementioned scholars and practitioners into his government, and a new crisis which occurred just as one of the two major wars of the post 9-11 world, in Iraq, was being wound down. Starting in late 2010, a series of popular uprisings known as the Arab Spring swept across the middle east like a tidal wave stretching from Tunisia to Egypt and as far east as Bahrain and Yemen. There was violent repression in many of these countries, but when the eastern half of Libya joined in the risings in February, 2011, that country's leader threatened, and began to implement what amounted to genocide against his own people. With the urging of regional groupings such as the Gulf Cooperation Council and the Arab League, as well as European partners, the U.S. initiated airstrikes in Libya with the purpose of alleviating the suffering of the rebel groups and disrupting Gaddafi efforts to attack them with his military. The U.S. slowly withdrew from the front lines of the effort, turning the lead over to NATO. In spite of this, however, the U.S. was involved to the end, which occurred after the death of Gaddafi in late 2011, brutally killed in a combined coalition air attack and rebel ground attack on his vehicle convoy.

While the operation seemed like a success at the time, later events, most notably the murder of the U.S. Ambassador to Libya and three other American citizens on September 11, 2012 cast the operation as a tragic failure.[5] In similar fashion to the pattern which followed Somalia, the U.S. is in another out cycle in terms of armed humanitarian interventions, actively choosing not to engage in one in Syria in 2013. It is always possible that the age of armed humanitarians is over,

---

[5] *The Washington Post*. "What Obama botched in Libya." May 5, 2014. http://www.washingtonpost.com/opinions/what-obama-botched-in-libya/2014/05/05/3aef7176-d47a-11e3-95d3-3bcd77cd4e11_story.html. Accessed May 5, 2014.

as the western world focuses on its economic woes, the U.S. moves toward conventional military engagement with the Islamic State in Syria and Iraq, and the rise of China and a militarily resurgent Russia draw U.S. attention. However, it is more likely that within the foreseeable future, another crisis which requires U.S. military forces to fight in defense of human rights and security will occur, and it is that likelihood which makes this study more than a look back at history, but a means to help predict how such a future intervention might come to pass. Furthermore, there is no reasons why the findings of the research cannot be applied to other types of interventions and even other fields of government decision making.

Current theories of foreign policy decision making and issue framing do not adequately explain the role that powerful individuals have on both processes. As Pollack notes, one reason for this problem lies in the preference of political scientists to look at systems, governments, and other phenomena that are easily observable and quantifiable, as the actions of individuals most usually are not, generating an aversion against the possibility of significant individual impact.[6] The filter of armed humanitarian interventions provides a useful prism through which to observe these processes and to demonstrate the centrality of the powerful individual to both of them. The two key research questions, then, focus on the role of the individual in the process, and whether that process has issue framing as a focus, or simply the reaching of the decision to intervene, with framing taking place later, or separately, if at all. To answer these questions, traditional foreign policy decision making models and framing models will be used, while a new model, the Decide/Explain model, which takes into account the role of the individual, decision making, and framing is tested.

Structure and Preliminary Results

This study follows a traditional research format, assessing the relevance of

---

[6] Pollack, Kenneth. "Let Us Now Praise Great Men: Bringing the Statesman Back In." *International Security*, 2001: 107-146. 3.

the study and establishing a literary and definitional framework for research and assessment. The case studies to be examined include those mentioned above as well as the decision not to intervene in Syria in 2013. In each case study the specific and world historical events will be provided, as well as an examination of the key players in the decision making process, what processes produced framing and intervention, how they reflect the models examined, and what implications the intervention had on future thinking on the subject, and future decision making efforts. The two non-interventions, Rwanda, and the review of the Syria case provided in the findings section of the work, show how the decision and framing processes fail when there is no powerful leader pushing for presidential notice and approval for operations, or the ability to frame such operations to stakeholder audiences, namely the media and the American people. Findings for the case studies follow them directly, and a broader section on findings brings the lessons of all of the case studies together into a coherent discussion.

In reviewing the case studies, the preliminary result of the research is that personality is always at the center of the decision making process for U.S. involvement in armed humanitarian interventions. With the exception of the Somalia intervention, each of the interventions studied showed the influence of a powerful agent or agents who pushed for the cabinet, and ultimately the president, to decide on combat as a better means than diplomacy to solve the crisis. In the cases where this was true, Kosovo and Libya, the powerful agent, or actor, was the secretary of state. In both cases it was she who ultimately convinced the president of the need to act. Where the cases differ, however, is that in the case of Kosovo, Secretary of State Albright was at the forefront of the decision making and framing efforts from the beginning. On the contrary, in the case of Libya, Secretary Clinton had to be personally convinced of the need to act, and once that happened, she became the decisive voice in recommending intervention to President Obama. The rapid onset of the Libya crisis versus the slow unfolding of the Kosovo intervention is also a significant factor in the decision making and framing processes for each, as well as the other case studies. The research shows that rapidly unfolding crises had significantly more difficult decision making and framing processes than slowly developing crises.

In terms of framing, the research shows that the same powerful actors who pressed for intervention also had a key role in framing the need for intervention to the American people. This was particularly true of Secretary of State Albright in Kosovo and Secretary of State Clinton in Syria. What is less clear from the empirical data available is if there were direct ties between the decision making and framing cycles, and if the need to construct frames to build stakeholder support for intervention was a key factor in any of the decision cycles examined. The only intervention which appears to show direct and lengthy framing, tied into the decision making process, was that in Kosovo in 1999, which saw systematic framing efforts over a period of months before the intervention, clearly tied in with ongoing diplomatic efforts, preparation for combat, and continued decision making. In the case of Libya, the reason for this is the rapid onset of the crisis, in Somalia because there was no solid enemy to frame against, and in a third case, the tragedy in Rwanda, it occurred because of the rapidity in which the crisis unfolded, and the lack of desire for intervention at senior levels of the administration.

So what difference does a study of past interventions make to current scholars and policy makers? The simple answer to that question is that this study is about more than humanitarian interventions. It is about decision making at the very highest levels. It is about the efforts leaders make to convince their stakeholders, ultimately us, the American people, of the correctness of their decisions. It is about where, when, and why the United States chooses to intervene in the internal affairs of other countries, particularly when its own core interests are not threatened. It is about the nature both of sovereignty and of security for the 21st century.

The study is also fundamentally about the cognitive challenge of foreign policy decision making and framing, in other words, the impact of the narrative on actual operations. The information environment, in many ways, has become the central battlefield of the 21st century, and there are examples in these case studies which clearly show how the narrative struggle was paramount, enabled by ever more pervasive and invasive forms of media.

Now, in 2018, decision making, planning, and framing literally move at the speed of twitter. With that in mind, perhaps taking the time to look at the background of decision making in a series of events linked in time can be a helpful preparation for students, thinkers, and policy makers. This research effort will have been worth it if it leads to deeper thinking on why these issues matter and how they can be implemented in a world of ever shrinking decision cycles and broadened stakeholder bases.

CHAPTER II - Studying Decision Making, Humanitarian Intervention, and Framing

The purpose of this research is to examine the decision making and framing processes for armed humanitarian interventions by the United States of America in the post-cold war era to determine the impact of powerful individual leaders on both. As noted in the introduction the study will apply a series of questions to determine this, including: How did such a change in U.S. policy making and political reasoning come about? What was the decision making process which led to the decision to intervene, and to explain that intervention in humanitarian, rather than U.S. security terms? Was it the result of a deliberative staff process, or that of the influence of a few key individuals? Furthermore, if the process recommended armed humanitarian intervention in some cases, does it always work? How does the decision making process used in each of the selected case studies of armed humanitarian interventions, such as the Somalia intervention under Presidents George H.W. Bush and Clinton, the 1998 Kosovo intervention, and the 2012 Libya intervention by U.S. forces compare with the others and with cases in which no intervention was undertaken? Furthermore, why did some efforts to frame interventions through a framing or strategic communications process succeed while others failed? And were those processes of deciding and framing linked?

As noted in the introduction, the hypothesis for the study is that armed humanitarian interventions occur when a powerful leader or small group of leaders dominates the decision making and framing process to force and explain such an intervention. In each of the empirical case studies we will seek to identify the decision making process which led firstly to the decision to intervene, and secondly to articulate that particular armed intervention in humanitarian, rather than other security terms. Research questions for each of the case studies are firstly, was the decision to intervene the outcome of a deliberative staff process, or that of the influence of a few key individuals? Drawing on the theoretical frameworks provided by Allison and others, such as the models of governmental politics as discussed in *Essence of Decision* as well as theories of framing and strategic communication as discussed by Entman in *Projections of Power*, the study will seek to confirm the hypothesis that strong individual leaders build consensus for, and frame, armed humanitarian intervention efforts.

Status of the Discussion

Prior to the commencement of this study, a thorough literature review sought to identify, consider and bring together a disparate set of criterion and arguments about the decision making process, framing, strategic communications, and the definition of armed humanitarian intervention. The reviewed works were linked to each other by theme, and organized in support of an examination to determine when, if, and how the interagency decision making process was effective, and, if not, what factors caused the differences for each situation as well as an effort to define media and communication framing and how armed humanitarian interventions were framed and marketed to critical stakeholders to generate support for intervention. Extant literature on the interagency strategic communications process was examined, with particular emphasis on the efforts of very senior leaders to sway the process.

The review highlighted the fact that there is little direct tie between the decision making process and specific framing efforts. There are significant conflicts between key interagency institutions and leaders which make consistent planning and messaging difficult. This appears to enable powerful personalities to make their wishes realities in terms of crafting responses to crises. Inferred, however, is the difficulty in synchronizing messages, or making "actions and deeds match" in such a decision-making environment, particularly in an environment increasingly dominated by the accelerated decision cycles brought about by technological improvements and the use of an ever wider array of social media platforms. With this in mind, one major task for the book is to help to fill that literature gap through the use of case studies on key interventions, as discussed below.

Research Approach

The emphasis of the research will be on a qualitative study based on primary sources, books, articles, public sources, and, where possible, on primary, on the record interviews. The methodology of the book is as follows: An examination of U.S. government interagency foreign policy decision making processes, as well as the framing development process; continuing into an examination of bureaucratic decision making theories, particularly those proposed by Allison in *Essence of Decision*; and moving into case studies which will bring the decision process and messaging cycle into focus.

The research methods used for this book are primarily qualitative in nature, relying on analysis of case studies for analysis due to the small number of cases and the nature of the data to be analyzed in order to ascertain the impact of key leader actions on the decision making and framing processes. During the course of the literature review, the author looked for the ways in which each author sought to engage the extant literature and theories to the work, as well as the purpose of the work and the approach taken to achieve that purpose. The design and findings of each study was examined as well as the methods, and instruments used in analysis.

Definitions

Common definitions of key terms such as armed humanitarian intervention and strategic communication and framing are necessary in order to narrow the focus of the research and provide a common framework for discussion in the context of this research project:

A: **Armed humanitarian intervention**, as defined in the extant literature, refers to "A coercive action by one or more states, in the legitimate context of an international organization, involving the use of armed force in another state without the consent of its authorities, and with the purpose of preventing widespread suffering or death among the inhabitants."[1] This could take the form of the use of armed forces to enter a sovereign territory for the purpose of protection of the human security of the inhabitants. It could also be to provide relief after a natural disaster or to protect one part of a populace from another, or from the government of the territory in question. The author's addition is that wide scale combat operations must be associated with the intervention for it to qualify. For example, the Haiti intervention of 1994, while involving forced entry by combat forces, did not result in significant combat operations, and varied only in small ways from the later 2010 earthquake intervention in the same country.[2]

B: **Framing and strategic communication** refer to the processes by which policy makers explain their actions and build credibility for decisions with their various stakeholder groups, but, with a focus for this project on three key groups, Congress, the Media, and the American people. Building from the military doctrinal definition of strategic communication (since 2013, the term has been changed to Communication Synchronization), it is defined as ensuring that words

[1] Pape, Robert A. "When Duty Calls: A Pragmatic Standard of Humanitarian Intervention." International Security 37, no. 1 (2012): 41-80. 44.

[2] U.S. Department of State Office of the Historian. "Intervention in Haiti, 1994-1995." http://history.state.gov/milestones/1993-2000/haiti. Accessed on 29 July 2014 at 0942.

and deeds match, and that cross government messaging is fully coordinated.[3] Framing is based on Entman's "Cascading Network Association Theory".[4] Since the government remains the primary source for information, this creates a system of asymmetric interdependence, but this can only be taken advantage of if there is unanimity in the message. Further, conflicting frames can be provided not only by the media, but by the party out of power and a variety of other formal and informal actors.

C: The "Powerful" or "Dominant" individual is someone whom Byman and Pollack would call a "Statesman." While the president sits at the peak of the decision making apparatus, and his power is undisputed, the term powerful or dominant, for purposes of this study, refers to a member or group of members of the decision making process who are A: Politically powerful, either because of their position in the cabinet, or other unique access to the president; B: Are sufficiently motivated by a particular cause to use their position to overcome the resistance of other members of the decision making apparatus to convince the president of the need to act; and C: Able to participate in framing efforts to build support among the wider stakeholder audience for decisions.[5] Yetiv notes that what he calls "Great Men" are a useful, but simplistic tool for analysis, and this study acknowledges that and seeks to place the role of these individuals into an overall decision making context.[6]

D: Foreign policy decision making: This includes planning and decision making by the senior most levels of the U.S. Government. For purposes of this research, it refers to the President of the United States, the members of the NSC, most important being the National Security Advisor, the Secretaries of State and Defense, and the Director of National Intelligence (or his predecessor, the Director

---

[3] Paul, Christopher. *Strategic Communication: Origins, Concepts, and Current Debates.* Santa Barbara, CA: Praeger, 2011. 8-9.

[4] Entman, Robert M. *Projections of Power: Framing News, Public Opinion, and U.S. Foreign Policy.* Chicago: University of Chicago Press, 2004. 9-13.

[5] Byman, Daniel L. and Pollack, Kenneth M. "Let Us Now Praise Great Men: Bringing the Statesman Back In." *International Security* 25, No. 4 (2001): 107-146. 134.

[6] Yetiv. 233.

of Central Intelligence) and other lead agencies such as the U.S. Agency for International Development. It also includes key Congressional leaders and the leaders of subordinate organizations such as the U.S. Mission to the United Nations, Ambassadors abroad, and military Geographic Combatant Commanders (GCCs). As provided by Graham Allison in *Essence of Decision*, two primary foreign policy and decision making concepts will be used to develop arguments on the role of the individual in decision making, and the resultant framing of interventions:

1. Rational Actor Model (RAM): Under the RAM, government actors assign values to their various courses of action, and pick the action that had the highest utility or payoff.[7]
2. Governmental Politics Model (GPM): In the GPM, a nation's actions are best understood through the prism of the personal politics and negotiations of key leaders. In this model even a shared goal can cause conflict because of the differing views of leaders based on the points of view of their parent organizations, personal interests, and backgrounds. In such an environment, even a paramount leader, such as the president, must seek consensus with his subordinates, if for no other reason than to prevent misunderstandings.[8] This invites a discussion of the role of transformational and transactional leaders into the discussion of decision making.

Description of Data Collection Tools and Study Procedure

As stated in the introduction, the challenge for this study is to demonstrate the impact that individual leaders have, or do not have, on the processes of decision making and framing as it pertains to U.S. armed humanitarian interventions. The literature review covered the key sources to be used for analysis. The research will consist of a qualitative study of those sources with emphasis placed on document

---

[7] Allison, Graham, and Zelikow, Philip. *Essence of Decision: Explaining the Cuban Missile Crisis, Second Edition.* (Longman: New York, 1999). 19-21.
[8] Ibid. 255-258.

studies, such as books, articles, public sources; and primary sources, including on the record interviews if possible as well as memoirs, first-hand accounts, and original reports. A review will be undertaken on the impact of public statements on the decision making process to determine the impact of framing efforts on the decision making process and vice versa.

Statistics: This study will rely on prolonged engagement and triangulation of sources in addition to positive and negative case analysis to ensure academic rigor of this research. The stress is on a deep investigation of the cases, or purposive/specific sampling rather than random sampling. This is due to the small number of cases to be examined (Five cases, three interventions and two non-interventions address the requirements mentioned previously). With this in mind, a deep dive, or saturation, of a small number of specific cases is more appropriate to the research.[9] Each case will also be subjected to a negative analysis in which reexamination of each case will attempt to determine if the themes which emerged from later cases apply to all of them. Due to the nature of the data and the limited number of cases, quantitative statistical analysis was not undertaken. The level of rigor involved ensures that the results of the research will be transferrable to other groups of cases in which similar events and decisions occur. An attempt will be made to identify, however tentatively, some of these cases.

Data collection: As previously described, data collection consists of primary source documents, books, peer reviewed articles, relevant media articles, and where appropriate and possible, interviews with subject matter experts (non-participant observation of conditions and processes relevant to the study) and participants in decision making. Archival research included both electronic and hard-copy issues of relevant journals, newspapers and other media and similar documents. There is a potential for incomplete records, recollections, and gaps in knowledge, however, the literature review the depth of research, and application of critical thinking are designed to remove that risk.

---

[9] Padgett, D. K. *Qualitative methods in social work research: Challenges and rewards*. Thousand Oaks, CA: Sage Publications, Inc., 1998. 52.

Intellectual Models and Frameworks

The following models will be used to test the case studies to determine the validity of the decision making and framing processes while examining the role of the individual in these processes:

Graham Allison's Refined Models

Graham Allison contributed two models for decision making which are most relevant to the research and were used to test the case studies. Allison's work relies on the Rational Actor Model (RAM) of government politics, decision making, and group dynamics.[10] The RAM posits that actors consider problems of policy in terms of largely implicit conceptual models that have significant consequences for the context of the thought. Its core concepts include: The ranking of objectives, discussion of alternatives, attachment of consequences to the alternatives, and a rational selection of the alternatives to act upon based on required goal completion.[11] Under the RAM, it is assumed that other world and domestic actors will follow the same rational system of decision making.[12] Further assumptions include the primacy of unitary states as actors, and the perception of the international environment as a self-help based "Hobbesean jungle," or anarchic world with no higher authority to moderate state action.[13] In such an environment, it is assumed that states will seek to act increase their security and power.

The second model to be used, underscored by rationality and the precepts of the RAM, is the Government Politics Model (GPM). In this model decisions are viewed as "outputs of large organizations functioning according to standards of behavior."[14] In this model, outcomes will be influenced by organizational, not

[10] Allison, Graham and Zelikow, Philip. Essence of Decision: Explaining the Cuban Missile Crisis. Vol. 2. New York: Longman, 1999. 13-16.
[11] Ibid.
[12] Bradford, Jeffrey Peter, "Political Aspects of Strategic Decision Making in British Defence Policy." PhD Thesis, Cranfield University, Royal Military College of Shrivenham, 1999. 9.
[13] Allison and Zelikow. 15-16.
[14] Ibid. 143.

individual, dynamics and cultures.[15] The various bureaucracies which make up the decision making process serve themselves first, then their higher authorities, which can cause the creation of gaps between the choices of leaders and the implementation capabilities and priorities of subordinate organizations.[16] Information is not easily or efficiently shared, resulting in potentially incomplete knowledge for decision makers. In this model even a shared goal can cause conflict because of the differing views of leaders based on the points of view of their parent organizations, personal interests, and backgrounds. In such an environment, even a paramount leader, such as the president, must seek consensus with his subordinates, if for no other reason than to prevent misunderstandings, and even a president's power may be curtailed by powerful subordinate bureaucracies.[17]

Because of these limitations, the personalities of key leaders and their propensity to fight for their views or acquiesce, even to the paramount leader, are central. This model can be heavily influenced by the power of key informed and motivated leaders to obtain their desired outcomes. Crucial to the model is the idea that "the leader's initial preferences are rarely a sufficient guide for explanation or prediction."[18] Bargaining takes place amongst agencies of varying relative power and interests, sometimes crippling the ability to make rational choices.

In *Explaining Foreign Policy*, Steven Yetiv broadens the tools developed by Allison by use of a new case study, that of the decision making process which surrounded the U.S. armed rejection of Iraq from Kuwait in 1991. One of his refinements of the Allison models was a Theory of Government Politics, by which key leaders acted as "pied pipers" and brought others along with them through persuasive power, particularly if the outlook of and relationships among the group members were similar and strong.[19]

---

[15] Allison and Zelikow. 255.
[16] Ibid. 257.
[17] Woll, Peter. *American Bureacracy.* New York: Norton, 1977. 206-207.
[18] Allison and Zelikow. 259.
[19] Yetiv, Stephen A. *Explaining Foreign Policy: U.S. Decision Making and the Gulf War.* Baltimore: Johns Hopkins University Press, 2004. 120. Referring to the Fairy Tale Character who uses music to entice children into following him.

The facets of Allison's models, with Yetiv's modifications, are shown graphically in Figure 1 below:[20]

Figure 1: Comparison of National Decision Making Models

Model	Level of Analysis	Theory	Result
RATIONAL ACTOR APPROACH	Government as unitary actor.	Theory of games as determinant of choice.	Rational choice among all actors
GOVERNMENT POLITICS (BUREAUCRATIC)	National Security Decision Making Organizations	Perceptions and solutions reflect organizational priorities	Operational routines are implemented.
THEORY OF GOVERNMENTAL POLITICS	National Security Decision Making Organizations and Leaders	Leaders with similar outlooks and priorities can be decisive.	Operational routines may be overcome.

Yetiv's model looks particularly useful for explaining the interventions in Kosovo and Libya, in which powerful actors, even though not in paramount roles, formulated their positions and drug other key leaders along, ultimately also participating in the public framing of the issues, although this is not discussed explicitly. Similarly, the role of outside pressures, such as those generated from the international community, other great powers, alliances such as NATO, and international organizations, particularly the UN, are also not addressed.

[20] Bradford. 39.

Expectations Based on Allison's Models

Case studies utilizing Allison's models should reveal several points of reference. The first is that one would expect all decision making actors to be rational, and to assume that other actors are also rational. The decisions made would resemble "outputs of large organizations functioning according to standards of behavior." Organizational, rather than individual dynamics and cultures, will drive a bureaucratic decision making style. The initial preferences of leaders, where known, do not sufficiently inform the eventual outcome, which is reached by a process of significant bargaining, which occurs among a variety of agencies of varying relative power and interests. Usually, these agencies are a set group, including the office of the president, the Department of State (sometimes with the US Mission to the UN as a separate actor) the Department of Defense, and the Intelligence Community. This bargaining may come at the expense of rationality.

Weaknesses of Allison's Model

The most important critique Allison models is that they were developed with a hyper-focus on a single event, the Cuban Missile Crisis, and its sub events. Similarly, Yetiv's take on the Governmental Politics Model has a deep focus on the approach to the first Persian Gulf War in 1990-1991.[21] As articulated by Bendor and Hammond, it is possible that the group of people and the specific events used by Allison may simply not be able to be replicated, thus making the work primarily descriptive rather than prescriptive or theoretical.[22] Jeffrey Bradford's theoretical approach focused the use of repeated games to look at issues such as UK annual

---

[21] Yetiv. 120.

[22] Bendor, Jonathan and Hammond, Thomas H. "Rethinking Allison's Models." *The American Political Science Review* 86, no. 2 (1992, June): 301-322. 302.

defense budget negotiations, providing an additional counterpoint to Allison's analysis. Bradford noted that Allison's original draft was handicapped by how recently it appeared after the events it described. With this in mind, one purpose of this book is to assess the ongoing validity of these models.[23]

Other issues are raised as potential weaknesses. Unfolding events may prove to be far more complex and far less linear that acknowledged by Allison. Further, operating rules and may be more numerous and complex than individual actors can process. In addition, the issue of hierarchy, or how smaller decisions/influencers fit into a larger picture, is not recognized in Allison's work.[24] Modern decision makers are not as uninformed as assumed (and may be quite specialized, although sometimes in the wrong ways) and modern bureaucracies are not as sluggish or staid as Allison proposed. Indeed, organizations can potentially bring more cognitive power to bear on issues than individuals. Unlike states, which are viewed as unitary actors, decision making groups are broken down into constituent groups, leading to questions of similarity of goals.[25] A further potential problem is the assumption that all players are rational, or if they will ever have adequate information on which to base decisions.[26] A lack of clarity in the model on the potential for multiple goals on the part of a single actor provides a challenge to Allison's definition of rationality, thus bringing the RAM into question.[27] Finally, the cases in Allison's study appear to be closed loops, a situation which may expose a potential flaw is Allison's seeming presumption that decisions taken at key points in time draw their decision cycles to an end.[28] This does not pay adequate note to the ongoing impacts of decisions, changes in circumstances, and the possible need for revisits of the same topics, which also points to events and crises as non-linear in nature.

---

[23] Bradford. 20.
[24] Bendor and Hammond. 306. The term they use is "Single Time Period" organization.
[25] Ibid. 302.
[26] Ibid. 305.
[27] Ibid. 302-303.
[28] Ibid. 303.

A major criticism of the GPM focuses on whether the highest levels of the government actually work in the manner described by Allison. Bradford questions whether goals of leaders at the cabinet level are actually so disparate, and both whether and why a president would have to bargain with his own appointees.[29] A common thread on this is that a president would try to avoid bargaining if possible, and that he would normally be in a paramount position to implement his or her desired course of action without doing so.

Between the Models: Linking the Foreign Policy Decision Making Process to Framing

The U.S. government uses an interagency process to decide on when and how the nation will intervene abroad. At some point in this process, and not necessarily concurrent to it, leaders frame and communicate their themes and messages concerning their opponents and world events. As noted in Christopher Paul's 2011 *Strategic Communication*, a successful framing or communication strategy calls for synchronizing messages with deeds.[30] Admiral James Stavridis, a noted military advocate of and expert on strategic communication, acknowledged the role of the national security apparatus and entreated leaders to "take an early and persistent role in deciding how ideas and decisions are shaped and delivered.[31] For Stavridis this need required a shared understanding of what strategic communications is and is not, particularly in an international context.[32] This is re-enforced by Nye (2005), who warned that "A communication strategy cannot work if it cuts against the grain of policy," reiterating the need for coordination of messaging at the highest levels.[33] As noted by Rodman and others, based on the

---

[29] Bradford. 18.
[30] Paul, Christopher. *Strategic Communication: Origins, Concepts, and Current Debates.* Santa Barbara, CA: Praeger, 2011. 8-9.
[31] Stavridis, James G. "Strategic Communication and National Security," *Joint Force Quarterly*, 2007: 4-7. 4, 7.
[32] Ibid. 7.
[33] Nye, Joseph. *Soft Power.* New York: Public Affairs, 2004. 110.

personality of a given president, and the constitutional seniority of the various cabinet members, the interagency process can be subverted by a powerful cabinet member.[34] Constitutional seniority in this case refers to the legal hierarchy of the cabinet, in other, words, that a powerful Secretary of State, the senior cabinet officer, will have more influence than a CIA director, or the Chairman of the Joint Chiefs of Staff. Well known examples of this include the role that Henry Kissinger played in the Nixon and Ford administrations, or that Vice President Cheney and Defense Secretary Rumsfeld played in the Bush administration. Richard Holbrooke, Madeleine Albright and Hillary Clinton also played this role in several instances, including the lead ups to the interventions in Kosovo and Libya, but no similar leader, including Secretary of State John Kerry, had the political clout to carry the frame through in regards to Syria or with Russia over its aggression against Ukraine. Inordinately strong leaders can either enhance or limit the effectiveness of the NSC and the interagency community to develop effective plans, to communicate them, or to get their plans cleared through the president.[35]

Even without the interference of personalities, however, a significant source of friction and conflict in the decision making process is the radically different institutional mindsets of the various interagency players, most specifically the Departments of State and Defense. A key point here is the ongoing gap in funding, crisis response methodologies, training, outlook, and expectations between these two most significant stakeholders in the decision making process, making such a process difficult to implement.[36] Where only one of the leading policy development organizations pushes a program, it is not likely to succeed, but when a key leader can convince other organizations, action becomes more likely. This would have ramifications for the attempt to intervene in Syria, since none of the cabinet leaders were in favor of military action.

---

[34] Rodman, Peter. *Presidential Command: Power, Leadership, and the Making of Foreign Policy from Nixon to George W. Bush*. New York: Alfred A Knopf, 2009. 53, 55-57.
[35] Nye. 29.
[36] Deutsch, John. "Strengthening the National Security Interagency Process." In *Keeping the Edge*, edited by Ashton Carter, 276-284. Harvard: Kennedy School, 2000. 270.

Framing and the Entman/Castells Model

Robert Entman provided a model for framing in *Projections of Power*, noting that the purpose of a frame is "to generate support or opposition to a political actor or policy."[37] This is what he calls the "Cascading Network Association Theory".[38] Since the government remains the primary source for information, this creates a system of asymmetric interdependence, but this can only be taken advantage of if there is unanimity in the message, particularly in a media environment which is prepared to conflate news with entertainment.[39] Manuel Castells drew upon and added to the concept in *Communication Power*, most particularly in his writing concerning Networks of Mind and Power. For this concept, Castells draws significantly on the models of framing developed by Robert Entman, who focuses attention on the efforts of the Government to frame key events, and the media's countervailing efforts to "counter-frame" them.[40] A graphic depiction of Entman's theory would resemble a downward spiraling ladder, showing the descent of information from on high. But it would also show lines back from the lower rungs to the higher ones, indicating the impact of framing and the upward, communicative impact of stakeholders on decision makers. According to Entman, the government is generally successful in framing when it can call on shared themes and ideals and get its themes in "early and often."[41] Yetiv provides an example of this theory in action by describing the methodology used by Bush in constructing an image of Saddam Hussein (who, in the summer of 1990, had just invaded and occupied Kuwait) as a new Hitler, and the overwhelming need to confront him rather than face a "New Munich," implying that appeasing, rather than

---

[37] Entman. 47.
[38] Ibid. 17-21.
[39] Bennett, Lance, and Entman, Robert. *Mediated Politics: Communication in the Future of Democracy*. Cambridge: Cambridge University Press, 2001. 166.
[40] Entman. 17-21.
[41] Ibid. 10.

opposing Hussein would have the same dire consequences that appeasement had in 1938, after which general war followed within a year.[42]

Castells' work focuses on a variety of communications issues, noting that power is based on the ability to form, shape and adjust networks and messages. This is referred to as "network power," which he calls the power to modify, change, or create networks.[43] To Castells, power lies within networked systems. Their operations, the interplay between them, and switching between them is a source of power to those who are able to implement the change. This ties directly back into the concept of framing, which can always be done by those with the power, information, and interest to do so.[44] According to Castells, "The framing of the public mind is largely performed through processes that take place in the media. Communications research has identified three major processes involved in the relationship between media and people in the sending and receiving of news through which citizens perceive their selves in relation to the world: agenda setting, priming and framing."[45] With that in mind, agenda setting seeks to delineate the terms of acceptable debate, while framing describes the manner in which the coverage provided emphasizes desired aspects of events in order to reach desired interpretations and outcomes.[46] Castells states that "Only those frames that are able to connect the message to pre-existing frames in the mind become activators of conduct… by finding resonance and increasing the magnitude of their repetition."[47]

In the cases to be examined, the government is the organization with the power and interest to establish, maintain, and capitalize on the power of communication networks in order to frame the debate on armed humanitarian interventions, and to persuade stakeholders of the need to intervene. Carrying this

---

[42] Yetiv. 94-95.
[43] Castells, Manuel. *Communication Power*. Oxford: Oxford University Press, 2009. 45.
[44] Nanabhey, Mohammed. "From spectacle to spectacular: How physical space, social media and mainstream broadcast amplified the public sphere in Egypt's 'Revolution'." *The Journal of North African Studies*. 2011: 573-603. 577.
[45] Castells. 157.
[46] Ibid. 158.
[47] Ibid.

argument one step further, it is highly placed, powerful individual actors who create the frames used to encourage intervention. According to Alex Mintz, decisions are "sold" to the public, or framed, in order that elites and decision makers can enhance their political standing and popularity, naturally preferring to have more support than opposition in the process.[48] Further, conflicting frames can be provided not only by the media, but by the party out of power, which has significant implications for the Libya case study and others.

Expectations Based on the Entman/Castells Model

A model drawing off the work of Entman and Castells would expect to see a concerted, planned effort by senior decision makers to set the terms of public discourse on a given issue, and to capitalize on the government's unique position as a single source for definitive information on key foreign policy and defense issues. Influencers outside of the foreign policy decision making process would be counteracted and refuted in order to maintain information primacy. Narratives would attempt to draw simple parallels to historical examples, not always contextually relevant, but well known and inflammatory at times. Control or influence on information networks would be established and increased so that messaging could be enhanced.

Weaknesses of the Entman/Castells Model

The Entman/Castells model describes a process by which power holders and decision makers monopolize information and attempt to use that monopoly to frame key issues both to enable decision making and to justify decisions that have been made. However, neither model describes the how of that process. Castells' is criticized for two reasons. The first is because of the negative linkages he draws

---

[48] Mintz, Alex. *Understanding Foreign Policy Decision Making.* Cambridge: Cambridge University Press, 2010.

with framing, network power, and free market capitalism however, the political side of his model is not central to its contribution in this case.[49]

The Combined Decide/Frame Model, Expectations, and Challenges

Inductive reasoning was used to develop the grounded theory on decision making and framing employed in this study. According to Strauss and Corbin, "A grounded theory is one that is inductively derived from the study of the phenomenon it represents. That is, it is discovered, developed, and provisionally verified through systematic data collection and analysis of data pertaining to that phenomenon."[50] Based on the hypothesis that armed humanitarian interventions occur when a powerful leader or small group of leaders dominates the decision making and framing apparatus to force and explain such an intervention, it is necessary to construct a theory that explains the concurrence or nexus of the decision making and framing processes. Relying on the literature review and a thorough examination of the Allison, Yetiv, Entman, and Castell's models, the following theory was developed and will be tested by the case studies; it could be suggested that when the foreign policy decision making process is dominated by powerful individuals with a motivation toward intervention, and the framing process is dominated by the same or similarly minded individuals, armed humanitarian interventions take place driven by this alignment.

A deciding and framing model would expect to see the decision making process dominated by key stakeholders with powerful interests in a given issue formed by their own experiences and pressures on them formed through their own participation in events, both in forcing a decision on a given issue (in this case, armed humanitarian interventions) and in framing that process and the associated

---

49 Taffel, Sy. "Manuel Castells' Communication Power." *Media Ecologies*. http://mediaecologies.wordpress.com/2010/05/31/manuel-castells-communication-power/. Accessed on July 10, 2014.

50 Strauss, Anselm and Corbin, Juliet. *Basics of Qualitative Research Techniques and Procedures for Developing Grounded Theory (2nd edition)*. London: Sage Publications: 1990. 23

decisions to the various stakeholders (in this case, the public, through the media). Such an explanatory model will face the same challenges that have been posed to its constituent models, however, it is believed that by unifying the two key processes (deciding and framing) into a single model, that weakness can in part be overcome. That, then, is the purpose for this study.

Case Studies and Case Study Selection

The method of research agglomeration for this book is selective sampling. Under selective sampling, a thorough literature review, which has been performed, is used to illuminate the various items (in this case, events) which form the overall sample, and to infer the strongest examples to be examined. While less than ideal for quantitative studies,[51] purposeful sampling is a key element in qualitative studies such as this book. In part, purposeful sampling was selected because of the very small size of the overall sample. As seen above, fewer than twenty total events, or cases, can be examined. Furthermore, the nature of the evidence to be analyzed, books, memoirs, and primary source documents lend itself to a purposeful sample. The cases also have similar background conditions, helping to control for third variable influences, or at least to acknowledge those differences, while avoiding the pitfalls and narrowness inherent in a single case study approach.[52] Finally, as Stephan van Evera notes, case studies can go farther in answering the question of how variables impact on each other more readily than quantitative tests.[53]

---

[51] Creswell, John W. *Research Design: Qualitative and Quantitative Approaches*. London: Sage Publications. 1994. 119.
[52] Van Evera, Stephen. *Guide to Methods for Students of Political Science.* Ithaca, NY: Cornell University Press, 1997. 52-53.
[53] Ibid. 54.

Explanation of Related Variables

Along with explaining why certain methods are used in the study, it is important to discuss variables, theories, and case studies which were not used in the study, and why they were judged to not be central to it. This will demonstrate the rigor of the research as well as the durability of the theoretical model described in the previous section, while incorporating or explaining competing factors in the decision making and framing processes.

The case studies were selected based on the following criteria: First, each intervention met the criterion established in the literature review, meaning that they were military, combative interventions, against the will of the host government, for purposes named as humanitarian. The interventions all took place after the end of the Cold War in 1991. This allowed a focus on U.S. power and capability little constrained by other powers, in other words, the so called "Unipolar moment."[54] In terms of the case studies adopted, it is clear that there are numerous interventions in the period from 1991 to 2013 that are not included. Notable U.S. interventions involving armed force in the period include: The Bush-Clinton interventions in Somalia from 1991-1993 (used), the Haiti intervention of 1994 (referenced but not used as a primary case study), the Rwandan Genocide (referenced in this work as a non-intervention), the end of the Yugoslav Civil War (used in terms of the lead up to the Kosovo crisis), the Kosovo intervention (used), the interventions in Afghanistan (2001) and Iraq (2003)(not used as they are better termed as conventional open warfare), Pakistan Earthquake (2005 and 2010) (not used), Indonesian Tsunami relief (2004) (not used), Lebanon Non Combatant Evacuations (2006) (not used), Operation Tomodachi/Pacific Passage, the simultaneous evacuation of U.S. personnel from and assistance to Japan following the Fukushima reactor meltdown (2011) (not used) and the Libyan intervention of 2012

[54] Krauthammer, Charles. "The Unipolar Moment." *Foreign Affairs*, Vol. 70, No. 1, America and the World 1990/91. 23-33.

(used). A key to the major U.S. interventions is provided below. There were numerous small scale deployments which are not included in this analysis. Figure 2 below shows the interventions, the years of the operation, the name of the president and his political party affiliation, and an area to note whether the operation met the definition of armed humanitarian interventions revealed by the literature review, and if the intervention would be one of the case studies for analysis.[55]

Figure 2: Selected List of U.S. Interventions, 1992-2013

Intervention	President	Party	Years	Region	Humanitarian?
Somalia 1	G.H.W. Bush	(R)epublican	1992-3	Africa	Y
Somalia 2	Clinton	(D)emocrat	1993-4	Africa	Y
Haiti	Clinton	D	1995	Caribbean	N
Bosnia	Clinton	D	1995-8	Europe	N
Rwanda	Clinton	D	1994	Africa	N
Kosovo	Clinton	D	1998-9	Europe	Y
Afghanistan	G.W. Bush	R	2001-14	Asia	N
Iraq	G.W. Bush	R	2003-11	Middle East	N
Pakistan Earthquake	G.W. Bush	R	2005	Asia	N
Indonesian Tsunami	G.W. Bush	R	2004	Asia	N

[55] Of course key data points from interventions not used in the case studies will be cited where appropriate.

NEOs in Lebanon and Georgia	G.W. Bush	R	2006 2008	Middle East Caucasus	N
Pakistan Flooding	Obama	D	2010	Middle East	N
Haiti Earthquake	Obama	D	2010	Caribbean	N
Japan	Obama	D	2011	Asia	N
Libya	Obama	D	2012	Africa	Y

Brief synopses of operations included in this chart help to illustrate the main points of the interventions and why they may or may not have been chosen for analysis.

Somalia 1 (1992) – Response to humanitarian crisis caused by failure and collapse of Somali Government. U.S. armed forces intervened as part of a UN effort to provide food, medicine, and humanitarian relief under President George H. W. Bush. [56]

Somalia 2 (1993) – Mission morphed under President Clinton into a manhunt for Somali Warlords, and failure in this effort led to shut down of the mission.[57]

Haiti (1994) – This intervention was undertaken to remove the administration of Raoul Cedras, which had overthrown the U.S. backed Aristide government. U.S. forces did land to provide security and humanitarian relief, but the issue was resolved diplomatically, and without significant use of Force.[58] Had the planned invasion taken place, then this intervention would have been included in those being analyzed.

---

[56] Weiss, Thomas G. *Humanitarian Intervention. 2 ed.* War and Conlict in the Modern World. Cambridge: Polity Press, 2012. 30-31.
[57] Ibid.
[58] Ibid. 10.

Bosnia (1992-98) – The Bosnian intervention took place near the end of multi-year Yugoslav Civil War. Operating under a UN Mandate, NATO forces arrived in Bosnia to assist with peacekeeping following the withdrawal of Bosnian Serb forces from the country.[59] Not included as a case study because the mandate was not humanitarian, and did not involve significant U.S. kinetics.

Rwanda (1994) – The most important non-intervention in the last century. Ethnic Rwandan Tutsis slaughtered over half a million Ethnic Hutus over the summer of 1994. In spite of some pressure from the UN, the international community remained largely inactive through the crisis.[60]

Kosovo (1999) – Provides one of the case studies. Military force used for the humanitarian purpose of protecting the Kosovar Albanians from Serb atrocities in winter 1999.[61]

Afghanistan (2001-2014) – Military intervention and occupation of the country as part of the counter-attack following the 9-11 attacks. Although some disaster relief and reconstruction activities have occurred since the invasion, in 2001, they were not the purpose for the intervention, and Afghanistan was rejected as a case study because of this.

Iraq (2003-2010) – Military intervention and occupation of the country for a variety of reasons, but with the stated objective of ending the Hussein government's support of terrorism and abrogation of treaties on the development of Weapons of Mass Destruction. Although some disaster relief and reconstruction activities have occurred since the invasion, in 2003, they were not the purpose for the intervention, and Iraq was rejected as a case study because of this.

Indonesian Tsunami (2004-2005) – Response to this 2004 Earthquake and Tsunami was provided by the armed forces, in part because of the remoteness of the stricken areas and the unique transport and response capability of the U.S.

---

[59] Hyland, William. *Clinton's World: Remaking American Foreign Policy*. West Port, CT: Praeger, 1999. 33.
[60] Hehir, Aidan. *The Responsibility to Protect: Rhetoric, Reality, and the Future of Humanitarian Intervention*. New York: Palgrave Macmillan, 2012. 30-34.
[61] Phillips, David L. *Liberating Kosovo*. Cambridge, MA: Belfer Center, 2012. 90.

armed forces. However, the operations were not inherently combative in nature, therefore, this intervention will not be considered as a case study.

Pakistan Earthquake (2005) – Response was provided by the armed forces, particularly given the proximity of major combat operations in neighboring Afghanistan, however, the operations were not inherently combative in nature, therefore, this intervention will not be considered as a case study.

Lebanon and Georgia Non Combatant Evacuation Operations (NEO) (2006 and 2008) – These operations saw U.S. forces used to help evacuate U.S. Persons from Lebanon as a result of the 2006 Hezbollah War and Georgia as a result of the 2008 Russian invasion. Since the purpose was to evacuate Americans, and not to impact the situation on the ground, these actions were not considered.

Pakistan Flooding Relief (2010) – Response to floods in the tribal areas of Afghanistan was provided by the armed forces, in part because of the remoteness of the stricken areas and the unique transport and response capability of the U.S. armed forces. However, the operations were not inherently combative in nature, therefore, this intervention will not be considered as a case study.

Haiti Earthquake (2010) – Response to the Earthquake in Haiti was provided by the armed forces, in part because of the level of infrastructure damage of the stricken areas and the unique transport and response capability of the U.S. armed forces. However, the operations were not inherently combative in nature, therefore, this intervention will not be considered as a case study.

Japan Earthquake (Operation Tomodachi) (2011) – Response to the earthquake in Japan was provided by the armed forces, in part because of the level of infrastructure damage of the stricken areas and the unique transport and response capability of the U.S. armed forces. Furthermore, U.S. bases and personnel were impacted, and evacuation was offered to all Americans who wished it. Since the purpose was specifically to evacuate Americans, with some lifesaving and search and rescue assets assisting the Japanese, and not to impact the situation on the ground, this intervention was not considered for a case study.

Libya (Operation Odyssey Dawn) (2012) – Provides one of the case studies. Military force used for the humanitarian purpose of protecting the Libyan civilians, particularly in the eastern part of the country, from attacks by regime forces.[62] This fits the qualifiers for intervention set out in the literature review.

A significant event is not listed on the table, the failure to intervene in **Syria (2013)** after the Assad regime repeatedly violated President Obama's "Red Lines," on the use of chemical weapons. This provided the catalyst for significant debate and diplomatic maneuvering surrounding a possible intervention in 2013, however, the intervention never took place. This book argues that one reason for this is that no powerful leader emerged in support of the intervention either in the decision making or framing cycles. By 2014, air strikes, not under humanitarian auspices, commenced against Islamic State targets in Syria, but this also falls outside of the types of interventions examined in the study.

With these thoughts in mind, three primary case studies have been selected for analysis to help determine the role of individuals in advocating and framing intervention decisions. The chosen case studies were selected on the basis of responses to natural as well as man-made disasters, government threats to human life, and attempts at genocide. They cover differing political administrations and one case study, Somalia, straddles a change in political administration. Geographic diversity is also ensured, with interventions in Africa, Europe, and the Middle East selected for study. This will allow a determination as to whether a particular region, ethnic, or religious group was treated significantly differently. The selected cases occurred during both Republican and Democrat administrations and provide a balanced sample for analysis, helping to rule out a partisan based intervention hypothesis. The Rwanda non-intervention will also be discussed since it provided the impetus for the development of current definitions and concepts of armed humanitarian intervention, while the decision not to intervene in Syria in August 2013 will be discussed as part of the findings.

---

[62] Hehir. 12-13.

Analysis of the case studies focuses on the following questions and themes. How did the case meet the criterion for humanitarian interventions as described in the literature review? What is the timeline of events, in other words, what caused the intervention, and what were the key decision and framing points in time? What was the decision making process? Was it implicitly tied into the framing process? Did the same people undertake each? Since the events examined take place in a time line, how did each armed intervention, or decision not to intervene, impact future choices?

Limitations of the Study and Intervening Variables

In examining the national security decision making and framing cycles, and the impact of the individual on them, there are several intervening variables which must be acknowledged for their potential impact on both cycles and leaders. Intervening variables to be discussed are: War weariness, public distraction, the attractiveness of the international narrative of R2P (where applicable in terms of the timeline), the lack of attractiveness of the narrative of other frames, such as chemical weapons abuse, geography and its impact on intervention, the timeline of interventions, and the efforts of allied or opposition countries to impact U.S. framing of armed humanitarian intervention efforts. The foundational beliefs of leaders can play a role, with leaders drawing on the Second World War era for their beliefs such as George H.W. Bush and Madeleine Albright, saw appeasement as something to be avoided, whereas those of the Vietnam generation, such as Clinton, saw internal dissent and defeat as a bigger problem.[63] Finally, the fundamental divide in America's view of itself as either a realist or liberal actor on the world stage must be considered.[64] The latter is, on one hand, a motivator for the leaders

[63] Albright interview on the McNeil/Lehrer Newshour, 10 June 1999. From Schnabel, Albrecht and Thakur, Ramesh. *Kosovo and the Challenge of Humanitarian Intervention: Selective Indignation, Collective Action, and International Citizenship.* New York: United Nations University Press, 2000. 89

[64] Kissinger, Henry. *Diplomacy.* New York: Touchstone Books, 1994. 43-45.

analyzed in the case studies, but can also be a significant factor in the public's support for or rejection of an intervention. This, in turn, becomes a planning factor for decision makers.

One intervening variable is the cumulative effect of events outside of the case studies. War weariness, for example, or the internal focus of the public following the world financial crisis of 2008 may be contributing factors in both the stance taken toward intervention in Libya in 2012, and the lack of interest in a similar intervention in Syria in 2013.[65] Lack of international support, or the active interference of a great power, such as Russia, China, or France, can also be a factor in decision making.

Further factors in the decision to intervene have included the discourse on chemical weapons usage, particularly on civilians, as well as a broader academic and practitioner discourse on humanitarian interventions in general, with a focus on R2P. Chemical weapons have been a source of international discussion and at least tacit agreement on their non-use since the First World War, while armed humanitarian interventions are relatively new and require discussion in terms of the narrative. In response to a series of man-made humanitarian disasters after the end of the Cold War, the principal arose that the international community has a responsibility to protect the lives of citizens whose sovereign governments were unable or refused to do so. The three principal events which brought this about were the killing of over a million Rwandans in 1994, the breakup of the former Yugoslavia from 1992 to the Kosovo air campaign of 1999, and the ongoing Darfur crisis.[66] A codification of the principal of humanitarian interventions came about as the result of the 2000 UN Millennium summit, and the subsequent International Commission on Intervention and State Sovereignty (ICISS) which officially coined the phrase "Responsibility to Protect" in its final report of the same name. R2P

---

[65] Dugan, Andrew. "Support for Syria Action Lower Than Past Conflicts." http://www.gallup.com/poll/164282/support-syria-action-lower-past-conflicts.aspx. Accessed on September 25, 2013.
[66] Bellamy, Alex J. "The Responsibility to Protect," in *Security Studies: An Introduction.* New York: Routledge, 2008, 422-37. 423.

implies that the security of individuals and groups of people is paramount over that of the state, when that state fails to account for that security, or actively acts against it.[67] Utilization of R2P provided networking power which enable framing to take place in Libya, while chemical weapons failed to provide the same for Syria.

Moral authority, or America's self-perception of its moral authority, as a final intervening variable in the decision to launch or not to launch a armed humanitarian intervention. In "Necessity or Choice? Securing Public Consent for War," John Schuessler discusses this as a problem of marketing, noting that the realist paradigm is in conflict with core American values.[68] This poses a problem in that any intervention or conflict must be framed to the American public as a war of necessity, forced on the nation by dire circumstances, or even by armed attack. When America acts, it should do so not for low goals, but with the goal of improving mankind's lot.[69] This is summed up by a quote from John Mearsheimer:

> "Americans tend to like (liberalism) because it identifies the United States as a benevolent force in world politics and portrays its real and potential rivals as misguided or malevolent."[70]

It is this struggle between the moral and the realist that creates challenges for decision making and framing. Richard Haass, writing in *Wars of Necessity and Wars of Choice*, there is a significant burden on the government to prove the benefits of its actions, particularly when American lives are at risk. This adds to the burden of both deciding on and explaining armed humanitarian interventions, which are, in the end, wars of choice, rather than necessity. For Haass, the benefits of such an intervention must outweigh the costs, while the net result must be positive, "If this test cannot be met, the choice will appear to be ill advised and

---

[67] Bellamy. 424

[68] Schuessler, John. "When Wars of Necessity Become Contested as Wars of Choice." In 2004 Annual Meeting of the American Political Science Association, 2004. 4.

[69] Ibid. 4.

[70] Mearsheimer, John. *The Tragedy of Great Power Politics*. New York. W.W. Norton and Company, 2001. 23-25.

most likely is."[71] Thus the "bang for the buck" test joins the other tests, motivators, and detractors for intervention which must be considered when examining each one, and which serve as intervening variables for the cases. In cases where there was no decision to intervene, it is often because the cost benefit analysis, or a perception of that analysis, comes up negative, meaning that the human, monetary, and political price of armed humanitarian intervention is simply not worth the perceived gains. The inference here is that framing acts of choice, such as armed humanitarian interventions, is a more difficult and time consuming act, less certain to succeed than is the case in wars of necessity.

A key point to be noted is that this study is focused exclusively on U.S. government decision making and framing processes. That is to say that any linkage to similar processes is coincidental. The nature of the U.S. political system is especially suited to the influence of the types of powerful leaders and framers discussed in the study. That said, it is reasonable to extrapolate that, where conditions in the political processes, institutions, and media of other countries are similar to those in the U.S., the lessons of this study could apply.

The limitations presented do not detract from the value of studying the role of the individual in foreign policy decision making and framing, whether for armed humanitarian interventions or other foreign policy endeavors. Rather, they augment and complete a picture of the foreign policy and framing processes which has heretofore been little explored. By bringing the literatures on decision making and framing together in a policy environment, this study expands the overall body of work on both fields, as well as on the case studies themselves. It also offers useful information to other researchers, policy makers and practitioners. Applicable implications focus on the linkages between policy making and framing, and the centrality of powerful motivators/spokespersons to each process.

---

[71] Haass. 10.

Conclusion

As will be seen in the case studies, the common factor underpinning each of the interventions discussed is the intervention and interaction of key leaders who could both push the decision making process and serve as spokespersons in successful efforts to frame the interventions. Similarly, in cases in which intervention did not occur, there was no clear spokesperson or mover with the political and framing cache able to provide the vital impetus for action. Having discussed the main themes of the literature on armed humanitarian interventions, the foreign policy decision making process, and the framing process, the purpose of this section of the book is to describe, in detail, the theoretical arguments of the book, and to define the tests that will be undertaken with the case studies to demonstrate the feasibility of the proposed theories.

The purpose of this research is to examine the decision making and framing processes for U.S. armed humanitarian interventions in the post-cold war era to determine the impact of individual transformational leaders on both processes. This section of the study reviewed the hypothesis that interventions occur when a powerful leader or small group of leaders dominates the decision making and framing apparatus to force and explain such an intervention, as well as the literature review which helped to frame it. Key definitions, particularly of armed humanitarian interventions derived from the literature review were discussed more fully, while the choice of qualitative over quantitative analysis was both described and justified in light of the small number of cases and the nature of the evidence, which is primarily anecdotal and not easily quantified. This section also discussed the cases, as well as rejected cases, and the rationale for their selection, noting a series of intervening variables and their potential impact on the findings. It also reinforced the utility of the study and its potential value to decision makers and other researchers. Preliminary findings of this study are that in armed humanitarian intervention situations, the existence of one or a few powerful leaders are required in both the foreign policy decision making process and the media framing process in order for such an intervention to take place. Where no powerful leader emerges to sway the opinion of other leaders and bureaucracies, in either the deciding or framing processes, interventions fail to occur.

CHAPTER III – George Bush and the Decision to Intervene in Somalia, 1992

> "The very real threat was that as much as one-fourth of all Somalia could starve to death before January, 1993."
> Dr. Phillip Johnston, Director of Care, 1994.[1]

In 1992, Somalia lay in ruins. Decades of civil war, inspired by a mixture of the influence of the Cold War, the rise of militant Islam, and the international drug trade had transformed the former Italian colony into the quintessential failed state. The epidemic of starvation which followed the end of the civil war on 1991 was so bad that by September, 1992, the media were reporting that 100,000 out of the population of six million had died, nearly half of starvation, with an amazing, and staggering 95% suffering from some form from illnesses related to malnutrition.[2] In December, 1992, the U.S. intervened with a massive military force designed at first to ensure safe food deliveries to the Somali people, and to defend those food shipments in an extremely hostile environment.

The U.S. armed humanitarian intervention in Somalia began in December, 1992, during the waning weeks of the presidency of George Herbert Walker Bush. While tragedy would strike the mission nearly a year later, with the battle of Mogadishu (of "Blackhawk Down" fame) and the graphic deaths of eighteen U.S. soldiers, the focus of this case study is rather on the decision making process which

---

[1] Johnston, Phillip. *Somalia Diary: The President of Care Tells One Country's Story of Hope.* Atlanta, GA: Longstreet Press, 1994. ix.
[2] Ibid. 2.

led to the initial intervention, an operation generally judged as a success in its mission to alleviate the suffering, and in particular, the starvation, of many of the people of Somalia.

The Somalia intervention, according to Andrea Talentino, marked the first military intervention by the international community into a civil conflict since the end of the Cold War.[3] This case study will describe the situation in Somalia which led to the U.S. decision to intervene, as well as describing the processes both for deciding on intervention and on the framing of the intervention in humanitarian terms. It will also describe the role played by key empowered individuals in both decision making processes. That process was dominated by President George H.W. Bush, and it is he who was the powerful leader whose actions led directly to the intervention. Unique among the cases examined, the Somalia intervention took place during a presidential election campaign, and the incumbent, who lost, proceeded with the intervention with the recognition and acceptance of his replacement, and undertook the operation during his lame duck session with the knowledge that it could well continue into the Clinton administration's first term.

Somalia in 1992, Background to Intervention

The first major rumblings that there was an international crisis brewing in Somalia came in March, 1991, with the announcement by Under Secretary of State for African Affairs Howard Cohen that Somalia was in the midst of "civil strife."[4] The U.S. Embassy in Mogadishu had been closed down in February of that year, with negative impacts for information gathering both by the U.S. Government and the media on the crisis.[5] The greater conflict in the former Italian colony has its

---

[3] Talentino, Andrea K. *Military Intervention after the Cold War: The Evolution of Theory and Practice.* Athens, Ohio: Ohio University Press, 2005. 95.
[4] Rutherford, Kenneth R. *Humanitarianism under Fire: The U.S. And UN Intervention in Somalia.* Sterling, Virginia: Kumarian Press, 2008. 14.
[5] Sommer, John G., and Collins, Carole C. "Humanitarian Aid in Somalia: The Role of the Office of U.S. Foreign Disaster Assistance (OFDA) 1990-1994." *Refugee Policy Study Group,*

roots in the Cold War, and is tied to the communist takeover in nearby Ethiopia. When that country's pro-western leadership was overthrown by communists in 1974, U.S. efforts in the region shifted to support of Sidi Barre's regime in Mogadishu, and included military basing in the port of Berbera through the end of the Cold War.[6] Barre had himself taken over by means of a coup in 1969, but he made some real progress in the development of the Somali state, driving up literacy and attempting to suppress clan-ism in favor of a wider Somali identity.[7] What he could not overcome, though, was the strong sense of tribalism within the country, as well as the pastoral nomadic system of agriculture.[8] With the ending of the Cold War, Barre proved unable to continue the suppression of dissent in the country, leading to a series of coups and upheavals.

By 1991, the country was largely lawless. Mogadishu itself was wracked with violence as two sub clans of the Hawiye clan, led by Mohammed Farrah Aidid and Ali Mahdi Mohammed struggled for control.[9] Aidid, the former foreign minister, and probably the strongest of the warlords, harbored significant animosity against both the universalist aspirations of the United Nations in general and with Secretary Boutros-Gali personally, since Boutros-Gali, an Egyptian, was in part responsible for Egypt's strong support for the former dictator Barre.[10] With nearly all vestiges of central government gone, the countryside fell victim to the drought and desertification which had famously afflicted Sudan and Ethiopia in the 1980s. Further, the epicenter of the clan violence was the main agricultural area of the country, meaning that even food that could be grown was either pillaged, not

---

November, 1994. 2. For over a year afterwards, OFDA remained the only U.S. Government Agency to remain in country.

[6] Cohen, Herman. *Intervening in Africa: Superpower Peacemaking in a Troubled Continent.* New York: St. Martin's Press, 2000. 197.

[7] Oakley, John L. and Hirsch, Robert B. *Somalia and Operation Restore Hope: Reflections on Peacemaking and Peacekeeping.* Washington DC United States Institute of Peace Press, 1995. 5.

[8] Ibid. 23.

[9] Rutherford. 16.

[10] Oakley and Hirsch. 19. He had served as Egyptian Foreign Minister and other positions before he became Secretary General of the UN in 1992.

harvested, or not distributed.[11] As a result of these factors, a UN report of 22 July 1992 claimed that Somalia would not be able to grow enough to feed more than half of its population for the following year.[12] Prices for food, when it was available, had increased by 1,200%, putting the purchase of food beyond the reach of many.[13] Death therefore stalked the land, both in the form of malnutrition and starvation related illness caused by constant warfare amongst the tribes aspiring to take over the country.

Early efforts by the UN to provide assistance to the people of Somalia were focused on food aid, and did little to attempt a political solution, which meant that, given the lack of force projection and protection capability on the part of UN forces, both UN and other Non-Governmental Organizations (NGOs) relief efforts came under frequent attack. Clark and Herbst documented the following major attacks in fall 1991 as listed in Figure 3:

Figure 3: Snapshot of Violence of Fall 1991

Date	Location	Incident	Victims	Organization
17 September	Mogadishu	Plane hit by missile		International Committee of the Red Cross (ICRC)
October	Somalia Wide	45 aid vehicles looted, workers robbed		International Committee of the Red Cross (ICRC)

[11] Rutherford. 16-17. According to the author, only 15% of the land in Somalia was arable in any case.

[12] UN Secretary General's report S/24343, 22 July 1992. http://www.securitycouncilreport.org/un-documents/document/Somalia%20S%2024343.php. Accessed on August 20, 2014.

[13] Natsios, Andrew. U.S. Foreign policy and the Four Horsemen of the Apocalypse: Humanitarian Relief in Complex Emergencies. Washington: Center for Strategic and International Studies, the Washington Papers, 1997. 21.

14 October	Mogadishu	Security Guards Attacked, attempted theft		Medicins San Frontieres
5 December	Mogadishu	Employee killed while distributing food	1 killed	CARE
9 December	Berbera	Employees killed, generator stolen	3 killed	Italian Cooperation
11 December	Mogadishu	Shot at Somali Red Crescent Headquarters	1 killed	ICRC
11 December	Berbera	Six gunmen robbed two employees	2 robbed	UNICEF

Source: United Nations High Commissioner For Refugees Situation Report[14]

By 1992 it was becoming more and more clear that the United Nations and the various members of the NGO community were unable to adequately respond to the Somalia crisis. By mid-1992, an estimated 3,000 Somalis were dying, primarily from starvation, each day.[15] Whereas such a crisis would have caused an outpouring of civil relief during the cold war, as seen by the response to the Ethiopia drought in the early part of the 1980s, the end of the Cold War meant that a more potent, military backed intervention might be contemplated. Furthermore, the desperate nature of the situation, and the failure of the international relief community to ameliorate the crisis, left a military response as the only solution which promised success.

[14] United Nations High Commissioner for Refugees Situation Report, Somalia Unit-Djibouti, October 31, 1991. In Rutherford. 17-18.

[15] Sahnoun, Mohamed. *Somalia: The Missed Opportunities*. Washington, D.C: U.S. Institute for Peace, 1994. 15-16.

The U.S. and the World in 1992, Context for Intervention

The central political fact of the early 1990's was the end of the Cold War and the increasingly unilateral role of the U.S. during an emerging unipolar moment. An optimistic mood prevailed, best personified by Francis Fukuyama's *The End of History and the Last Man*, which appeared in 1992, and posited that the U.S. victory over communism meant that liberal democracy had permanently displaced it. In this era of triumphalism, however, the country, and the world, were led by the same politicians who had finished the Cold War, and were in fact still cold warriors. This was borne out through the first two years of the Somalia crisis, 1990 and 1991, in which the U.S. had a consistent stance, namely, that the problems of Somalia were internal in nature, and that therefore, the U.S. would stay out of them.[16] In 1992, the U.S. was just beginning to contemplate, if not to understand, the implications of the end of the bi-polar world that was the product of the Cold War, which had come to an end with the collapse of the Soviet Union the year before.

Washington was, in effect, left holding the bag for a world in which the control and stability provided by bi polarity and the gravity of the Cold War ideological conflict was rapidly devolving. The centerpiece for this decay was not in Africa, however, but the devolution of the Yugoslav Socialist Republic into its constituent parts, and the efforts of the Serbian government in Belgrade to prevent this. It was the breakup of Yugoslavia which most concerned the U.S. and its allies, as well as its former enemies, in the first years of the decade, and which received the most attention from the media as well as politicians.

As important as the growing war in Yugoslavia was, there were a host of other international issues to occupy the Bush team through 1992. Russia, the former enemy of the Cold War, was also trying to adapt to the new reality, and efforts to assist the new Russian President, Boris Yeltsin, to stabilize his country

---

[16] Talentino. 106.

through economic measures such as Most Favored Nation Status were priorities.[17] The U.S. international aid community was also focused on providing humanitarian assistance across the new states which rose up across the former Soviet Union.[18] In the Middle East, Israel's efforts to absorb an influx of Jews from the former Soviet Union caused demographic instability in the region, while the development of new settlements on Palestinian land caused political upset.[19]

Even in Africa, there was competition for attention for the administration. In South Africa, the most important country on the continent, the political fallout of the fall of the apartheid regime occupied significant attention. In Angola, the post-Cold War settlement was still working itself out in the form of a continued civil war. In Mozambique, civil war also loomed as a major distractor for the administration. Even in a year that was not going to be a "Year of Africa" there was little reason to think in January 1992 that by December Somalia would be a leading foreign policy issue with U.S. troops on the ground.

In terms of domestic politics, the impending November, 1992 presidential election was the key event of the year, with the slow crawl out of economic recession a prime issue.[20] As early as March, Bush expressed growing concern of the right of center third candidate Ross Perot and his capacity to swing the election in favor of a Democrat challenger by stripping away Republican votes.[21] By May, Bush's approval rating had dipped down to 40%, while his disapproval rating had reached 53%.[22] While Bush dismissed fears of Perot and disapproval at the time, his correspondence indicates that the election came to take on increasing amount of his and his team's time, particularly in the critical period after the Democrat National Convention in July. Personnel changes came along with this, most notably as James Baker, the capable Secretary of State, was moved to the more political

[17] Bush, George H.W. *All the Best: My Life in Letters and Other Writings.* New York: Scribner, 1999, 2012. 396.
[18] Sommer and Collins. 3.
[19] Bush, 2012. 397.
[20] Powell, Colin L. *My American Journey.* New York: Balentine Books, 1996. 559.
[21] Bush, 2012. 403.
[22] Powell. 553.

position of White House Chief of Staff and senior counsel to the president.[23] Somalia became a key part of the electoral debate, with candidate William Jefferson Clinton accusing Bush of a major foreign policy failure for choosing not to intervene in either Bosnia or Somalia.[24]

One result of the attempt to overcome the recession was a planned reduction in the expenditures across the foreign policy apparatus. On one hand, the Department of State had cut back its funding and staffing of embassies.[25] The Chairman of the Joints Chiefs of Staff Colin Powell reported that, in 1992, the Department of Defense was in the process of a Post-Cold War draw down of 25% of its manpower.[26] At the same time, it was deeply involved in military assistance to the Iraqi Kurds, who were in the process of fighting off efforts by the Saddam Hussein regime to conquer their homeland. Indeed, in spite of its defeat and humiliation in the 1991 Persian Gulf War, Iraq remained a high priority for the administration, and another potential distraction from events in Somalia. In an era in which budgets still mattered, the Pentagon, which had already seen a billion dollars siphoned off to Post Gulf War Operations in support to the Iraqi Kurds, was leary of further potentially open ended and costly commitments. Whenever Robert Wolthuis, Deputy Assistant Secretary of Defense for Global Affairs, brought the money point up in interagency planning meetings, he was countered by Cohen, who continually reminded the group that Somalis were dying while they deliberated.[27]

The Bush Team in Its Second Half, Leadership, Processes, and Strong Voices

In *Presidential Command*, Peter Rodman gives us a snapshot of an administration that was the closest thing to a finely oiled policy making machine as

---

[23] Bush, 2012. 409.
[24] Krieg, Andreas. *Motivations for Humanitarian Intervention: Theoretical and Empirical Considerations*. Berlin: Springer Science and Business Media, September 3, 2012. 76.
[25] Lofland, Valerie J. *Somalia: U.S. Intervention and Operation Restore Hope*. Newport: The United States Naval War College, 2012. 55.
[26] Powell. 548.
[27] Poole. 9.

any in U.S. history. He describes the Bush leadership team as "the most collegial and smoothest run" of the administrations he reviewed in his study.[28] The key leaders in the administration had worked with one another before, and in varying hierarchical situations. For example, Colin Powell was National Security Advisor while Bush was Vice President, and Bush had been Director of Central Intelligence when Richard Cheney was White House Chief of Staff. According to Steve Yetiv, who covered the same team and their decision making process for the First Gulf War, George H.W. Bush was one of the most knowledgeable and prepared foreign policy presidents in the history of the Republic,[29] noting that he was often better informed and educated on key issues than his cabinet subordinates.[30] On the other hand, while this was invaluable in the case of the Gulf War, it must be noted that none of the senior members of the administration were Africa hands, and by natural processes this tended to push African issues down in level of apparent importance. Bush himself cites his military service as something which helped to inform his decision making, and this is significant considering that he is the last U.S. President to have served in combat.[31] Bush's leadership team were nearly all supportive of him first and their bureaucratic identities second. The sense of camaraderie and common purpose among the Bush team were so strong that confrontations between them were inevitably the result of poor information sharing on decisions rather than on purposeful deception or disagreement.[32]

Brent Scowcroft, Bush's National Security Advisor, came to embody the position, having held it before during the Ford Presidency. He is described as being wholly the president's man, but he was also an innovator, establishing the NSC Principals Committee, which regularly consisted of the full NSC without the

---

[28] Rodman, Peter. *Presidential Command: Power, Leadership, and the Making of Foreign Policy from Nixon to George W. Bush*. New York: Alfred A Knopf, 2009. 180.
[29] Yetiv, Steve. *Explaining Foreign Policy: U.S. Decision Making and the Gulf War. 1 ed.* Baltimore: Johns Hopkins University Press, 2004. 9.
[30] Rodman. 180.
[31] Bush, 2012. 441.
[32] Rodman. 181.

president.[33] Such a gathering of senior leaders allowed for stronger, more final results than the already existing Deputies Committee. Scowcroft also brought the intellectual strength and organizational prowess to successfully help Bush to coordinate the activities of his two principal subordinates, Defense Secretary Cheney and Secretary of State James Baker, both of whom were powerful personalities, but also known for their absolute loyalty to the president. Cheney, in particular, is described by Rodman as being "The classic example of a cabinet secretary acting as the president's man at the head of his department, imposing the president's agenda, not as the spokesman to the president of his department's institutional agenda."[34] Secretary Baker is seen in a similar light in terms of his loyalty to the president. Although by the time of the events in question, Baker had left the Department of State, his temporary successor, Lawrence Eagleburger, continued in a similar vein to his predecessor.

Jon Western, in "Sources of Humanitarian Intervention: Beliefs, Information, and Advocacy in the U.S. Decisions on Somalia and Bosnia," describes the main group of decision makers in the Bush Administration as "selective engagers" who were able to build a frame of the situation in Somalia as being based on such deep seeded historical enmities that the U.S. intervention would be ineffective and dangerous.[35] Because of their paramount positions in the administration, this group had superior access to information and influence to get their point of view across, and this explains why they were able to delay their selection of option to intervene. In this analysis, one reason for the resistance to intervention by the administration was that, with the end of the Cold War, the Horn of Africa, which had been a significant flashpoint in the struggle between east and west, had significantly diminished in importance generally and as a threat to U.S.

---

[33] Rodman. 183.
[34] Ibid. 185.
[35] Western, Jon. "Sources of Humanitarian Intervention: Beliefs, Information, and Advocacy in the U.S. Decisions on Somalia and Bosnia." *International Security*, Spring 2002, Vol. 26, No 4, 112-142. 117.

national security specifically.[36] The opposing group, which eventually won out and drove through the implementation of intervention, are termed "Liberal Humanitarians," and include some in government but primarily the consist of non-governmental organizations focused on human rights and food issues. This argument concludes that it was collusion with the media that allowed the liberal humanitarians to win out and secure intervention on humanitarian lines.[37]

Key to any intervention would be the Department of Defense (DOD). Following the end of the Cold War, the department was operating under the so called Powell Doctrine, which was adopted from a similar Reagan era policy championed by then Secretary of State Caspar Weinberger. Under this doctrine, the U.S. would only intervene militarily in situations in which it could quickly commit overwhelming force on a rapid timetable for mission completion and success. Leaping into civil wars, or seemingly unending commitments, was anathema to the spirit of the doctrine, and it was adhered to adamantly by DOD officials until the remarkable turnaround of November 1992.[38] Even with the change in DOD opinion, the influence of the Powell Doctrine is still clearly visible in the form in which the decision to intervene was made, and its mandate that the mission was only one of providing food aid in Somalia rather than acknowledging the political nature of the disaster, and also in the initial proposal that the intervention last no longer than Inauguration Day, January 20, 1993.[39]

The end of the Cold War was also forcing a review of structures, organizations, and outlook in the Department, under the leadership of Richard Cheney, as Secretary, and Colin Powell, the Chairman of the Joint Chiefs of Staff. There was a sense that the U.S. should not "go it alone" in countering threats, but should do so as the leader of a coalition of friends and allies. The Defense Planning Guidance for 1992 emphasized that the U.S. must be willing to continue to provide

---

[36] Western. 118.
[37] Ibid. 117.
[38] Powell. 557.
[39] Poole, Walter S. *The Effort to Save Somalia.* Washington D.C.: Joint History Office, Office of the Chairman of the Joint Chiefs of Staff, 2005. 2.

the decisive leadership for such coalitions and missions.[40] This would be borne out when President Bush decided to intervene in Somalia with a military force.

Who Is Behind the Wheel? Drivers for Intervention

In the early days of the crisis in Somalia, leadership from within the Bush administration was primarily provided by a group of junior level leaders, primarily in the Department of State. Herman Cohen states that this was because of an ongoing budget crisis and a feeling of conflict fatigue, with over a dozen U.S. commitments around the world since the end of the Cold War.[41] In spite of this, Congress, became the strongest and most consistent supporter of relief aid, and, later, intervention in the struggling country.[42] Although the final decision for U.S. intervention was made relatively quickly, the groundwork for the ultimate decision stretched out over the whole of 1992. In January, the UN passed Security Council Resolution 733, which provided for armed intervention, imposed an arms embargo on the country, called for a cease-fire, and mandated the deployment of unarmed cease fire monitors. Ironically, as it would turn out, the resolution passed in this form in spite of efforts by the U.S. delegation to the UN to weaken its provisions.[43] The U.S. would continue to classify the crisis in Somalia as a food issue through the decision making process and well into the intervention, which had the benefit of securing support across the interagency community, but would have significant consequences when the intervention was well underway.[44] Indeed, it was only the insistence on starvation rather than politics as the central issue in Somalia that eventually made military intervention possible, since the DOD would never have

---

[40] Cheney, Richard. *In My Time: A Personal and Political Memoir*. New York: Simon and Schuster, 2011. 236.
[41] Cohen. 207.
[42] Clarke, Walter and Herbst, Jeffrey. *Learning from Somali*a. Boulder, Colorado: Westview Press, 1997. 191.
[43] Natsios. 1. This was because the U.S. was concerned about payments for UN peacekeeping operations, of which there were already 12 at the time.
[44] Interview with Ambassador Herman Cohen, May 12, 2004, in Rutherford. 22.

agreed to intervene, nor would the president have directed them to, had Somali politics have seemed to be paramount.[45]

Meanwhile, the Department of State, and particularly the Africa Bureau under Cohen, began a push to raise awareness of the Somalia issue in the government, with an opening step being to steadily increase the number of meetings on the Somalia issue.[46] This desire for greater attention was echoed by other key players on the international aid and development scene at the Assistant Secretary level, most notably Andrew Natsios of the Bureau for Food and Humanitarian Assistance (OFDA), and later the director of the U.S. Agency for International Development (USAID). In a congressional hearing in January, 1992, Natsios called the crisis in Somalia the "Worst in the world, with up to 90% of children under age five were malnourished."[47]

In terms of international pressure to act, the primary motivator for overall action was UN Secretary General Boutros Boutros-Gali, who as an Egyptian saw the crisis in Somalia as a personal issue and one which he would expend much capital to have solved. Boutros-Gali was closely associated with several of the key players mentioned above, such as Cohen, and Undersecretary of State for International Security Affairs Frank Wisner.[48] In addition to the personal nature of the conflict for the UN Secretary General, he also suffered from a case of UN triumphalism. Boutros-Gali believed that the post-Cold War world was the time of the UN, which he called "the central instrument for the prevention and resolution of conflicts and the preservation of peace."[49] Further, he expected the membership of the UN, more specifically the members of the Security Council, and very specifically the US and the other Cold War winners to bear more burdens in support

---

[45] Talentino. 113.
[46] Cohen. 205.
[47] U.S. House of Representatives Select Committee on Hunger. "Humanitarian Tragedy in Somalia: Hearing Before the Select Committee on Hunger." 102nd Cong., 2d Sess, report serial No. 102-120, 30 January, 1992. 5. Testimony by Andrew Natsios.
[48] Interview with Ambassador Herman Cohen, in Rutherford. 22.
[49] Boutros-Gali, Boutros. *Agenda for Peace.* New York, United Nations, June 1992. http://www.cfr.org/peacekeeping/report-un-secretary-general-agenda-peace/p23439. Accessed on October 10, 2014.

of the UN, famously calling out the west for its willingness to engage what he called a "rich man's war" in European Bosnia while ignoring the plight of Africans, and in particular Somalis.[50]

It is worth noting that all voices in the Department of State were not unanimous as to the sources and primary nature of the problem in Somalia. While the Africa Bureau, with the backing of USAID, consistently pointed to the food crisis as the paramount issue in the country, the Bureau of International Organization Affairs, led by John Bolton, continued to insist that the primary problem was the political infighting in the country and its impact on the security situation.[51] At the time of the intervention, significant media sources seemed to side with the position of Bolton, with the New York Times in particular emphasizing the need to disarm the Somali warlords as part of the intervention.[52] The most significant resistance to a focus on Africa came, however, not at the deputy level, but at the top, where Secretary Baker was little focused on the issue, but increasingly dominated by the presidential campaign which he left to join in August 1992.

The U.S. Congress, and in particular the Congressional Black Caucus and key Senate leaders such as Nancy Kassebaum and Paul Simon, were central in pushing, in an increasingly louder tone, for increased U.S. action in Somalia. According to the Congressional Record, there were 162 events in with Somalia mentioned, covering both the Senate and House of Representatives, during the 102nd Congress. To demonstrate the increase in importance of the issue, 44 of those events took place over all of 1991. 118 occurred in 1992, and 86 of those are from June onwards.[53] In June, 1992, for example, a note to Bush signed by 88 House

---

[50] Boutros-Gali, Boutros. "Remarks in the UN Security Council, July 23, 1992." *Facts on File*, Vol. 52, No. 2700. 623.
[51] Cohen. 207.
[52] Bonner, Kaymond. "Buy up the Somali's Guns." *New York Times*, December 2, 1992. http://www.nytimes.com/1992/12/02/opinion/buy-up-the-somalis-guns.html. Accessed on August 20, 2014.
[53] Congressional Research Service. "Congressional Record of the 102nd Congress." http://thomas.loc.gov/cgi-bin/thomas2. Accessed on 9 October, 2014.

members implored the president to increase Somalia to the highest priority for U.S. attention and action, calling the situation "an unprecedented humanitarian disaster."[54] They find no evidence that any media report induced the administration to launch the airlift, rather that the airlift announcement incited the uptick in coverage.[55] Acting Secretary of State Eagleburger stated that it was congressional pressure, rather than the media, which generated support for the airlift. His term for what did work was "...intense pressure from key members of congress." In his estimation Senator Kassebaum's visit in July was the turning point, and was undertaken specifically to engender media pressure.[56] On July 22, her trip report appeared in an ABC Evening News story which directly prompted President Bush to meet with Secretaries Cheney and Baker to discuss and commence the airlift.[57]

In response, the Senate went directly to the source of U.S. relief operations, requesting that USAID immediately step up its support for relief efforts, including further mobilization of the Office of Foreign Disaster Assistance (OFDA).[58] OFDA Administrator James Kunder notably echoed Andrew Natsios' statements on the dire situation in Somalia.[59] A series of seven hearings began in the spring in several House committees right up through the decision to intervene, with queries and requests for action sent from the Congress to all of the U.S. players, Secretary General Boutros-Gali, relevant international organizations, and even several of the Somali faction leaders to raise awareness, garner support, and urge action.[60]

This is not to say that the voice of Congress was unanimous, as significant resistance existed, based on several factors. The major cause of complaint was the perceived price of the operation.[61] Another was a reluctance to have the UN take

---

[54] Office of U.S. Foreign Disaster Assistance. "Situation Report No. 10, 'Somalia-Civil Strife'" 23 June 1992. 3.
[55] Livingston, Stephen and Eachus, Todd. "Humanitarian Crisis and U.S. Foreign Policy: Somalia and the CNN Effect Reconsidered." *Political Communication* 12, 1995: 413-429. 425.
[56] Interview with Secretary Eagleburger on May 12, 1995, Livingston and Eachus. 425.
[57] Livingston and Eachus. 426.
[58] Rutherford. 39.
[59] Livingston and Eachus. 424.
[60] Clarke and Herbst. 6.
[61] Oakley and Hirsch. 37. At this time the U.S. already owed the Security Council over a $100 million for the support of peacekeeping operations.

charge of such a massive, but delicate issue as the resupply effort. Some democrats resisted on the principal that the whole problem in Somalia could be traced back to republican led actions in the Reagan administration in support of the Barre regime, although this was refuted by the administration.[62]

By July, 1992, pressure from all of the aforementioned sources increased to the point that the White House began actively pressuring the Department of State to develop an array of policy responses for Somalia, under the leadership of Herman Cohen and the Department's Africa Bureau. President Bush, although beginning to feel some pressure to act, did so at this time only on the pretext of developing ways to better assist the UN mission.[63] As a result of these pressures to intervene somewhere in the world, which openly manifested themselves at the 1992 Republican National Convention, President Bush announced on August 14th one week before the start of the convention, that the U.S. would commence the transport of relief supplies to Somalia.[64] The airlift was undertaken with the support of Kenya, but America's traditional allies in Europe remained focused on events in Russia during 1992.[65] Notably, this was the last major administration decision on Somalia before the November elections. This decision was undertaken so quickly that the Kenyan government was not notified beforehand, which was significant since the neighboring country would necessarily be a location from which relief efforts would be launched.[66] The airlift was, in hindsight, the fundamental policy shift that set the administration on the road to full intervention, and yet it was not decisive, since the main player in any intervention, the DOD, was still not

---

[62] Oakley and Hirsch. 37. The source of this complaint was Democrat Howard Wolpe of Michigan.

[63] Brent Scowcroft, as interviewed by Western. 125. Western quotes Scowcroft on the mechanism for this decision, also noting that it was the Hempstone cable from Kenya, and it's posting in the Washington Post, which inspired the response.

[64] Fitzwater, Marlon. "Statement by Press Secretary Fitzwater on Additional Humanitarian Aid for Somalia." Washington, D.C. August 14, 1992. http://bushlibrary.tamu.edu/research/public_papers.php?id=4676&year=1992&month=8

[65] Lofland. 58.

[66] Hempstone, Smith. *Rogue Ambassador: An African Memoir*. Sewanee, TN: University of the South Press, 1997. 21.

compelled to cooperate beyond the airlifts, in spite of Department of State proposals that troops also be used to guard the supply distribution centers.

While the airlift did succeed in significantly increasing the amount of food on hand in the crisis areas, the fact that the aerial ports of debarkation were not secured meant that the local militants were able to seize a growing amount of relief aid for themselves, with OFDA claiming that the amount of aid actually reaching Somalis fell by nearly half during this period due to corruption and violence.[67] Furthermore, with the onset of the 1992 election, interest in Somalia by the senior leaders of the Bush administration was at a low ebb. However, interest was maintained, and increased, through some portentous moves the secondary level of decision making, such as the appointment of Frank Wisner, a known advocate for African Affairs, as undersecretary of State for International Security Affairs, with a specific brief to develop strategies for Somali relief.[68] Wisner and the NSC Deputies Committee, with Walter Kansteiner serving as Scowfcroft's eyes and ears there, would have to struggle between the competing distractions of the political campaign, Bosnia, and other, seemingly more threatening and promising events in Africa, such as the planning for free elections in South Africa as well as the increasingly violent civil wars in Mozambique and Angola.[69] With all of this in mind, the Deputies Committee, through September and October, came to the conclusion that the airlift should be ended by December, and that a brigade sized force of approximately 3,000 personnel would be needed to secure the supply areas from corruption and pillage. They strongly encouraged greater UN involvement both in the supply and security operations, and offered to transport the multi-battalion UN force which was promised for Somalia on 4 November.[70]

---

[67] OFDA Situation reports numbers 13, 14, and 18, covering September 16, October 1, and November 6, 1992. In Oakley and Hirsch. 25.
[68] Ibid. 41.
[69] Interview with Walter Kansteiner, National Security Council Africa Desk Officer, March 29, 1999. Western. 134.
[70] Poole. 12-13.

President Bush began to get personally and deeply involved in the Somalia issue in July, 1992, in response to pressure from Congress and media reports on the situation in the country, and with Somalia already emerging as a campaign issue. He provided direct comment as well as a series of personal follow up questions to a report based on OFDA Director James Kunder's visit to Somalia on 2 August and a report from the U.S. Ambassador to Kenya, Smith Hemptsone, which provided a description of how the unrest in Somalia was bleeding across their shared border.[71] His "A Day in Hell" cable was so powerful and moving that Brent Scowcroft ensured that it was seen by the president.[72] Bush was described as acting with a "burst of energy" by Herman Cohen in his memoirs on his time working with Africa issues.[73] This increased interest culminated in a move by the administration to encourage the UN to markedly increase the number of peacekeepers allocated to Somalia by 3500, up from the 500 currently allowed.

From August onwards, the administration's focus was dominated by the 1992 presidential electoral campaign, which the Bush administration lost by the largest margin of an incumbent president since 1912.[74] The campaign saw the challenger, William Clinton, repeatedly accuse the administration of complacency for its failure to act in either Bosnia or Somalia.[75] While Bush continued to show interest in the Somalia crisis, it was not until after the election that his interest returned and indeed peaked, and within days after the polling ended Bush increased the frequency and intensity of his questioning and directed his staff to come up with viable options to ease the suffering.[76] This level of planning for action would primarily take place at the Pentagon, which, for reasons of bureaucratic structure, was pushed down to a secondary level (being handled at first by SOLIC, the Special

[71] Kunder, James. "Testimony before the U.S. Senate Committee on Foreign Relations Subcommittee on African Affairs." September 16, 1992.
[72] Livingston and Eachus. 425.
[73] Cohen. 208.
[74] Greenstein, Fred I. *The Presidential Difference: Leadership Style from FDR to Barack Obama, 3rd ed.* Princeton: Princeton University Press, 2009. 169.
[75] Oakley and Hirsch. 35.
[76] Interview with Richard Clarke, NSC head of international programs on July 16, 1994, in Rutherford. 66.

Operations and Low Intensity Conflict directorate), which recommended that any action be done as part of the UN mandate and not as a unilateral U.S. action.[77] This recommendation, in modified form, influenced the decision to couch the U.S. intervention strictly in terms of the UN mandate. However, reporting from the CIA warned that a UN only approach was not feasible due to the high vulnerability of lightly armed UN forces to lethal attack from the forces of the warlords.[78] This meant that better armed U.S. forces would be required at some point.

Public Opinion and the Somalia Intervention

Direct comparisons were made between the unfolding humanitarian disaster in Somalia and the other major concurrent international issue, the devolution of Yugoslavia, and in particular the privations in Bosnia-Herzegovina.[79] It must be kept in mind that the Somalia intervention, unlike the other case studies, took place without significant coverage by public opinion surveys and polling, particularly during the initial decision to intervene, although that would change near the end of the operation.[80] Television coverage of the conflict in Somalia was non-existent into the first quarter of 1992, while newspaper coverage among the major papers was also extremely limited.[81] Media interest in Somalia remained slight until mid-summer, when it increased in intensity and frequency of coverage. From June 1992 on, however, print coverage steadily rose, and by August, over 100 articles per month were appearing, along with twenty to twenty five television news pieces.[82]

---

[77] Coll, Alberto R. *The Problems of Doing Good: Somalia as a Case Study in Humanitarian Intervention.* Washington, D.C.: Pew Case Studies in International Affairs, Institute for Study of Diplomacy Publications, Georgetown University, 1997. 4.
[78] Lofland. 59.
[79] Robert Gallucci, Assistant Secretary of State for Political Military Affairs, said that "The memo said: Somalia – Low Risk, High Payoff, Bosnia – High Payoff, in an interview with Rothkopf, David. *Running the World: The inside Story of the National Security Council and the Architects of American.* New York: Perseus Group, 2005.
[80] Klarevas, Louis J. "The Polls-Trends: The United States Peace Operation in Somalia." *Public Opinion Quarterly* Volume 64, 2000: 523-540. 524.
[81] Livingston and Eachus. 419.
[82] Ibid.

Louis Klarevas notes that the decision by Bush to start the airlift raised public attention somewhat during the fall, but also said that news coverage peaked only twice, once in December, 1992, when the intervention began, and once near its end after the Battle of Mogadishu in October, 1993.[83] This polling data puts further lie to the idea that the media created the main pressure for the intervention, in spite of the statements of some analysts, such as George Kennan, to the contrary.[84] After the election in November, 1992, and Bush's defeat, the drumbeat for intervention focused on the need to act before the inauguration of Bill Clinton as President in January.[85] Was there an effort by the administration to build a frame for the public in support of intervention? One would expect there to be, particularly since, as stated by Martin Linsky and Jonathan Moore, government leaders consider the media to be central in both policy implementation and agenda stetting with the public.[86] The media therefore inform an audience which cannot possibly be fully informed on all issues, and policy makers must take account of the opinions of the audience and the various tools for reaching those audiences.[87]

Based on the records of media coverage on Somalia and the key media pieces mentioned in this case study, it does appear that the U.S Government was able to successfully dominate the discourse on its intervention in Somalia, particularly when broadcast news is considered, at the outset of the crisis, although there is no evidence that it purposefully did so. The true deluge of broadcast news stories about the events in Somalia followed, rather than led, significant government decisions. This was not the case with print media, however. In the

[83] Klarevas. 524-525. Limited polling performed in September, 1992, revealed that only 11% of the polled audience followed Somalia closely, and a combined 35% showed any interest at all in the crisis. Kiarevas 529. Livingston noted that these numbers steadily increased through the fall, but did not exponentially rise until after the announcement of intervention after Thanksgiving, 1992. Livingston and Eachus. 420-422.

[84] Livingston and Eachus. 413. Kennan (1993, September 30) is quoted as saying that there is no doubt that the media and images of suffering were the primary motivators.

[85] Bell, Peter. "The Tragedy in Somalia can't wait for Clinton." *The New York Times*, November 5, 1992. A note from the chairman of CARE, posted in the New York Times, noted that waiting until January might cost the lives of 100,000 Somalis.

[86] Linsky, Martin, Moore, Jonathan, O'Donnell, Wendy, and Whiteman, David. *Impact, How the Press Affects Federal Policy Making.* New York, W.W. Norton, 1986. 7.

[87] Ibid. 11.

case of Somalia, in many instances the media relied on government for key information based on initial ignorance of the press corps, and the public writ large, on the region and the issues.[88] A lack of diplomatic representation in the country helped to keep background interest low, since journalists relied on such sources for access and information.[89] However, as public attention to the crisis grew, the lawlessness which was at the core of the problem in Somalia made basic access to the country by third parties, such as the media and humanitarian aid agencies significantly easier than was the case in besieged Bosnia. This meant that it was possible for these agents to report more directly on issues in Somalia, and to, especially in the case of the aid agencies, eventually become agents of change in their own right.[90]

Models and the Somalia Decision Process

Writing about the Persian Gulf War, Yetiv notes that the Rational Actor Model could not adequately explain some things, such as how President Bush would, on certain issues, act out seemingly impetuously in response to actions by Saddam Hussein.[91] It appears that Bush's decision to intervene in Somalia, and the Pentagon's switch from refusal to acceptance of the mission, should be seen in this light as well. Indeed, if one takes the position, as Bush and DOD did through November 1992, that armed intervention in Somalia (or, for that matter, Bosnia) was an irrational act, then further evidence, both of Bush's centrality to the decision making process, and the non-rationality of the decision to intervene, is the result.[92] From a perspective of national security, the decision is not rational, since the events in Somalia, as they were known at the time, did not impact the vital security of the

[88] Livingston and Eachus. 415.
[89] Ibid. 417.
[90] Western. 124.
[91] Yetiv. 8.
[92] Ibid. 9.

U.S.[93] It is the impact of personal politics that makes Bush's actions rational. The airlift decision, when placed in the context of the political campaign, and falling as it did immediately before the Republican convention, is rational in that light. The final intervention decision, taken by a defeated president choosing to take on an operation that seemed achievable (Somalia) versus one that did not (Bosnia) is also a rational decision. DOD's seeming flip flop in support for the operation was a result of the power of the president, and the congenial relations between the senior Bush leaders described above. Powell knew his boss well, and reacted to his desires as a good subordinate does. Once divining the commander in chief's intent, the Joint Staff then offered a series of approaches, from minimalist to maximum effort, and it was the maximal option that President Bush chose, while also agreeing to Powell's suggestion that former Ambassador to Somalia Robert Oakley be recalled to lead the diplomatic side of the operation.[94]

Furthermore, the Governmental Politics Model appears to be in operation throughout the Somalia decision making process. As could be expected, the DOD officials took a similar, common stance on intervention, as detailed in the description of the Powell Doctrine, which Somalia most definitely did not fit. This view changed as the key defense leader in the case, Colin Powell, began both to believe the mission was achievable, and that there was solid political benefit in doing so.[95] The National Security Advisor adhered to the desires of his boss, the president. OFDA and USAID favored intervention, as one would expect given the institutional mandates of their organizations to provide aid and humanitarian assistance to those in need, regardless of danger. The Department of State response was subdivided by relevant section, with those leaders and offices directly involved in Africa in favor of intervention, and some of those with other or wider foci against, which does affirm the GPM in which what leaders say and do depends upon which agency they come from more than any other factor.

---

[93] Cohen. 201.
[94] Poole. 20.
[95] Lofland. 59. Powell had visited Somalia in October, and this may have also impacted his thinking, although he himself does not comment on this in his memoirs.

In terms of the question of government framing of the crisis, during the summer debates and leading into the fall, there is limited evidence that either pro or con intervention forces attempted to use the media to frame the debate.[96] There were some exceptions, including Natsios, who did turn to the media in an effort to secure funding and support for interventions. This, of course, does not apply to outside of government figures. Secretary General Boutros-Gali and representatives from numerous humanitarian aid organizations turned to the media, particularly the editorial pages of the major papers, in an attempt to influence the debate.[97] By fall. 1992, Boutros-Gali was pushing for a U.S. or international intervention under the auspices of Article VII of the UN Charter.[98] Natsios openly believed that government framing was needed in order to secure intervention and he actively courted the media, being quoted over 50 times over the course of 1992.[99] Up until the switch by DOD, then the GPM seems to hold, but then it fails to provide a satisfactory result, such result which can only be applied by examining the role of the powerful actor to sway decision making and opinion. In this case, it happened that the powerful actor also happened to be the most powerful actor, President Bush.

From the time of the airlift decision in August, 1992, the Bush administration, with increasing pressure from within, in the form of continued and increased meetings and statements from Department of State and USAID leaders, and from outside, in the form of Congressional and UN statements, began to push for more international support for a larger intervention. Both relief agencies and foreign governments asked for U.S. support to move supplies and peacekeepers in in accordance with UNSC 767, while the U.S. sought the assistance and involvement of other major powers, particularly the UK and France. 45,000 metric tons of relief supplies were delivered over the course of the airlift, but the reports

---

96 Livingston and Eachus. 422.
97 Ibid. 422.
98 Cohen. 210.
99 Livingston and Eachus. 424.

from the media, NGOs, and fact finding missions continued to paint a bleak and monetarily costly picture of Somalia.[100]

Meanwhile, the U.S. media, which had been remarkably quiet on the Somalia issue, began to make itself heard, particularly with a New York Times piece on July 31 which detailed the failure of the UN to adequately deal with the food crisis.[101] Other New York Times pieces that week specifically called out the administration and began to demand action. Media interest and pressure dovetailed with increasing demands from NGO's for assistance with the mission.[102]

Decision making for intervention now fell to a traditional interagency process, chaired by the National Security Council, with a Deputies Committee chaired by Admiral Jonathan Howe in his role as Deputy National Security Advisor. In the meetings which followed, each deputy brought his own department's plans and options to the table, in accordance with Allison's models. In this case, however, Howe was able to override departmental prerogatives and develop a unified strategy.[103] This was, in part, because of a turnaround in the position of the Department of Defense on the intervention, especially given that the conditions that General Powell and the Department of Defense laid down as essential for a successful intervention, namely that the mission be well defined, were no closer to being met than they had been throughout 1992. A formal working group on Somalia was established under Ambassador Brandon Grove, which came to the

---

[100] Sommer. 22-23.
[101] Rutherford. 45. The article, from the New York Times, was entitled "U.S. Says Airlifts Fail Somali Needy…". Up to that time, the author notes that the major television networks only mentioned Somalia 15 times in the first half of 2014, and most of those mentions were brief. That would change in the second half of the year.
[102] Rutherford. 67.
[103] Clarke, Walter and Herbst, Jeffrey, Somalia and the Future of Humanitarian Intervention. Foreign Affairs, March/April 1996. http://www.foreignaffairs.com/articles/51844/walter-clarke-and-jeffrey-herbst. 73. Members of the Committee included: Howe as Deputy National Security Advisor, Wisner and Cohen for the DOD. The Department of Defense sent Admiral David Jeremiah, Vice Chairman of the Joint Chiefs of Staff. The Office of Foreign Disaster Assistance sent its director and senior staff.

rapid conclusion that a forceful, armed intervention would be required in order to provide the relief that Somalia needed.[104]

Building on what it claimed were its keys to victory in the Persian Gulf War, meaning a tightly defined mission, with a solid timeline for implementation, the Department of Defense resisted efforts to push for an armed humanitarian intervention in Somalia on the grounds that the mission was ill defined and had no definite timeline. The main point of the argument was that the issue in Somalia was a lack of a solid political basis for decision making or consensus building. By definition, this would create a situation where, if U.S. troops did intervene, one side or the other of the political continuum would resist, forcing the Coalition to choose sides in a mission that was supposed to be about feeding people.[105] This combined with difficult terrain features (interesting for an armed force that had, a year prior, successfully completed full combat operations in far worse terrain in Saudi Arabia, Kuwait, and Iraq) and a perception that it would be very difficult to distinguish friend from foe in an environment where the combatants did not wear uniforms. The DOD remained the main hold out against intervention, not wanting to have to "fix the civil war," as its senior leaders believed they were being told to do by the NSC.[106] As late at the 20th of November, the Deputies meeting on Somalia paid lip service to intervention while focusing on providing monetary and logistical support, but not military assistance, to the small cadre of UN peacekeepers on the ground in the country.[107]

The deputies meeting on 21 November, 1992 became pivotal for the decision making process. Admiral Jeremiah, speaking for his lead, Chairman of the Joint Chiefs of Staff Colin Powell, switched the Pentagon's former position, stating that his department was capable of accomplishing the food aid and relief

---

[104] Natsios, Andrew. "Humanitarian Relief in Somalia: The Economics of Chaos." In Clarke and Herbst, 1997. 78. Natsios was present when Bush related this information.
[105] Interview with Kansteiner, 1999. Western. 116.
[106] Oakley and Hirsch. 37.
[107] Interview with Herman Cohen, March 30, 1999. Western. 136.

mission if so requested.[108] The caveats were that there be no mission creep beyond the food operation and that the operation be short in duration, given the doctrinal mission of the forces to be used (The Marines).[109] Furthermore, Powell sought to explicitly opt out of a Bosnia intervention in return for acceding to the Somalia intervention.[110] At this time, three use of force options were provided by the Pentagon, with each recommending a greater military footprint. With this advice given, President Bush decided to act two days later, and to select the option that utilized the strongest military force recommended.[111]

The DOD switch had come after the election, when, concurrent with a return of focus by President Bush, Scowcroft, Cheney, and Powell began discussions to reverse the DOD policy, in coordination with General Hoar, at that time Commanding the relevant regional combatant command, US Central Command.[112] CENTCOM, as part of its doctrinal planning process, had already developed some plans for interventions in the Horn of Africa region, and had gone so far as to designate the First Marine Expeditionary Force (I MEF) based in Camp Pendleton, California, as the primary unit for potential armed humanitarian interventions.[113]

Given that Bush is reported to have made his decision to intervene after a briefing of under an hour on 23 November, 1992, the question of why the change of position must be asked. Several reasons reveal themselves. While not a factor in his August decision to start the airlift, media pressure, in the form of television news footage of the victims of starvation in Somalia, is cited as a reason for Bush's November decision both by acting Secretary of State Eagleburger and by Colin

---

[108] Oakley and Hirsch. 43.
[109] Cohen. 211-212. Cohen remembers that the strongest choicer was selected because the intermediate option, a UN led operation, would have taken six months to implement.
[110] Strobel, Warren P. *Late Breaking Foreign Policy: The News Media's Influence on Peace Operations*. Washington D.C.: U.S. Institute of Peace, 1997. 139.
[111] Clarke and Herbst, 1996, 9.
[112] Oakley and Hirsch. 42. A note on Combatant Commands. At this time military oversight of U.S. affairs in Africa was divided, with Africa outside of the Horn of Africa falling under command of U.S. European Command, based in Germany, while the Horn of Africa, which included the countries relevant here, namely, Somalia and Kenya, fell under U.S. Central Command, which had a as its primary interest the Middle East.
[113] Ibid.

Powell.[114] Political pressure from Congress and from liberal activists in the lower tiers of the administration is one reason, along with pressure from the UN, the NGO community, and increasingly by the media.[115] Another is that the Bush administration, in seeking to establish its legacy in the aftermath of electoral defeat, wished to go out with a positive act on the world stage. Jon Western noted in an interview with National Security Advisor Scowcroft that Bush became more and more personally effected by the reporting coming from Somalia.[116] Beneath the façade of the Cold Warrior, Bush was actually predisposed to action by events in his vice presidency under Ronald Reagan. During the Sahel crisis of the early 1980s (made famous in part by the "We are the World" USA for Africa fundraising effort), Bush visited a CARE camp attempting to feed the dying, and he witnessed the suffering and death of victims in very similar circumstances to those reported to him from Somalia. In a more pragmatic vein, intervening in largely Muslim Somalia would allow him to reject pressure to do so in Muslim Bosnia coming from the Arab world, particularly Saudi Arabia. Similar pressure was exerted over the race of the victims in Somalia, allowing the administration to deflect cries of racism and differential treatment of white Europeans in Yugoslavia over black Africans. [117]

Another concern for Bush was that the incoming president would be little inclined to act with decisiveness abroad, so that getting the intervention going before he took office would lock him into continuing it. On one hand, this seems to be disputed by Bush's statement that the intervention would be wrapped up by inauguration day, and by the statement he made to Powell that "I don't want to stick Clinton with an ongoing military operation."[118] On the other hand, Powell, Scowcroft, and Cheney all replied that there was little chance that the intervention

---

[114] Powell. 564.
[115] Natsios. 44. The author reports that when Bush addressed the nation announcing the operation, he held in his hand "a letter signed by eleven U.S. based NGOs imploring him to act."
[116] Interview with Brent Scowcroft, April 29, 1999. Western. 136.
[117] Clarke, Richard, Director of the DOD Office of International Programs, interview with the authors. July 16, 1994. Clarke and Herbst, 1996. 78.
[118] Powell. 565.

could be wrapped up in such a short time, with Bush agreeing to the operation regardless.[119] With the decision to act somewhere in mind, there were two choices for action, Bosnia and Somalia. To paraphrase a statement by later Secretary of Defense Donald Rumsfeld, Bosnia was a "known known," and what was known was ugly. Bosnia was guaranteed to be a quagmire in terms of money, manpower, and national reputation. Somalia, although also known to have significant problems, seemed to be by far the easier of the two missions to accomplish militarily, while also getting the benefit of defusing the increasing calls from the UN and the media for intervention somewhere. Some in the DOD may have thought that intervention in Somalia would be cheaper, quicker, and less of a burden than a similar intervention in Bosnia.[120]

President Elect Clinton, whose own actions had helped to bring about his electoral victory and increased pressure on the administration to act, continued that pressure after the election, pushing for intervention in Bosnia but accepting of the Bush decision to do so in Somalia.[121] This is all the more interesting since it marked a sea change in how lame-duck presidents could be empowered to act.[122] In his own memoires, Clinton stated that he did not feel that he had been entrapped, that "Bush had been very helpful," and that "I felt that he wanted me to succeed as president."[123] Given that Bush's failure to act in Somalia or Bosnia was a key facet of Clinton's campaign against him, he could hardly have said otherwise when Bush did act.

On December 3rd, 1992, The UN Security Council enacted resolution 794, which laid the framework for the establishment of a multinational relief force under U.S. direction. The following day, President Bush congratulated Boutros Gali on

---

[119] Powell. 565.
[120] Talentino, 115.
[121] Western. 136. Western notes that the Joint Chiefs very much wanted to avoid intervention in Bosnia, and that Powell's reversal came after a transition meeting with Clinton, and in part was the Pentagon opting for what it thought was the lesser of two evils.
[122] Western. 135. Customarily, significant Presidential Activity ceased between the election and the innaguration of the incoming Chief Executive.
[123] Clinton, William J. *My Life*. New York: Knopf, 2004. 484.

the resolution, pledged his support, and reiterated the humanitarian nature and expected short duration of the proposed U.S. intervention.[124] Operation Restore Hope (The U.S. aspect of UNITAS) was also announced on December 4th 1992, and on December 9th, U.S. Navy Seals and Marines landed on the beaches south of Mogadishu, to a media circus, and UNITAF, the United Task Force implementing the operation began.[125] As mandated by UNSCR 794, U.S. forces assumed command of the operation, and provided 25,000 out of 37,000 personnel. In accordance with Bush's planning guidance that the operation be a coalition, 28 partner nations contributed to the effort. Within days of the launch of the operation, Pentagon leaders were already mandating the seizure of weapons and disarming of combatants.[126]

By March, 1993, UNITAF was converted into UNISOM II, ending the period of the case study. Viewed purely in terms of UNITAF's mandate to alleviate starvation in Somalia, the operation was a success, with approximately 100,000 lives saved by all means deployed. But the fundamental issue of a political settlement to underwrite the aid was never adequately addressed. In another example in which the failure to plan for a long term operation manifested itself, eight to ten reserve civil affairs units were to have been deployed, but were cancelled because the operation was supposed to only last six weeks.[127] Similarly, since food was the focus, there was no clear vision of how reconciliation should proceed.[128] However, the lack of a peaceful resolution to the conflict led President Clinton to accept the transition to UNOSOM II, the force which ultimately met its demise following the events portrayed in "Blackhawk Down," in which eighteen U.S. service personnel were killed a running battle with Aidid henchmen, creating

---

[124] Bush, 2012. 416.
[125] The Pentagon encouraged this as a follow up to Powell's request to the White House to help build public support for the operation. Interview with Kansteiner, 1999. Western. 138.
[126] Sciolino, Elaine, "Mission to Somalia: The Big Job Ahead." *The New York Times*, December 4, 1992. A 23.
[127] Clarke and Herbst. 1996. 77.
[128] Ibid. 78.

a media circus as their bodies were seen to be drug through the streets of Mogadishu. U.S. forces were withdrawn soon afterwards.

Conclusion

> "The first step in planning for humanitarian peace-enforcement operations must be the articulation of an integrated humanitarian-political-military strategy that responds to the immediate humanitarian crisis while outlining a longer-term process designed to resolve the underlying political issues that may have brought on the crisis in the first place. These actions must be consistent with international values and standards of conduct."
>
> Walter Clarke and Jeffrey Herbst, 1997.[129]

This case study set out to examine the decision to intervene in Somalia, with several questions in mind. It laid out the timeline of the crisis, to include its causes as well as the key decision points, who made and influenced them, and how those decisions played out in the final act, the intervention of December 1992. Although there was significant action by lower level members of the decision making cycle, in the case of the Somalia intervention, none of them had the power to compel President Bush to act singularly. It is clear from the evidence presented, and from his known style of governing, that the decision to intervene came from the top, as only the president, at the top of the decision cycle, could have compelled a clearly unwilling Department of Defense to change its mind on intervention. Even Powell's apparent horse trade of Somali intervention with avoiding the same in Bosnia with President Elect Clinton came after the election, at a time when Bush was already seriously considering an expansion of the U.S. role in Somalia as it became clear that the airlift was not working as expected. We cannot, of course, know if his defeat impacted the decision making process, or if a victorious Bush would still have decided for intervention, however, based on statements by Powell and Eagleburger that it was pressure from the media and NGO's that prompted

---

[129] Clarke and Herbst. 1996. 4.

Bush, it is reasonable to believe that he would have acted in the same way even if he'd have won. If his reaction was purely to secure his legacy and to compel Clinton, then the operation might have been different in time and scale if Bush had won, but it would likely still have taken place. Further, if media and Congressional pressure were the key drivers, then a returning Bush may have not been able to resist the mission creep and change in focus that eventually doomed the operation.

In terms of framing, the evidence presented shows that the media largely followed the lead set by the government. While some of the key players used the media to facilitate their own efforts to force decisions on key issues, such as the airlift decision, there is no evidence that framing by the government was undertaken in a systematic way, or that such decisions were an implicit part of the decision making cycle for the decision to intervene in Somalia. In spite of the lack of a conscious decision to frame, decision makers did frame the media. This took place more because of the primacy of the government as an information holder and broker, and because of the unique nature, and high danger, of the situation on the ground, which put the government in the position of having a monopoly on the information needed by the media to go to press in an accurate fashion.

U.S. policy toward interventions changed as a result of the perception of failure of the Somalia intervention, with a significant reduction recommended for future interventions. [130] Had Bush been reelected, and been able to resist the pressure to change the initial mission, this might not have been the case. The first major intervention after the Cold War lead to significant questions on what armed humanitarian intervention meant, when they were appropriate, and what goals were appropriate for future efforts. Gone was the idea that a large military force, intervening in a sovereign nation, could do so in an apolitical fashion, without taking sides in the dispute at the heart of the crisis. [131] OFDA proposed that the U.S. aid community and the DOD develop an early warning system for humanitarian crisis which might allow for pre-emption, an early U.S. move toward

---

[130] Clarke and Herbst. 1996. 70.
[131] Ibid. 82.

what would later become the concept of Responsibility to Protect.[132] Even UN Secretary General Boutros-Gali, in his "Agenda for Peace", published in 1995, showed the negative impact of the failed mission in Somalia, with a dampened ardor for intervention. Congress too had its enthusiasm for intervention dampened significantly, with the total price in dollars, lives, and political capital lost proving to be more than could be borne.

All of these factors would have repercussions for future interventions, most particularly for the failure of the international community to react adequately to a crisis which was brewing south-west of Somalia, and which in fact came to prominence just days after the Mogadishu battle. The genocide in Rwanda, which began soon after the end of the Somalia mission, would redefine the terms of western armed humanitarian intervention and shape future discussions of state sovereignty, failed states, and human security.

[132] Sommer and Collins. 4.

CHAPTER IV – Clinton 1994: Rwanda and Its Impact on Humanitarian Intervention

> "It (The U.S.) led a successful effort to remove most of the UN peacekeepers who were already in Rwanda. It aggressively worked to block the subsequent authorization of UN reinforcements. And even as, on average, 8,000 Rwandans were being butchered each day, U.S. officials shunned the term "genocide," for fear of being obliged to act. The United States in fact did virtually nothing "to try to limit what occurred." Indeed, staying out of Rwanda was an explicit U.S. policy objective."
>
> Samantha Power, "Bystanders to Genocide (2001)."[1]

Somalia, and the failure there, as described in the previous case study, burned the Clinton administration badly. It was a foreign adventure that they had not chosen, but had warmly supported, and when the mission failed the White House quickly withdrew U.S. forces and sought to distance itself from the decision to intervene and from the principle of armed humanitarian intervention. But the world had not changed, and Yugoslavia, the mission that no one in the Bush administration wanted to tackle, still loomed ever larger in the international calculations. But before the Yugoslav crisis reached its crescendo, there was a terrible international crisis which changed the way interventions, national sovereignty, and human security would be seen in the future. The genocide in

---

[1] Power, Samantha. "Bystanders to Genocide." The Atlantic Monthly, September, 2001. http://www.theatlantic.com/magazine/archive/2001/09/bystanders-to-genocide/304571/. Accessed on April 20, 2014.

Rwanda, which saw between half a million and a million Rwandans killed in the 100 day period between April and June 1994, and to which there was little western or U.S. reaction, was the catalyst for change.

This section will discuss the non-intervention in Rwanda, with several objectives. One is to show the negative impact of the way in which the Somalia intervention ended on decision making moving forward. Another is to introduce a new leadership team with a quite different dynamic, both in relation to each other and to their outlook on decision making, framing, acceptable use of the armed forces, and humanitarian interventions in general. Yet another is to show how a different international environment, in other words, more international involvement, might impact decision making and framing efforts. Background information on the Rwandan genocide, the UN and U.S. response, and the impact of the Rwandan genocide on future thinking will be provided, linking this shorter study to the larger study of the Kosovo intervention which follows.

Rwanda and the World in 1994, Background to Non-Intervention

Rwanda's ethnic divide, between Tutsi and Hutu tribes, had been a source of division and occasional violence since the departure of the Belgian colonial regime in 1960. The Belgians had favored the Tutsi minority during the colonial era, which caused indignation among the majority Hutu population. A civil war between the Tutsi and moderate Hutu peoples on the one hand and the hard line conservative Hutus on the other had been underway since 1990, with a cease fire and power sharing agreement known as the Arusha Treaty imposed by the international community in 1993 and the establishment of a UN peacekeeping force, (UN Mission in Rwanda or UNAMIR) in October, 1993.[2] Unfortunately the

---

[2] Albright, Madeleine. *Madam Secretary, a Memoir*. New York, Harper Collins, 2013. 148. According to a memo to the US UN staff, the U.S. made it clear when it voted for the resolution, which took place two days before the events in Mogadishu, that its support did not include the deployment of U.S. forces. Original Document from 15 April 1994 in Ferroggiaro, William, Ed. "The U.S. and Rwanda, 1994, Evidence of Inaction." George Washington University.

force was lightly armed, had a disjointed command structure, was undermanned, and in fact became victims of the violence, with the Belgians, the best armed, trained, and knowledgeable of the various contingents, withdrawing early on after they began to take casualties in the violence. A ceasefire in the civil war, agreed to President Juvenal Habyarimana, was viewed with skepticism and trepidation by Hutu extremists, resulting in the shoot down of the presidential aircraft on April 6, 1994, while on approach to the airfield at Kigali, Rwanda. Although blamed on the Tutsi rebels, the shoot down was undertaken by Hutu extremists in retaliation for Habyarimana's relatively moderate stance toward the rebels. Notably, the area from which the pair of rockets which destroyed the aircraft was fired was controlled by the Presidential Guard, which was in turn controlled by the extremists.[3] Massacres of Tutsi and moderate Hutu elements began on the very next day, in what was clearly an orchestrated slaughter, perpetrated at first by Hutu police and military leaders. The national identity card system imposed by the Belgian colonial administration decades before became a chooser of the dead, as checkpoints were set up all over the country, and those with the wrong identities were killed. By late April, 1994, the International Committee of the Red Cross estimated that up to a half a million people might have been killed in what many in the humanitarian aid community were terming a case of genocide.

The Rwanda crisis flared, and ended in catastrophe, within a three month period from April to June in 1994, beginning when the ceasefire between the Tutsis and Hutus ended, and ending when the Hutus completed their reign of terror and re-established their undisputed rule.[4] While there were warnings and indicators that a crisis was brewing before it began, this still represents a significantly shorter

---

http://www2.gwu.edu/~nsarchiv/NSAEBB/NSAEBB53/ Accessed on 14 October 2014. A collection of Declassified Original documents on the information known and the decision making process.

[3] United Nations. "Report of the Independent Inquiry into the actions of the United Nations during the 1994 Genocide in Rwanda." December 15, 1999. www.un.org/news/ossg/rwanda_report.htm. Accessed on September 15, 2014. This and other reports were not available at the time of the decision making in 1994.

[4] Talentino, Andrea K. *Military Intervention After the Cold War: The Evolution of Theory and Practice.* Athens, OH: Ohio University Press, 2005. 279.

decision making time frame than that for the Somalia and Kosovo case studies, and similar in length to the Libya cycle. In terms of the other cases examined, Talentino notes that there was at least six months of lead time for the Somalia intervention (and in that case the crisis was known about for another 18 months before that) and two years of decision making time before the Kosovo intervention of 1999.[5]

Furthermore, historical rivalries among the great powers involved clouded the issue and delayed actions that might have mitigated the violence. Albright notes that the French support of the Hutu government and leadership went so far as to say that they had been provoked into the violence by Tutsi and moderate Hutu reprisals after the presidential aircraft shoot down, and included arms shipments before and during the crisis.[6] Herman Cohen was not as harsh, calling the French victims of poor judgment in continuing support of the Tutsis, and focusing on perceived threats from nearby Uganda rather than internal violence.[7]

In terms of the UN Security Council, veto carrying members France, Russia, and China came down on the side of state sovereignty and declared the crisis an internal matter. The U.S. also leaned in this direction, with a bias toward non-interference in a sovereign state. Belgian efforts to cover their own failure to prevent the attacks, and withdrawal of their forces, by pushing for a complete international withdrawal also helped to confuse the issue. Rwanda's recognized government made no request for, nor appeared receptive to, international intervention.[8] Given that the government was dominated, and then fully taken over, by the conservative Hutu elements who perpetrated the genocide, this is not surprising, but it meant that another voice which might have urged intervention was silent.

---

[5] Talentino. 279.
[6] Albright. 150. See also Cohen, Jared. *100 Days of Silence: America and the Rwandan Genocide.* Lanham, Maryland, Rowan and Littlefield Publishers, 2007. 2.
[7] *Intervening in Africa: Superpower Peacemaking in a Troubled Continent.* New York: St. Martin's Press, 2000. 179.
[8] Weiss, Thomas G. *Humanitarian Intervention.* Cambridge: Polity Press, 2012. 7.

Finally, there was a large scale information gap, both from intelligence, diplomatic, and journalistic sources. With most embassies evacuated (The U.S. mission was evacuated early in the crisis), the remoteness of the country, and the level of danger involved, it was extremely difficult to ascertain the details of events in country, and therefore to formulate appropriate responses.[9] Those who were expert on the ground, such as Bushnell and other foreign service staff in the Africa Bureau, had become callous about the numbers of dead in various disturbances over the years. In the previous year's fighting in Burundi, for example, 25,000 had perished. Significant massacres of Tutsi and moderate Hutu had occurred on nine different occasions from 1990 to January 1994. While these experts knew that something was wrong, they were shocked and numbed by the enormity of the unfolding catastrophe.[10] President Clinton, who had more information than most, said that "We did not fully appreciate the depth and speed with which Rwanda was being engulfed by this unimaginable horror."[11]

In an effort to save face and cover up their own ignominious withdrawal, the Belgians wished to see a complete withdrawal of UN forces on April 20th.[12] This was in contrast to African members of the UN Security Council, who according to US Mission to the UN deputy David Scheffer, with a clarity provided by proximity to information on the crisis, wanted UNAMIR to be reinforced.[13] Belgium's stance, which included influencing the U.S. as a NATO ally, was a major factor in the U.S. decision to refrain from intervening militarily in the Rwandan crisis, in spite of efforts by Albright to alter this stance.[14] The Council, as a result, both ignored intelligence provided by the UNAMIR commander, Canadian General Romeo Dallaire, warning of the violence, and minimized the circulation of his early

---

[9] Albright. 149.
[10] Power, 2001.
[11] CBS Evening News. Text of Clinton's Rwanda Speech. March 25, 1998. CBSnews.com. Accessed on 14 October 2014.
[12] Albright. 150.
[13] Scheffer, David. "Lessons from the Rwandan Genocide." *Georgetown Journal of International Relations,* Summer/Fall 2004. 127.
[14] Albright. 150.

reports on the extent of the massacres.[15] In spite of his appeals for more troops and a stronger mandate, the strength of the force he had was cut down to nearly nothing, from 2700 to 250 personnel, and he was censured by the Security Council for making the suggestion.[16] As it happened, Dallaire actually kept about 500 troops on the ground, and it is estimated that they were able to save approximately 25,000 potential victims, a sign of what could have been accomplished had there been adequate international will power applied.[17]

As was the case with the deterioration of Somalia in 1991-1992, the world was an ugly place, with a series of other crises that Albright noted tended to drown out what warnings there were about rising violence in Rwanda.[18] Foremost among them was the ongoing violence in Yugoslavia. In his memoirs, President Clinton noted that the NATO bombing of Bosnian Serb forces surrounding the ethnic Muslim city of Gorazde began on the same day as the Rwandan presidential aircraft shoot down, and absorbed his attention.[19] The U.S. was still heavily involved in operations in the Middle East, still instigated by an intransigent Saddam Hussein and Iraq. Economic and political reform in Russia still dominated the attention of the U.S. at this time. Another political and humanitarian affairs distraction came in the form of the U.S. response to political unrest in Haiti. The U.S. reaction began with embarrassment but ended with an ouster of the dictator Raoul Cedras under the threat of U.S. military force (The threat was real, as U.S. forces were actually on the way to Haiti when the political deal took place).[20]

---

[15] Original January 11, 1994 in Ferroggiaro.

[16] Okechukwu, Groupson-Paul. "Politics and Failures of Ethics of Humanitarian Intervention in African Conflicts." *Journal of Alternative Perspectives in the Social Sciences*. Volume 3, No. 3, 2011, 581-606. 592.

[17] Power, 2001.

[18] Albright. 19. Among them were numerous warnings from the UNAMIR commander, including the January 11, 1994 memorandum already cited.

[19] Clinton, William. *My Life*. New York: Knopf Doubleday, 2004. 584. Specifically, Clinton says that he was "Preoccupied with Bosnia."

[20] Halberstam, David. *War in a Time of Peace*. New York: Scribner, 2001. 273. The embarrassment was the turnaround of a U.S. military ship carrying relief supplies to the country. The ship, the Harlan County, was turned away by armed militants shouting taunts about Mogadishu to the U.S. Sailors and Marines aboard.

The DOD, in the throes of post Cold War downsizing, was still wedded to the Powell Doctrine, all the more so after the tactics of the "Blackhawk Down" incident seemed to verify the Powell precept of overwhelming force. In response to the debacle in Mogadishu, the U.S. was in the midst of developing a formal White House doctrine on peacekeeping, under the leadership of Richard Clarke, a special assistant to Clinton known to be highly proficient in the bureaucratic maneuvering necessary for such a position. The resulting Presidential Decision Directive, PDD 225, named sixteen factors that policymakers needed to consider when deciding whether to support peacekeeping activities: seven were linked to U.S. support of UN votes to start operations, even if no U.S. soldiers were involved. Another six, stricter criteria would limit the role of U.S. forces in such operations, while three more, stricter still, would limit combat roles. The criteria were described as "zero degree of involvement, and zero degree of risk, and zero degree of pain and confusion."[21] The implementation of this peacekeeping doctrine in May, 1994 would virtually guarantee that the U.S. would not get involved in Rwanda.

Senior U.S. leaders, stung by the failure in Mogadishu, simply did not wish to act; even though a U.S. led international force may have been the only force with the international respect to pull off an intervention.[22] Scheffer told reporters in October, 1993, that "We should not rush into each and every humanitarian affairs catastrophe, deflecting thoughts of an early involvement in the crisis.[23] Albright notes that the lessons of Somalia, and of other African crises such as violence in Burundi in 1993, were simply not applicable to the situation in Rwanda, and that sticking to those lessons led to inactivity in the face of levels of violence which were extreme and unexpected.

New Players: The Clinton Team and New Directions in Foreign Policy

---

[21] Congressman David Obey, Quoted in Power.
[22] Albright. 152.
[23] Scheffer. 123.

If the administration of George H.W. Bush was one of the most prepared for foreign policy decision making in the history of the Republic, than that which followed, the William (Bill) Clinton administration was nearly exactly the opposite. First and foremost, the new group of leaders was not a team, as such, at the outset of the administration. Unlike the Bush cabinet, the new group had not all worked together in the past, and because of this were not accustomed to how each worked, or how changes in hierarchy might change the dynamic of their relationships. The new administration brought with it both a new outlook on decision making and foreign policy, but also a new team with a new outlook on what the U.S. role in the world should be. There was a significant discussion in the Clinton Administration over what direction U.S. policy should take in a post-Cold War era. In spite of this, they did build on some Bush team practices, with a sense that U.S. power should be used in accordance with U.S. Allies and interested parties, and where possible under the auspices of the United Nations.

Clinton himself had received an education which exposed him to foreign policy matters, having studied them at Georgetown's School of the Foreign Service before spending time as a Rhodes Scholar and as a staffer on then chairman of the Senate Foreign Relations Committee, William Fulbright.[24] Balancing this, he was highly risk averse, and desired actions that could be guaranteed to succeed rather than potentially fail and cause a loss of popularity for him and his administration.[25] In contrast to Bush's passionate focus on foreign policy (to his political detriment) Clinton's entry argument for his presidency was that he would take direct control of the domestic agenda, and in particular the economy, while allowing expert foreign policy staff take care of the international issues to be faced.[26] This approach was criticized by Cold War historian John Lewis Gaddis, who said that Clinton was "...at fault for allowing an illusion of safety to produce a laissez-faire foreign and

---

[24] Hyland, William. *Clinton's World: Remaking American Foreign Policy.* West Port, CT: Praeger, 1999. 15.
[25] Ibid. 203.
[26] Halberstam. 193. The author claims that Clinton saw Foreign policy as "an inconvenience" which would get in the way of his true passion, domestic affairs.

national security policy."[27] Criticism aside, this mindset can be clearly seen in the foreign policy team he assembled in 1993.

As a result, Clinton tapped the foreign policy leaders of past Democrat administrations. Twelve years separated his administration from the last Democrat, Jimmy Carter. Nevertheless, second tier Carter veterans formed the first cadre of Clinton's foreign policy leadership team.[28] Warren Christopher, who had served as Deputy Secretary of State under Carter, is the chief example of this. Les Aspin, the incoming Secretary of Defense, seemed to be the one example of a purely political choice, although his knowledge of defense issues was widely known.[29] His replacement after Mogadishu by William Perry meant that an untried, if capable leader, would be in charge of the Defense Department during the Rwanda crisis. In a continued role of prominence, Colin Powell remained as Chairman of the Joint Chiefs of Staff until the end of his nominative term of office. None of these leaders were strong activists for U.S. military intervention, which left those initiatives to other administration personalities. In that regard, this is not significantly different from the way the Bush team had looked two years earlier on Somalia, with deputies and department heads rather than principals taking first note of critical events.

One significant change in the power of the foreign policy leadership team was the return of the U.S. Embassy to the U.N. to a seat on the cabinet. Having served in that position, George H.W. Bush had demoted it for the course of his presidency, but it was returned to prominence by Clinton, and the person appointed to the job, Madeleine Albright, would rise to prominence in the second term of the administration.[30] Albright, along with National Security Advisor Anthony Lake, and Strobe Talbot, who served as special Ambassador to Russia, provided the intellectual guidance for the administration's foreign policies.[31] Unlike Scowcroft

---

[27] Gaddis, John Lewis. *Surprise, Security, and the American Experience.* Cambridge, Massachussetss: Harvard University Press, 2004. 77.
[28] Hyland. 18. Hyland notes that Clinton specifically avoided senior cabinet officers in favor of their deputies to avoid having them overshadow his own presence.
[29] Ibid. 19.
[30] Ibid.
[31] Ibid. 20.

and the Bush National Security Council, the primary drivers for the new team were to craft strategies that attempted to solve Clinton's political needs and desires, while avoiding a new Vietnam-like (or Munich, in the case of Albright) entanglement.[32] The team, however, did keep the basic processes of its predecessors, in that Lake met with the Clinton daily, and the Principals and Deputies' Committees continued to function. However, according to Rodman, the president's role, which he described as "unstructured" meant that both groups were weaker than they had been under Brent Scowcroft's guidance.[33]

As noted by Hyland, the new team inculcated the administrations polices with a set of key tenets, namely that: Balance of power politics were outdated; in their place, the U.S. needed to pursue more noble, humanitarian goals; that the use of force should be used to these ends, and that the best test of the validity of a policy lay in the support that could be gathered for it both domestically and internationally.[34] The first two of these goals were a definite change in outlook from the Bush administration. This leadership team would bring about a changeover toward a Wilsonian worldview, pressing for a much broader set of collective security solutions to international problems under UN leadership.[35] The new leadership team and their new outlook set the stage for significant changes in how the U.S. would operate, and this would be seen in the Haiti intervention of 1994, and later in Bosnia in 1995 and Kosovo in 1999. But first, the Rwandan tragedy would strike, and in response, the new team would do… nothing.

---

[32] Rodman, Peter. Presidential Command: Power, Leadership, and the Making of Foreign Policy from Nixon to George W. Bush. New York: Alfred A Knopf, 2009. 206.
[33] Ibid. 208. On page 209, Rodman quotes Clinton as directly saying that he did not wish to be "confined by formal structures," preferring to "forage around himself."
[34] Hyland. 21.
[35] Ibid. 23.

Who Is Behind the Wheel? Drivers for Non-Intervention

Deputy Assistant Secretary of State Prudence Bushnell was one of the first to send up warning signals immediately following the plane crash which killed the Rwandan and Burundian Presidents, claiming that "widespread violence" could follow, an opinion which was supported by Rwanda observers outside the government, most especially the group Human Rights Watch and other non-governmental organizations.[36] This was supported by the intelligence community, which continued with its routine missions in spite of the difficulties in information gathering in the region. By April 26, only weeks into the genocide, elements of the intelligence community identified the planned nature of the atrocities and the names of the perpetrators. This was reinforced by a Defense Intelligence Agency (DIA) report from 9 May on the directed nature of the attacks, using the term genocide to describe the events.[37] There is, however, no evidence in the literature examined that the various intelligence agencies as a community took a stance on intervention. Jared Cohen describes executive level intelligence reporting as being designed more to cover the agencies equities than to encourage action.[38]

Following the evacuation of the American Embassy, official U.S. notice of events faded quickly. According to National Security Advisor Lake, Haiti and Bosnia were his primary foci for the period.[39] In an interview to Ivo Daalder, he said that "it was almost literally inconceivable that American troops would go to Rwanda."[40] The Principals committee of the NSC never met to discuss Rwanda. Thus Lake, who was an Africa expert, was not engaged, whereas his deputy, Clarke, crafter of the non-interventionist intervention policy, was most closely connected

---

[36] Interview with Bushnell from Power. Her Original report is included in Ferroggiaro.
[37] April 9 Report is included in Ferroggiaro.
[38] Cohen, Jared. *100 Days of Silence: America and the Rwandan Genocide.* Lanham, MD: Rowan and Littlefield, 2007. 29.
[39] Interview with Anthony Lake, 2001, in Power.
[40] Anthony Lake interview with Daalder. Ivo, and Destler, I.M. *In the Shadow of the Oval Office: Profiles of the National Security Advisors and the Presidents They Served - from JFK to George W. Bush.* New York: Simon and Schuster, 2009. 241.

with events, followed a predictably non-interventionist course.[41] The Deputies Committee did meet to discuss the situation, as did a series of interagency working groups and task forces, which were dominated by Clarke and his staff. Familiar faces, such as Frank Wisner, represented the DOD in the Deputies group, but Wisner had already been prepped by his staff in an April 11 memo which stated clearly that there would be no U.S. involvement on the ground until after the end of the conflict.[42] Much like Sate Department Leaders, he had juniors, such as Donald Steinberg, the Africa desk officer, who were knowledgeable, but he did not avail himself of the advice offered. Congress similarly maintained its distance. Democrats, while in the majority, were on the defensive against a resurgent Republican party with a dominant domestic agenda. No one wanted to go near a situation which might turn into another Mogadishu during a congressional election year. An examination of the Congressional Record for the time frame in question, September 1991-May 31, 1992 (this date was selected because after this point the bulk of the atrocities had already been committed), shows much less interest than had been the case with Somalia. During this time frame, the 103rd Congress had 44 events, hearings, or resolutions mentioning or related to Rwanda, and of those, only five of the events (hearings in this case) specifically discussed the ongoing atrocities there.[43] On 13 May, Senators Jim Jeffords of Vermont and Paul Simon of Illinois sent a letter to Clinton urging an arms embargo, sanctions, and an increase in the strength of UNAMIR, however, did not request the involvement of U.S. forces.[44]

Madeleine Albright, who at the time was the U.S. representative to the United Nations, summed Rwanda up with the sad, but accurate statement that "I had become defensive and cautious about UN peacekeeping in general and didn't

---

[41] Power. 2001.
[42] Original memo in Ferroggiaro.
[43] Congressional Research Service. Congressional Record of the 103rd Congress. http://thomas.loc.gov/cgi-bin/thomas2. Accessed on 9 October, 2014.
[44] Original letter in Ferroggiaro.

see any practical way for the UN to restore order at that point."[45] According to Albright, the Pentagon was against an intervention, arguing first that it would be impossible to create a coalition with the requisite resources to intervene, and then that the logistical difficulties of intervention in a land locked country were too high. Ultimately, she says, military leaders "said bluntly that they were not prepared to do it."[46] While these debates raged, both in Washington and New York, the killing and dying in Rwanda continued.

On 22 April, 1993, the White House Press Secretary released a statement noting the survival of a prominent Rwandan Human rights monitor, Monique Mujawamarija, who had previously met with President Clinton, and about whom he had specifically asked as the news of the slaughter became known.[47] The statement went on the call for the Tutsis and Hutus to return to cease fire negotiations, and for the leaders of the Rwandan Army to end the violence in the country. It also called for the continuation of the UNAMIR mission, although, significantly, not asking for the strengthening of the mandate of UNAMIR or the forces assigned to it.[48] This statement was the most significant U.S. effort to respond to the crisis, but, predictably, its impact was minimal. Equally ineffective were contacts made by Bushnell to contacts in the Rwandan Defense Ministry on 27 April. She noted that the "world did not buy" the official line, that the killings had been started by Tutsis, and appealed personally to the Rwandan Defense Cabinet Director to "do the right thing" and stop the violence. Unsurprisingly, this lower, ministerial level effort to bring an end to the crisis also failed to achieve results.[49]

---

[45] Albright. 150.
[46] Albright. 153.
[47] Original document from Ferroggiaro.
[48] Ibid.
[49] Ibid.

Public Opinion and the Rwanda Non-Intervention

Beginning immediately after the start of the massacres, the media began to cover events, mainly based on eyewitness accounts from contacts on the ground. Notable coverage included front page stories in the April 9th and 10th editions of the Washington Post, one on the 10th in the *New York Times* citing a Red Cross source that "tens of thousands" had died. Other front page stories appeared on April 14th, 19th, and 24th. The April 19th report, which cited information from Human Rights Watch, specifically called for use of the term "genocide."[50] Meanwhile, the Washington Post Editorial Board had spoken against U.S. intervention, in effect towing the government line on the issue.[51]

The Rwandan crisis happened at time when foreign policy was on the decline as a point of interest for the American public and media. According to James Lindsay, a 50% drop in major network coverage of international stories occurred between 1985 and 1995, but this trend was starting to reverse itself by the time of Clinton's reelection.[52] The Rwandan crisis would engender a similar response. In June, even after the details of the killings were well known, CBS public opinion polling, asking the question "In order to stop the killing in Rwanda, do you favor or oppose the United States sending in ground troops?" revealed only 28% in favor and 61% against such action.[53] This fits with Entman's proposition that a split in public opinion over an issue will serve to generate opposition to action among elites and decision makers.[54]

The Rwandan genocide followed shortly after the inglorious retreat from Africa which followed the Battle of Mogadishu and the withdrawal of U.S. forces

---

[50] Power, 2001.
[51] The Washington Post Editorial Board. "One, Two, Many Rwandas." *The Washington Post*, April 17, 1994. A15.
[52] Lindsay, James. "The New Apathy." *Foreign Affairs* 79, No. 5, September/October 2000. 2-8
[53] Wittkopf, Eugene. *The Domestic Sources of U.S. Foreign Policy*. Lanham, MD: Rowman and Littlefield Publishers, 2004. 103.
[54] Entman, Robert M. *Projections of Power: Framing News, Public Opinion, and U.S. Foreign Policy*. Chicago: University of Chicago Press, 2004. 18.

from Somalia. This left a bad taste in the mouth of policymakers and an unwillingness to commit forces to a part of Africa that was even more remote and unstable than coastal Somalia. Media coverage of the crisis was evident, but since there was no decision to intervene, there was no ready government source of information, and the media reporting was not desirous of action in the way that it had been in the case of Somalia.[55] Since the crisis area was so remote, this meant that information was simply unavailable to the media, and therefore the public, which meant that there was no public groundswell of support. For example, in the most dangerous week of the massacres (and most crucial decision making in the U.S. and the UN), only one question was asked about Rwanda during the Department of State daily briefing.[56]

Models and the Rwanda Decision Process

According to Cohen and Power, there was never a pivotal moment, a debate, an argument about intervention. Lake, Christopher, and Perry never met with President Clinton about it.[57] The failure of the outside world to intervene in the Rwandan genocide was not only a failure of U.S. policy makers to act. In each of the earlier interventions of the decade, Somalia, and Haiti, the U.S. had acted under a firm UN mandate, even if the U.S. took on a disproportionate role or command of the interventions. A key failure, and one which influenced others in the case of Rwanda was that of the United Nations to reach a consensus on intervention in a timely fashion. Given that the U.S was not, under the George H.W. Bush or Clinton White Houses, inclined to act without UN authority in these cases, this was a critical failure.[58] According to Hehir, this was a result of a conscious decision by the P5 (The five permanent members of the UN Security Council; the U.S. UK, France,

---

[55] Talentino. 40.
[56] Albright. 154.
[57] Cohen. 5.
[58] Hehir, Aidan. The Responsibility to Protect: Rhetoric, Reality, and the Future of Humanitarian Intervention. New York: Palgrave Macmillan, 2012. 30.

Russia, and China).[59] That failure, while a significant factor, still allows for a discussion of the decision making processes which kept the U.S. to its position to act multilaterally if at all (In this case, to not act).

In his memoir, Bill Clinton reiterated that there was simply little interest in an overseas deployment of U.S. forces to central Africa in 1994. Clinton later expressed deep regret for this, but he reiterated that due to domestic pressure against deployments, and the other world issues pressing at the time, he and his team were "inadequately focused" on the possibility of sending troops to stop the atrocities in Rwanda.[60] Decision making for the non-intervention seemed to follow the bureaucratic Governmental Process Model of Allison. Institutional interests and bias were the order of the day when determining the fate of Rwanda. The DOD stuck its prevailing doctrine, and since it was not ordered to change its stance by President Clinton, it did not do so.[61] At the Department of State, Secretary of State Christopher knew so little about the area that an atlas was required to bring him up to speed, and he showed a general lack of interest in the issue.[62] Naturally, the specific bureau of interest, the Africa Bureau, brought key knowledge to the table, but, as had been the case with Somalia, were unable to overcome the biases of their organizational leaders. Unlike Somalia, however, no one at the senior cabinet level, least of all President Clinton, was willing to take on the cause and push through and frame an intervention, and little domestic pressure existed to overcome the fact that administration leaders simply did not perceive Rwanda as a national security priority. With that in mind, the administration can be said to have acted rationally in deciding not to intervene.

There is, interestingly, evidence of framing as part of the justification for non-intervention in Rwanda. This can be found in part in the staunch refusal of the

---

[59] Hehir. 31.
[60] Clinton. 584.
[61] This was confirmed by the Joint Staff in an interagency conference on the situation on 11 May. Original notes in Original document from Ferroggiaro.
[62] Power, 2001. The author quotes the Belgian Foreign Minister Willie Claes, who was infamously told by Christopher that "I have other responsibilities" when discussing the situation.

Clinton administration to use the term genocide in identifying the crisis.[63] Not only did the administration not want to act, since it would be obligated by the 1948 Genocide convention to do so, but it did not want to be seen as calling out an aggressive act without being willing to do anything about it. [64] The resultant potential loss of legitimacy weighed heavily on the minds of Department of State lawyers and NSC staffers such as Susan Rice, who openly questioned the impact of using the term might have on the upcoming mid-term elections.[65] The U.S. did not, in fact, even hint at genocide in a general fashion until May 21, six weeks into the crisis, and well after most of the killing had taken place.[66] This was a result of a series of consultations involving the Africa Bureau, the International Organizations Bureau, and the Legal Department at State, which approved the statement that "Acts of genocide had occurred," even though those acts were still ongoing at that date.[67] As late as June 10th, a Department of State spokesperson still refused to openly use the term, and it was on that date that Secretary of State Christopher finally used the term publicly. Thus, the only significant framing of the crisis was to actively frame the effort not to respond to the crisis in Somalia. To be fair, however, this appeared at the time to be a bold move, considering that the UN itself did not refer to the situation in Rwanda as genocide until over a month later, in July.[68]

Conclusion

> "America's new peacekeeping doctrine, of which Clarke was the primary architect, was unveiled on May 3, and U.S. officials applied its criteria zealously. PDD-25 did not merely circumscribe U.S. participation in UN missions; it also limited U.S. support for other

---

[63] Talentino. 127.
[64] Halberstam. 273.
[65] Rice quoted in Power, 2001. Although she later denied memory of the statement, it was corroborated by other members of the working group on the conference call.
66 Power, Samantha. A Problem From Hell: America and the Age of Genocide. New York: Harper Collins. 2002. 366.
[67] Original Memo in Ferroggiaro.
[68] Sheffer. 130.

> states that hoped to carry out UN missions. Before such missions could garner U.S. approval, policymakers had to answer certain questions: Were U.S. interests at stake? Was there a threat to world peace? A clear mission goal? Acceptable costs? Congressional, public, and allied support? A working cease-fire? A clear command-and-control arrangement? And, finally, what was the exit strategy?"
> Samantha Power, 2001.[69]

No senior leader wanted intervention in Rwanda strongly enough to force the issue. This was true both at the UN and in the U.S. and its allies. As the springtime of slaughter continued, there was simply no leadership provided by the White House, and no member of the top foreign policy hierarchy was motivated enough to bring their political cache to bear on the Rwanda issue. As then Lieutenant General Wesley Clark, who was working on policy issues at the Pentagon put it "The Pentagon is always going to be the last to want to intervene. It is up to the civilians to tell us they want to do something and we'll figure out how to do it."[70] While this opinion is not always true, what is the case is that with no senior leaders arguing for intervention, the next tier down, the deputies and department heads, were not going to stick their own necks out in favor of a troop deployment into combat operations in the middle of Africa. And so, the status quo reigned supreme.

The findings in the Rwanda case can be simply stated. In terms of the process used in decision making, the models provided by Allison and Yetiv stand up well. Cabinet departments defaulted to their institutional positions, and no senior leader chose to break the deadlock. In fact, the institutional biases, and that of President Clinton, against action were so strong that no serious effort was made to have the senior level discussion that might have led to action. Due to this, the idea of the powerful individual is negatively verified, in that, lacking a strong, well placed motivator or spokesperson, no intervention took place. Similarly, other than the discussion and debate on using the word genocide, there was no attempt to

---

[69] Power, 2001.
[70] Clark interview with Power, 2001.

frame an intervention, rather the opposite, as events in Rwanda were repeatedly downplayed by government spokespersons. Unfortunately for the people of Rwanda, the arithmetic was quite simple. No consensus and no framing meant no intervention.

This chapter described the genocide in Rwanda and the decision not to intervene. It noted the new set of personalities and different decision making dynamic of the first Clinton administration, and the impact of a perceived failure in the Somalia intervention on the possibility of involvement in the Rwandan Civil War and genocides. This study stands as a stark example of a situation in which no powerful decision maker is motivated to force government decision making and framing efforts for armed humanitarian intervention. Without either, there was no motivation among key stakeholders, namely Congress and the American public, for intervention. Ultimately, the genocide in Rwanda would spark a discussion on human security and the meaning of state sovereignty when human rights and security were endangered. The resulting thought process in the international community was that states which did not adequately address human security needs might have their sovereignty abrogated by the international community, the core of the idea that would become the doctrine of Responsibility to Protect (R2P). That discussion would help to fuel future armed humanitarian interventions, most particularly the remaining two case studies, the Kosovo intervention of 1999 and the Libya intervention of 2011.

CHAPTER V – Kosovo – "Madeleine's War": March, 1999

"The Balkans produce more history than they consume'"
Winston Churchill[1]

"Ambassador Frank G. Wisner… laments that the U.S. Department of State has a "very thin" understanding of history's role in shaping politics and state policies in Southeast Europe."[2]

"Ending this tragedy is a moral imperative."
President Bill Clinton, March 24, 1999.[3]

The U.S. led NATO military intervention in Kosovo began on March 24, 1999. It continued through June, consisting primarily of an increasingly intense series of airstrikes intended both to convince Serbia to cease its internal persecution of Kosovar Albanians and to materially degrade its capability to do so.[4] According to Houghton, approximately 1,000 aircraft, mostly American, flew 38,000 combat missions as part of the intervention.[5] This included contributions from 18 of the 19

---

[1] Phillips, David L. *Liberating Kosovo: Coercive Diplomacy and U.S. Intervention*. Cambridge, MA: Belfer Center, 2012. 3.
[2] Excerpt from interview with Frank Wisner, August 31, 2010. Phillips. 4.
[3] Clinton, William J. "Excerpt from transcript of the President's Address." University of Virginia, March 24, 1999. http://millercenter.org.scripps/archive/speeches/detail/3932. Accessed October 15, 2014.
[4] Clinton. William J. *My Life*. New York: Knopf, 2004. 941.
[5] Houghton, David P. *The Decision Point: Six Cases in U.S. Foreign Policy Decision Making*. Oxford: Oxford University Press, 2013. 195.

members of NATO at the time.[6] The decision to intervene in Kosovo has its roots both in the early incidents of the Yugoslav Civil War from 1991-1996 and the interventions and non-interventions which preceded it, including the Somalia intervention and the Rwanda non-intervention. It came at a time when the international community, stung by its failure to prevent the massacre in Rwanda, began to seriously discuss human security and its relevance, and potential dominance over traditional concepts of state sovereignty. This would eventually lead to the development of the concept of Responsibility to Protect (R2P), which will be discussed more fully in the context of the third case study, the Libya intervention.[7] In fact, the air campaign in Serbia and Kosovo marked the first time that an armed humanitarian intervention would take place in an internationally recognized, undisputedly sovereign state, a fact in which it differs from the Somalia case study.[8]

This chapter examines the historical precedents for the intervention, noting the historical factors which caused the crisis and the intervention. It will also examine the changes in the second Clinton administration which helped to facilitate the intervention. One notable leader and two strong supporting actors took the lead both in the process. Secretary of State Madeleine Albright, special envoy Richard Holbrooke, and General Wesley Clark acted as powerful leaders in pushing the decision making cycle, and as powerful spokespersons in the framing process for the intervention. The study will also examine the role of President Clinton and presidential politics (in particular, ongoing effort to impeach Clinton over the Monica Lewinsky scandal), the UN, Congress, NATO and the media both on the decision making process and as each was impacted by the decision making and

---

[6] Greece was the only holdout. Also noteworthy is that the operation saw the first participation in external operations by the German Air Force since the end of the Second World War.

[7] Hehir, Aidan. The Responsibility to Protect: Rhetoric, Reality, and the Future of Humanitarian Intervention. New York: Palgrave Macmillan, 2012. 30.

[8] Talentino, Andrea K. *Military Intervention After the Cold War: The Evolution of Theory and Practice.* Athens, OH: Ohio University Press, 2005. 242-243.

framing processes.[9] Significantly, alliance politics were present in Kosovo in a way that they were not before, and the role of a powerful international ally, the UK, will be considered. Lessons learned from the intervention, including how the Kosovo intervention impacted future humanitarian interventions, will also be discussed.

Kosovo and Yugoslavia, 1989-1999 Background to Intervention

Through the early and late 1990s, Yugoslavia and the deteriorating situation there were at the forefront of world politics. As noted, the brief, bloody interlude in Rwanda did little to distract from concurrent events in the Balkans. And it was the failure to intervene in the African nation which would ignite a renewed discussion of intervention, and a greater readiness on behalf of the international community and the U.S. to militarily intervene in humanitarian affairs crises in the future. [10] The NATO intervention in Kosovo would be an example of this increased zeal. By 1998, Kosovo remained as one of the last unresolved ethnic disputes resulting from the breakup of Yugoslavia.[11] With two million inhabitants, it was, although nominally a part of Serbia, 90% Albanian in ethnic makeup.

Serious persecution of the Kosovar Albanians had commenced with the ascension to power of Slobodan Milosevic in 1987, and continued with increasing severity throughout the period of the breakup of Yugoslavia, an event which overshadowed it in the eyes of the western media.[12] The primary pro-Kosovar leader, Ibrahim Rugova, had, since 1992, led a non-violent campaign on behalf of his people, but he was increasingly sidelined as Serb hostility bred a hostile

---

[9] Rothkopf, David. *Running the World: The inside Story of the National Security Council and the Architects of American Power Public Affairs*. New York: Perseus Group, 2005. 373.
[10] Talentino. 127.
[11] The other remaining flashpoint in Serbia is the Hungarian dominated province of Vojvodina, north of Belgrade. The remaining disputes focus on outside claims to various pieces of former Yugoslav states, and semantic issues such as the name of Macedonia, which is disputed by Greece. Hill, Christopher R. Outpost: Life on the Frontline of American Diplomacy – a memoir. New York: Simon and Schuster, 2014. 448.
[12] *Independent International Commission on Kosovo Report.* Oxford, Oxford University Press, 2000. 38-39.

Kosovar response. Kosovar Albanians were surprised by their seeming abandonment by the west, as their leaders had expected the negotiations which led up to the Dayton Peace Accords in 1996 to include favorable resolutions to all remaining territorial disputes, including their own.[13] According to DiPrizio, this occurred as an implicit tradeoff to Serbia on Bosnia, since the Serbs would never have agreed to a linkage between the two issues.[14] On the other hand, Albright notes that the Kosovar Albanians were well aware that they were nearly alone of Yugoslavia's ethnic groups in not achieving independence from Serbia.[15]

In the spring of 1998, an extensive, systematic attack on Kosovar Albanians began, with two results. The first was a wave of thousands of refugees, eventually rising to 750,000, which fled to whichever country would accept them.[16] The second was an increase in the power, and effectiveness, of the Kosovo Liberation Army (KLA). Since its inception in November, 1997, The KLA eschewed the non-violent means of Rugova, and actively sought the means to retaliate against the Serbs in any way it could, eventually be classified as a terrorist organization by the U.S.[17] Following economic unrest in Albania in 1997, the KLA received, through theft and direct aid, enough Albanian military weapons to seriously destabilize the situation.[18] Its actions caused a violent thought loop by blurring the nature of the Serbian response between legitimate police and counter terror action and its own barbarous acts.[19] The U.S. envoy, Robert Gelbard did not help the situation by quickly branding the KLA as a terrorist group, which could be seen to legitimize the Serb response.[20] By summer, 1998, attacks on ethnic Albanians had escalated to the point that U.S. interest began to peak, with a pivotal report by Julia Taft,

---

[13] Holbrooke, Richard. *To End a War.* New York: The Modern Library, 1999. 273.
[14] DiPrizio, Robert C. *Armed Humanitarians: U.S. Interventions from Northern Iraq to Kosovo.* Baltimore: Johns Hopkins University Press, 2002. 218.
[15] Albright, Madeleine. *Madam Secretary, A Memoir.* New York: Harper Collins, 2013. 383.
[16] Blair, Tony. *A Journey: My Political Life.* London: Knopf, 2010. 252.
[17] Zenko, Micah. "Coercive Diplomacy Before the War in Kosovo, Case 252." Washington: Georgetown, Walsh School of the Foreign Service, 2001. 3.
[18] Hill, Christopher R. Outpost: Life on the Frontline of American Diplomacy – a Memoir. New York: Simon and Schuster, 2014. 101.
[19] Albright. 389.
[20] Hill. 104.

Assistant Secretary of State for Population, Refugees, and Migration. Discussing a recent investigative mission to Kosovo, she notably described a region on the precipice of genocide.[21]

Given the general consensus not to involve ground troops in the intervention, the administration decided to press on the diplomatic front. The lead negotiator for the region, Gelbard, proved to be incapable of dealing adequately with Milosevic.[22] In October, 1998, therefore, Richard Holbrooke, although not currently holding an appointed government office, was therefore sent to Belgrade to negotiate on Kosovo, armed with the threat of air strikes.[23] Christopher Hill, the American Ambassador to Macedonia, was sent to accompany him due to his expertise in the region and the fact that Holbrooke had been a private citizen and uninvolved in the peace process since Dayton.[24] Their efforts seemed to be successful in the short term, but the Racak massacre proved that Milosevic's promises were not trustworthy. Much as the loss of the 1992 election served as the catalyst for President Bush's volte face on Somalia, Racak proved to be the turning point on intervention in Kosovo. By late January, 1999, the impeachment proceedings were over, and while the Clinton White House certainly lost some moral authority as a result, the end of the trial meant that Clinton could not look on Kosovo with an undistracted eye. With this in mind, Albright personally galvanized her fellow cabinet members into action, particularly over a 4 day period beginning on January 19th.[25] Even though they were known to be opposed just weeks before the start of operations, Albright's rhetoric drug her peers along.[26] Keeping the aversion to ground invasion in mind, she convinced Defense Secretary

---

[21] Department of State News Briefing, Julia V. Taft, Assistant Secretary of State, Bureau of Population, Refugees, and Migration, and Eileen Malloy, Deputy Secretary of State for European and Canadian Affairs, September 9, 1998. Included in Zenko. 3. Her exact description was "An Erie Landscape, teetering on the brink."

[22] Hill. 100. Gelbard was see to be "Too honest and blunt" for the job, treating Serb leaders as though there were Latin American crime lords as a result of previous work in that region.

[23] Clinton. 940. He notes that air strikes were threatened by NATO on 13 October.

[24] Ibid. 104.

[25] Albright. 397.

[26] Gellman, Barton. "The Path to Crisis: How the United States and its Allies Went to War." The Washington Post, 18 April 1999, A1.

Cohen, National Security Advisor Berger, and Chairman of the Joint Chiefs Air Force General Hugh Shelton to agree on a set of guiding directives for negotiation and intervention.[27] These were agreed to by the main players, and consented to by a newly interested Clinton.

This agreement, to back diplomacy with the threat of force, to include NATO, and to force the two parties to meet under the auspices of the International Contact Group, which included the U.S., UK, France, Germany, Italy, and Russia. The meeting, which occurred under British and French leadership at Rambouillet, began on February 6, 1999, and lasted for a month, but neither the Serbs nor the Kosovar Albanians could be made to accept mutually agreeable terms, in spite of a renewed embargo on Serbia, and the threat of a naval blockade of the Albanian ports through which the Kosovar Albanians imported the majority of their military supplies.[28] Morton Halperin, Department of State Director of Policy Planning, noted that as the negotiations drug on, U.S. intelligence services noted a significant buildup of Serb forces in and near Kosovo, after pressuring the removal of the observer team provided by the Organization for Security and Cooperation in Europe (OSCE), the Serbs launched an ethnic cleansing campaign in Kosovo.[29]

In direct terms, the failure to reach an agreement on the status of Kosovo at the Rambouillet conference led to the U.S. led military intervention in Serbia, although key leaders such as Albright, Clark, and Solana expected both the diplomatic failure and the subsequent intervention. Serbian intransigence at the negotiating table strengthened western resolve to act, and to follow the lead of a U.S. government that, due to Albright's efforts, already say military intervention as the only way to compel compliance from Belgrade.[30] The conference ended on 18

[27] Gellman, "The Path to Crisis: How the United States and its Allies Went to War." The Washington Post, 18 April 1999, A1.
[28] Clinton. 940. The Albanians eventually agreed to terms, but they were not accepted by the Belgrade government. Clinton thought that he could work with Rugova, but not the KLA.
[29] Halperin, Morton. "*Winning the Peace,*" from Buckley, William Joseph. *Kosovo: Contending Voices on Balkan Interventions*. Grand Rapids, MI: William B. Eerdmans Publishing Company, 2000. 227.
[30] Talentino. 261.

March, the final foreign policy meeting, at which the definitive decision for intervention was taken, occurred on the 19th, and the bombing began one week later.[31]

The European members of NATO, having concluded the rest of the Yugoslav Civil War, and having endured a series of public embarrassments, such as the failures to protect Muslim minorities in Srebrenica and Gorazde, had little stomach for further conflict with Serbia, and would have to be led into any intervention by the United States. Tony Blair, the UK Prime Minister, worked hard to personally change this stance from January, 1998 onwards, and during the intervention would work closely with Clinton, splitting the duty of coalition cheerleader.[32] Furthermore, with NATO forces already on the ground in Bosnia as a result of the Dayton Accords, where they would be vulnerable to Serb reprisals, it was unreasonable to expect there to be no NATO voice in decision making.[33]

Notably among the cases examined, and in U.S. post-Cold War interventions in general, there was no specific guidance, in the form of a resolution, from the United Nations Security Council on the events in Kosovo. The U.S., and NATO, would, in effect, be acting bilaterally on the issue. This was due to the question of Russia and how it perceived the intervention in Serbia. Historically, Russia had seen itself as the protector of the Slavic peoples. This feeling was so powerful that in 1914, Russia had mobilized its army against the Austro-Hungarian Empire in retaliation for Austrian attacks on Serbia, an act which helped bring about the First World War. U.S. envoy to Russia Strobe Talbot called the Kosovo decisions and intervention "the most severe, dangerous, and consequential crisis in U.S.-Russian relations in the post-Cold War period.[34] Russia's stance, according to Talbot, was that western involvement in a traditionally Russian sphere of

---

[31] Clinton. 940. Clinton emphasized that he approved of the Airstrikes.
[32] Blair. 252.
[33] Gellman. A1.
[34] Talbot, Strobe. *The Russia Hand: A Memoir of Presidential Diplomacy*. New York: Random House, 2003. 334.

influence would critically damage pro-western reform efforts in the country.[35] Twice, during the October threat of attacks that led to the final Holbrooke agreement, and once, in late March, 2008, the Yeltsin government threatened the U.S. over Kosovo. It was Serbian intransigence, and continued flaunting by Milosevic of attempts to negotiate, that allowed Moscow its way out, and there was a tacit agreement that Russia would not bring the intervention to the UN Security Council because of this.[36]

The United Nations, unlike previous humanitarian interventions in the 1990's, was not a leading player in Kosovo, in part because Serbia's patron, Russia, sat on the UN Security Council ready to use its veto to protect Belgrade. Sanctions and projects for humanitarian assistance, but not intervention, were approved by Security Council Resolution (UNSCR) 1160 in March, 1998.[37] The strongest UN statement on the issue came in September 1998, with Security Council Resolution (UNSCR) 1199. The resolution did recognize the threat that Kosovo posed to "peace and security in the region," but went no farther, and did not authorize action.[38] A follow on measure, UNSCR 1203, passed on October 24th, 1998, led to the OSCE support of the Kosovo Verification Mission, which was supposed to monitor the ceasefire that Holbrooke had brokered, but the mission was ill defined and coordinated, and in any case the ceasefire that it was supposed to monitor was tenuous at best.[39] As part of the deal, Milosevic also pledged political conciliation and the chance for displaced persons to return to their homes, but these agreements were never kept.

---

[35] Talbot. 348.
[36] Ibid.
[37] United Nations Security Council. "Resolution 1160." New York: March 31, 1998. http://unscr.com/en/resolutions/1160. Accessed on October 16, 2014.
[38] United Nations Security Council. "Resolution 1199." New York: September 23, 1998 http://unscr.com/en/resolutions/1199. Accessed on October 16, 2014.
[39] University of the West of England. "Kosovo Documents." Bristol, UK. www.ess.uwe.ac.uk/kosovo/kosovo-documents7.htm. Accessed on October 16, 2014.

The U.S. and the World in 1999, Context for Intervention

In every case of foreign policy decision making, the decisions made have to be taken in the context of the broader state of the U.S. and the world at the time of the crisis. For the Clinton administration, the implosion of the Russian economy and the economic collapse of the Asian Tigers was a number one priority for attention and effort. [40] Within months, the economies of Thailand, Indonesia, Malaysia, the Philippines, Hong Kong, and South Korea spun out of control, undoing years of double digit growth, and dragging Russia along with them. Similarly, the rise of China as a serious economic competitor was underway. Clinton would fly to China in 1998, followed by visit by the Chinese premier Zhu Rongji to discuss Chinese entry into the World Trade Organization. Details such as arranging for Clinton to avoid Tiananmen Square, the site of the brutal 1989 civil rights crackdown, absorbed time and attention.[41] Meanwhile, North Korea demonstrated its capability to launch a multi stage rocket, increasing its ability to threaten U.S. interests in East Asia.[42] Further south, India shocked the world by conducting a nuclear test which was mirrored weeks later by Pakistan.[43]

Perennial problems in the Middle East and Africa continued. The death of King Hussein of Jordan caused concern over the succession to the Hashemite throne, while the Middle East peace process was at a standstill.[44] Saddam Hussein continued to cause trouble for the U.S., while in Africa, war broke out between Ethiopia and Eritrea, and ongoing civil wars in Zaire and Sudan also competed for attention. Al Qaeda inspired attacks on U.S. embassies in Kenya and Tanzania occurred, and taken with the decision making surrounding the retaliatory cruise missile attacks on Sudan and Afghanistan, this served to push events in the Balkans

---

[40] DiPrizio. 135.
[41] Daalder. 251.
[42] Albright. 354.
[43] Clinton. 867.
[44] Ibid.

further to the back burner of public awareness.[45] Cuba was in the news, according to Albright, when a Papal visit to the communist island state raised the possibility of political change there, and with that possibility came attention from the administration.[46]

Europe provided a positive glimmer, but the source of the good news was not in the Balkans, or in Russia, but rather in violence plagued Northern Ireland. According to Clinton, the negotiation of the Good Friday Agreement in May, 1998, largely ending three decades of sectarian violence in the province, drew considerable attention just as the conflict between Serbs and Kosovar Albanians was entering a deadly phase.[47] Events in Russia, which was still in the throes of unrest in Chechnya tempered this positive news and created more work for the Clinton Administration. Russia came to see the Kosovar Albanians as Serbia's version of the Chechens, and, given its violent response to Chechen rebels in 1995, Moscow's tendency was to let Belgrade deal with the Kosovar Albanians in a similarly brutal fashion.[48]

Domestically, a primary, and, indeed, overwhelming preoccupation of the administration was the Monica Lewinski affair and the impeachment proceedings which stemmed from it. From August, 1998, when Lewinski testified to a grand jury on the president's sexual activity, to January, 1999, when the impeachment ended, the affair dominated the attention of the media and the White House.[49] Ivo Daalder cites the combination of the end of the Lewinsky affair, and its coincidence in time with the Racak massacre, as the two events which brought Clinton fully on board intellectually with the Kosovo intervention discussions, which had hitherto been handled nearly exclusively by Berger (to the dismay of Albright).[50]

---

[45] Albright. 363. She described the day of the attacks, August 7, 1998, as the "worst day of her life."
[46] Ibid. 334-336.
[47] Clinton. 867.
[48] Talbot. 348.
[49] Albright. 352.
[50] Daalder. Ivo, and Destler, I.M. *In the Shadow of the Oval Office: Profiles of the National Security Advisors and the Presidents They Served - from Jfk to George W. Bush*. New York: Simon and Schuster, 2009. 254.

Furthermore, a pre-election financial scandal, the Whitewater affair, was nearing its own completion and this also absorbed presidential attention. Ken Starr, the independent prosecutor assigned to the case, was publically tracking down leads throughout 1998, and is frequently mentioned in the Clinton memoirs.[51] A glimmer of redemption and relief on this issue would not come until the acquittal of Susan MacDougal, one of the defendants, on April 12, 1999, in the midst of the Kosovo War.[52] These pressures forced Clinton, who had grown considerably in his effectiveness as a foreign policy president, to return to the strategy of his first years in offices, in other words, to let his delegates handle international crises. This would not, at first, bode well for Kosovo.

The Evolving Clinton Administration: Leadership, Processes, and Strong Voices

1994 was a key year for the administration. The Republican congressional victory in November of that year brought the administration under repeated attacks from key opposition leaders on the direction, or lack of direction, that administration policies undertook.[53] While his chances for a second term were in question after these mid-term elections, Clinton beat Senator Robert Dole handily in 1996, and became the first Democrat president to be reelected to a full term since Franklin Roosevelt.[54] While the Dayton Peace Accords of 1996, which brought an end to the main actions of the breakup of Yugoslavia, gave the administration a solid foreign policy victory on which to hang its reputation, the rhetoric of weakness continued and would be a factor in future administration decision making.[55]

---

[51] Clinton. 920.
[52] Ibid. 942.
[53] Hyland. 139.
[54] Daalder. 251.
[55] Hyland. 145. In the fall elections, the Republicans took control of the U.S. House and Senate for the first time since 1952.

The years between 1994 and 1998 saw significant changes both in the outlook of the Clinton Administration and in its leadership. In terms of personal growth, the events in Somalia, Rwanda, and elsewhere had taught President Clinton that he could not simply delegate foreign relations to his subordinates, but would have to take a steady, consistent role in the national security decision making process, and he became more comfortable doing so.[56] Clinton had also emerged as one of the world's senior statesmen, not only in the obvious power of the U.S., but in terms of his own time in officer and personal growth in that office.[57] According to Henry Kissinger, Clinton and many on his staff were still too keen to conflate foreign and domestic policies, and to see the former as an extension of the latter.[58] At his core, he remained far more pragmatic and less moralistic than his subordinates, particularly Madeleine Albright, who was now Secretary of State.[59]

Albright, the first female Secretary of State, brought a strong awareness of the need of her new role, having moved up from her previous position as Ambassador to the UN. Her formative years were dominated by experiences surrounding the Second World War, and the parallels she drew to the situation in the Balkans referred back to Hitler, Munich, and appeasement. By 1998, Albright had been part of the leadership team since the beginning of the administration, and was a powerful advocate for a number of causes, one of which became Kosovo. She distinctly lamented the failure to act in the Rwandan genocide, and was quick to use her position of new found importance to ensure that neither another Rwanda nor another Munich or Auschwitz would happen on her watch.[60]

Completing the diplomatic side of the leadership trio which pushed for intervention was Richard Holbrooke. Holbrooke had a deep history in the Department of State going back to the Vietnam War, `and an equally deep

---

[56] Houghton. 201.
[57] Albright. 350.
[58] Kissinger, Henry. "Kosovo and the Vicissitudes of American Foreign policy. Doing Injury to History." *Newsweek*, April 15, 1999. From Buckley. 296.
[59] Houghton. 213.
[60] Albright. 386. She pointedly reminded Berger when discussing Milosevic in April, 1998, that she was Secretary, not Ambassador, and could not be dismissed now as she had been previously.

commitment to the concept of Atlanticism and the value of maintaining peace in Europe.[61] While he saw the need for UN approval for interventions, he was also willing to press for armed humanitarian interventions without the UN if need be.[62] Holbrooke brought with him a close working relationship with two people who would prove to be critical in the Kosovo crisis. The first was Slobodan Milosevic. Holbrooke had forged a relationship with and understanding of Milosevic which made him the go to diplomat for dealing with him, as well as the acknowledged expert on how to deal with him. Second was Wesley Clark, who worked with him on the negotiation of the Dayton Accords and with whom he would work on both the diplomatic front of the Kosovo crisis as well as pressing for military intervention when those negotiations failed.[63]

With the departure of Anthony Lake, his deputy, Sandy Berger took his place. Berger's primary goal was to provide advice that fit his intense awareness of Clinton's political needs at a given moment.[64] However, Berger was positively described as being highly analytical, incisive, and working well with the other members of the cabinet, as well as having near identical feelings on events as his presidential supervisor.[65] Albright describes their relationship, which would be central to the successful push for intervention, and not always perfect, but better than it could have been, and they were in frequent communication.[66]

Berger's style was a significant, but logical changeover from that of Lake. He established strong rules for behavior, emphasizing the need for team work, and particularly by avoiding "policy debate via press conference."[67] According to Ivo Daalder, he made better use of the Principal's committee on the NSC to generate

---

[61] Chollet, Derek, and Power, Samantha. *The Unquiet American: Richard Holbrooke in the World.* New York: Public Affairs 2012. 165.
[62] Holbrooke, Richard. "Speech at the National Press Club, November 2, 1999." From Chollet and Power. 253.
[63] Clark, Wesley. *Waging Modern War.* New York: Public Affairs, 2012. 122.
[64] Rodman. 207.
[65] Halberstam, David. *War in a Time of Peace.* New York: Scribner, 2001. 409.
[66] Albright. 350-351. She notes that their shared telephone line was used "a dozen times a day or more."
[67] Daalder. 250.

well thought out and debated recommendations for President Clinton to consider. Very little actually reached him without having been considered in this way.[68] Furthermore, he gave voice to key leaders, such as Holbrooke, CJCS Shelton, and CIA chief George Tenet by having them join the senior group for meeting twice a week. This came to be known and the ABC lunches, with the acronyms standing for Albright, Berger, and Cohen.[69]

Like his predecessors, Les Aspin and William Perry, William Cohen, the new secretary of defense, was not inclined to fight against the customary uniformed military reluctance to use force.[70] Having voted against the interventions in Bosnia which led to the Dayton Accords, Cohen now sought to protect U.S. forces there by staying out of further military entanglements with Serbia.[71] Furthermore, the uniformed leadership of the military, even six years into the administration, still bore a fundamental mistrust of Clinton and his senior cabinet officials, a mistrust that was largely reciprocated by the civilian leadership in the White House.[72] In contrast to the earlier interventions, in which the Secretary of Defense and the Chairman of the Joint Chiefs took the lead, however, the key mover in breaking the deadlock in the Department of Defense turned out to be the commander on the ground, General Wesley Clark, the NATO and U.S. European Command leader who described himself as "a greater activist than most of the people in the military."[73] Clark had been closely connected with Holbrooke, working with him in the negotiation of the Dayton Accords in 1996.[74] Like Albright, his view of Milosevic and the threat he posed to the peace of Europe was harsh.[75] Wearing, as he did, two military hats, that of a U.S. regional commander and that of a NATO coalition headquarters, Clark was uniquely situated to understand the impact of

---

[68] Daalder. 248.
[69] Ibid. 249.
[70] Rodman. 208.
[71] Zenko. 5.
[72] Halbertsam. 418.
[73] Blumenthal, Sydney. *The Clinton Wars*. New York: Farrar, Strauss and Giroux, 2003. 640.
[74] Rodman. 224.
[75] Ibid. 224. According to Halberstam, p. 395, he viewed Milosevic as "A pathological Liar always playing for time."

action, or inaction, on the alliance, which would be engaging in what was only its second combat operation in the fifty years of its existence.[76] Unlike his military peers, he dealt with civilian leaders with some level of comfort, if not ease, and was therefore trusted by them, while on the other hand many of his military peers found him to be abrasive and a source of resentment.[77] Like Albright, he was willing and able to establish direct linkages to the president and to the National Security Advisor rather than have his role be limited by his direct superior, Cohen.[78] He was regularly in contact with Berger directly, a fact which actually stiffened the bureaucratic stances of his DOD leadership, such as Chairman Shelton, against him and against the intervention.[79]

The Clinton team, having now been together, by and large, for six years by the time Kosovo became a critical issue, had indeed gelled and matured in a way that was not and could not have been true during the Rwandan Crisis. In spite of this maturation, however, it would never be the type of team that the George H.W. Bush had led during his Presidency. Indeed, such a team would have been impossible to create, given Clinton's path to the White House from a small state governorship. Further, its focus on domestic policy and partisan combat were in stark contrast to the Bush administration (who, it must be countered, lost their bid for reelection in part because of the lack of domestic focus.) However, it was at least a team experienced with the hard knocks of foreign and domestic policy, and of partisan politics. It was also a team that, according to Albright, was friendly and socially active with each other.[80] In Berger, Clinton had a perfect foil, and well understood the capabilities and foibles of his senior cabinet team, most particularly Albright.

---

[76] Clark. 77-79.
[77] Halbertsam. 433.
[78] Clark. 113. He was called to task by Shelton for some of the advice which he provided Holbrooke, which the Chairman and Secretary thought was out of order, and in their purview.
[79] Rodman. 223-224. Doctrinally, Clark, as a Geographic Combatant Commander, reported directly to the Defense Secretary, not to the Chairman of the Joint Chiefs. The CJCS does not, as such, give orders to or direct the military, but acts as a planning and advisory body to the Secretary of Defense and the President.
[80] Albright. 351.

Who Is Behind the Wheel? Drivers for Intervention

> "When we were fighting against Hitler, it wasn't just Hitler; it was fighting against fascism... and when we're dealing with a now indicted war criminal such as Milosevic, it isn't just him. It is struggling against a concept, which is that it is not appropriate, possible, or permissible for one man to uncork ethnic nationalism as a weapon."
>
> Secretary of State Madeleine Albright, 10 June, 1999 interview on MacNeil Lehrer News Hour.[81]

Before the Dayton accords in 1995, Bosnia stood out as a symbol of failure for the Clinton administration's foreign policy initiatives, and NATO credibility became an issue just as important, if not more, than the situation on the ground in Kosovo.[82] NATO intervention and the positioning of U.S. forces in Bosnia helped to secure the region and limit the ability of Serbia to continue aggressive acts there. Kosovo, however, was a different case, as the embattled region was a province of Serbia itself, and not a separate region of the former Socialist Republic of Yugoslavia. The province, which was overwhelmingly populated by ethnic Albanians, held a central position in the Serbian psyche because of the battle which was fought there against the Ottoman Empire on June 28, 1389.[83]

As early as December 1992, then President Bush had warned the Belgrade regime that the U.S. would not tolerate a Serb crackdown on Kosovo, in what was known as his "Christmas warning". The newly elected President Clinton confirmed this warning, following which Kosovo promptly dropped off the international or domestic U.S. radar screens, since it was an internal matter, and seemed to pale in

---

[81] Albright interview on the McNeil/Lehrer Newshour, 10 June 1999. From Schnabel, Albrecht and Thakur, Ramesh. *Kosovo and the Challenge of Humanitarian Intervention: Selective Indignation, Collective Action, and International Citizenship.* New York: United Nations University Press, 2000. 89.

[82] Kelley, Michael. Surrender and Blame, The New Yorker, December 19, 1994. http://www.newyorker.com/magazine/1994/12/19/surrender-and-blame. Accessed on 15 October 2014.

[83] Hyland. 45.

significance compared to other issues, such as Somalia, Rwanda, and nearby Croatia and Bosnia-Herzegovina.[84] In 1996, Kosovo, which had heretofore emphasized non-violent action to achieve independence from Serbia, began to see an uptick in armed resistance. The U.S. seemed to reinforce this in tacit ways, for example, by opening a U.S. Information Agency information center in Prishtina, the capital of Kosovo, in July, 1996, which was considered to be a de-facto embassy in the province.[85] By spring, 1998, with the aforementioned events having been resolved, the western governments began to focus on the Kosovo issue, although the fact that there had been no game changing event, such as the Siege of Sarajevo, or the destruction of Srebrenica, to galvanize around, not would there be until the Racak massacre in January, 1999.[86] Racak proved to be the game changing moment that allowed Albright to bring her full persuasive power to bear on the situation. William Walker, head of the OSCE Verification Team, who called Racak a crime against humanity in a Prishtina press conference that was not approved by the White House, while an aide remembered that Wesley Clark said that, as a result of Racak, he "had them where he wanted them," meaning that force would now be on the table.[87]

Madeleine Albright emerged as the most senior, and powerful administration voice in favor of military intervention in the Balkans in general and in the Kosovo crisis in particular, in this they were joined by the Vice President, Al Gore.[88] Richard Holbrooke became assistant secretary of state for European affairs, and special envoy to the Balkans. It was his efforts which brought about a successful conclusion to the Dayton Peace Talks and put him in a key position to influence the Kosovo intervention. Holbrooke was trusted by U.S. leaders for his seeming ability to force Milosevic to comply with their demands, similarly, the

---

[84] Talentino. 256.
[85] Remarks by R. Nicholas Burns, Department of State Press Briefing, June 5, 1996. From Phillips. 66-67.
[86] Talentino. 257.
[87] Halberstam. 410.
[88] Rodman. 222.

Serbian leader seemed to respect Holbrooke as a negotiator.[89] He had arranged a meeting between Milosevic and the Kosovar leader Rugova which took place in May, 1998, but nothing meaningful came of the event.[90] A meeting between the two in October, 1998, led to a ceasefire, but this had little meaning since the KLA were thereby emboldened to increase their attacks on Serb forces, which simply encouraged greater Serb intervention and an intensification of the spiral of violence.[91] Furthermore, the negotiations had been explicitly underpinned by a NATO threat to begin air strikes within four days if no agreement was reached.[92] Clinton made his decision to approve intervention when Serbia failed to sign on the Rambouillet proposals.[93] When Holbrooke returned to Belgrade in March, 1999, after the failure at Rambouillet, his presence was more of a last ditch effort to inform Milosevic of the threat of force than a serious peace mission.[94] This is the one example from the case studies that seems to fit with the "implemental mindset" discussed as part of Dominic Tierney's "Rubicon Model" meaning that there was not going to be a backing down from attack by that point.[95]

Albright continued in her role as the hawk in terms of NATO intervention in Kosovo, and she was skeptical that any diplomatic course that was not backed by force could be ultimately successful.[96] Her position became so outspoken that Berger, now the National Security Advisor, frequently prevented communications from her reaching President Clinton, a situation which remained nearly constant

---

[89] Phillips. 60. Phillips reports the incident in which Holbrooke, having just been married, continued to lobby for bombing of Serbia, during his honeymoon, in the events which led to the 1995 Dayton Peace accords.
[90] Interview with Ambassador Richard C. Miles, Charge d'Affaires, U.S. Mission to Serbia. In Phillips. 71.
[91] Talentino. 260.
[92] Statement to the Press by NATO Secretary General Javier Solana on 27 October 1998. http://www.nato.int/docu/speech/1998/s981027a.htm. Accessed on 15 October 2014.
[93] Scolino, E., and Bronner, E. How a President, Distracted by Scandal, Entered the Balkan War. The New York Times. 1A. April 18, 1999.
[94] Talentino. 260.
[95] Johnson, Dominic, and Tierney, Dominic. "The Rubicon Theory of War: How the Path to Conflict Reaches the Point of No Return" *International Security* 36, No. 1 (2011): 7-40. 15.
[96] Houghton. 208.

until the Racak massacre.[97] In congressional testimony on the intervention given approximately one month after it began, Albright laid out the reasons for the U.S. actions. She noted historical importance of the Balkans as a cultural and religious crossroads remembering that the First World War started there. She noted the proximity of the region to key U.S. Allies such as old NATO members Greece and Turkey, and new ones such as Hungary and the Czech Republic. She emphasized that the intervention allowed the U.S. and NATO to live up to their "highest ideals, and hoped that the intervention would become "a turning point in European history."[98] In stark contrast to the decision making process for the Somalia intervention, the Principal's Committee in the NSC repeatedly deadlocked on the issue, with the Departments of State and Defense at loggerheads over the potential responses.[99] Racak, and the Serbian slaughter of 45 ethnic Albanians there broke the political deadlock and set U.S. leaders onto the path of intervention and allowed Albright, Holbrooke, and Clark to sway the other key decision makers.[100] Over a four day period, from January 19 to January 23, 1999, the Principals Committee engaged in the debate that would ultimately set the U.S. on the path to intervention. As described by Albright, she convinced the other Principals that a further ultimatum, backed by the threat of force, should be placed on the table, and it was this threat which brought about both the peace conference at Rambouillet and the armed humanitarian intervention which followed.[101] During the October crisis, Clark had developed an air campaign which was never implemented, and proposed a similar military response now.[102] Nevertheless, neither President Clinton nor his Vice President, Al Gore were interested in deploying troops into Kosovo, although the events in Rwanda and Bosnia seem to have convinced them that some military action could work.[103] They seemed to collectively forget that the supposed

[97] Rodman. 222.
[98] Halperin, in Buckley. 224.
[99] Rodman. 223.
[100] Houghton. 208.
[101] Albright. 397-398.
[102] Clark. 118.
[103] Houghton. 201, 213.

effectiveness of air strikes in compelling Serbia to negotiate at Dayton failed was explicitly linked to ground offensives into the region.[104]

In contrast to the Somalia intervention, in which pressure from Congress was directly cited as a source of pressure to intervene, there was little outright support for military coercion of Serbia. Albright noted that key leaders, such as Senators Biden and Lugar, from the Senate Foreign Relations Committee, and Speaker of the House Dennis Hastert, were in general support of the air strikes, and that the vote in the Senate supporting them was respectable, at 58 in favor, 41 against, while the vote in the House of Representatives was 219-191, both indicators of bipartisan support for the air strikes.[105] However, Congressional leaders were strongly opposed to the possibility of the use of ground forces in Kosovo, a fact which significantly influenced the decision to intervene and the planning for the implementation once intervention was agreed upon. The Kosovo crisis covers two Congresses, the 105th and 106th. The 105th Congress, which lasted from January, 1997 to December, 1998, mentioned Kosovo 461 times, with seven hearings specifically focused on intervention, and one, that of 5 October 1998 specifically enjoining the U.S. not to intervene. From January to April 28, 1999, there were 42 Congressional events about or mentioning Kosovo, with a pivotal hearing recommending against the use of ground forces on March 10th 1999.[106] Neither Clinton nor his political allies wished to embark on a major invasion while the presidency was under attack, with impeachment proceedings underway following the Monica Lewinsky sex scandal.[107] Furthermore, they did not want an extended campaign, particularly a ground campaign, to last into the fall, when it would potentially cause problems for Al Gore's campaign for president.[108]

---

[104] Talentino. 258.
[105] Albright. 408.
[106] Congressional Research Service. Congressional Record of the 105th and 106th Congresses. http://thomas.loc.gov/cgi-bin/thomas2. Accessed on 9 October, 2014.
[107] Clinton. 805, and Houghton. 202.
[108] Redd, Stephen B. "The Influence of Advisors and Decision Strategies on Foreign Policy Choices: President Clinton's Decision to Use Force in Kosovo." *International Studies Perspectives*, Volume 6, 2005. 137.

Congress came to support the attack decision, but was unwilling to commit ground forces. This is reflected by two key votes which took place on the first day of the air strikes. According to Clinton, the Senate voted 58-41 in support of the air strikes. The House also supported them, but was careful to place limits on them. Voting 219-191, the House stated that ground troops could only be used in Kosovo after a cease fire, and only with Congressional approval.[109] So throughout, Congress remained reluctant on a total combat solution to the problem. In April, as pressure to introduce ground forces grew, Congress again voted to deny their use.[110] Congressional reluctance transferred itself over to Secretary of Defense Cohen, who had come to his position directly from Capitol Hill, voted against action in Bosnia, and now felt caught between the activists and the non-interested.[111]

The Pentagon, as it had been in previous cases, was against the intervention and particularly against the deployment of ground forces in Serbia and Kosovo, with one study estimating that 100-200,000 troops would be needed to properly enforce NATO's will on the Belgrade regime, and the CIA noting that ethnic cleansing had already begun there.[112] Clearly these forces would be primarily supplied by the U.S., something which the Pentagon was unwilling to do. Buckley notes the dichotomy that, nearly to a fault, the players pushing for military interventions were all civilians whose outlooks were shaped by the Vietnam War, while the military, also remembering Vietnam, were by and large against intervention.[113] Support was bipartisan, according to Hill, with key conservative figures such as Paul Wolfowitz, a neo-conservative and later an architect of the U.S. Global War on Terror, in support of U.S. efforts to resolve the Kosovo issue

---

[109] Clinton. 940.
[110] Ibid. 942.
[111] Rodman. 226.
[112] Harris, John F. "Advice did not sway Clinton on Airstrikes." *The Washington Post*, 1 April 1999. A1. http://www.washingtonpost.com/wp-srv/inatl/daily/april99/clinton040199.htm. Accessed on 16 October 2014.
[113] Buckley. 266.

forcefully.[114] In a manner reminiscent of the Vietnam Era, once the bombing began, Clinton insisted on personally signing off on targets, a process which would limit the flexibility and effectiveness of the attacks.[115]

The most significant international leader pushing for intervention in Somalia had been UN Secretary General Boutros-Gali, but there was no UN pressure for Kosovo, as has been discussed. Instead, international pressure for intervention in Kosovo would come from two key sources. One, very public voice, was the UK Prime Minister Tony Blair. In response to the events which led to the fall, 1998 Holbrooke mission, Blair, in a speech to the UN General Assembly, called the situation in Kosovo an "Impending humanitarian affairs disaster."[116] Blair notes that what he calls his "political awakening" over Kosovo came over the course of 1998, fueled by UK intelligence reporting over the rising death toll in the province.[117] Blair had developed a close working relationship with Clinton, which he says was put to the test, particularly over the issue of ground intervention, of which Blair was outspokenly in favor.[118] But Blair also understood that there could be no NATO intervention without the U.S., which would bear 85% of the military burden of the intervention. The relationship stood the test, and the "political soul mates" continued their collaboration afterward.[119]

The other, who exerted pressure primarily through NATO military commander Clark, was that organization's Secretary General, Javier Solana. Solana was supremely aware of the need for successful operations in building NATOs reputation after the Cold War. One of his first directive to Clark was to absolutely ensure that the NATO piece of the effort which brought Serbia to the

---

[114] Hill. 108.

[115] Houghton. 202-203. President Johnson had adopted a policy of personally clearing attacks in North Vietnam, in an effort to avoid antagonizing the Soviet Union and Communist China. Clinton is known to have been deeply impacted by Vietnam.

[116] Blair, Tony. "Address by Tony Blair to the United Nations General Assembly, 21 September 1998." http://news.bbc.co.uk/2/hi/events/clinton_under_fire/latest_news/169395.stm. Accessed on October 15, 2014.

[117] Blair, Tony. *A Journey: My Political Life*. London: Knopf, 2010. 252. The death toll over the time frame of the crisis rose to 200,000.

[118] Ibid. 252.

[119] Ibid.

table at Dayton succeeded.[120] He carried that determination forward into the Kosovo planning, imploring Clark to make sure that whatever operation be carried out be done under NATO auspices, particularly after NATO was shut out of a role in the enforcement of the October agreement in 1998.[121] In common with the White House, the overwhelming preference for NATO was that there be an air component of the operation with no NATO ground forces until after a peace deal had been forced.[122] This was in contrast to the view of military leaders in the Pentagon, who questioned the utility of an air only operation, while simultaneously strongly resisting the idea of putting boots on the ground.

Support among the NATO allies was varied. UK and French support for air operations stayed in the 60-70% range through the conflict, with the French showing a similar taste for ground operations.[123] In the UK support for ground operations never rose above 50%. [124] In Germany, on the other hand, support never rose above 30%.[125] According to Blair, Solana and Clark welcomed Blair's assistance in gathering support for the intervention, which he was happy to give.[126] He also helped to deflect calls for an early cease fire, particularly from the Italians and Germans.[127] In Germany, a political upheaval had just occurred, with new Chancellor Gerhard Schroeder, a Social Democrat, leading the first non-Christian Democrat government since 1982. The leaders of the new government, in particular Schroeder and the Green Party foreign minister, Joschke Fischer, openly supported the operation, but Schroeder was well aware that the German people were not prepared at first for entry into a conflict.[128] With this in mind, Schroeder deployed German military forces into frontline combat operations for the first time

---

[120] Clark. 80.
[121] Ibid. 139.
[122] Ibid. 134.
[123] Auerswald, Donald P. "Integrated Decision Model of NATO Policy in Kosovo." *International Studies Quarterly*, Issue 28, 2004, 631-664. 640.
[124] Ibid. 640.
[125] Ibid.
[126] Blair. 266.
[127] Ibid. 266. Also Clark 228.
[128] Schroeder, Gerhard. Entscheidungen: Mein Leben in Der Politik. Hamburg: Ullstein, 2006. 85.

since the end of the Second World War, saying that the operation was "not a war, but the imposition of a peaceful solution" to the crisis.[129] Germany was keen to reassure its allies that a Social Democrat Germany could be a reliable military partner.[130] However, the bombing campaign revealed a rift in the German left between former West Germans who supported the military operation, and former East Germans, in particular members of the PDS, old German communist party, who were decidedly against the intervention, noting that it had no UN mandate, threatening to break apart the new coalition government and return the Christian Democrats to power.[131] Schroeder later used his position as the rotational president of the EU council to help broker an end to the conflict.[132]

As Wesley Clark described it, there were four objectives for the air offensive with the overall goal of halting and reversing the ethnic cleansing campaign and facilitating the return of the refugees who had already fled. First, it should be as nearly casualty free as possible. Second, it should be focused on the Serb forces actively engaged in ethnic cleansing. Third was the principle of minimal collateral damage. Fourth, targets would be chosen with the aim of maintaining the alliance's cohesion.[133] Though the initial agreement was for a few nights of bombing at most, as the campaign began it proved to easier to continue it than it had been to negotiate it in the first place. [134]

---

[129] Schröder, Gerhard. "Erklärung von Bundeskanzler Gerhard Schröder zur Lage im Kosovo." Stichworte zur Sicherheitspolitik, March 24, 1999. 41.
[130] Schröder, Gerhard. "Deutsche Sicherheitspolitik an der Schwelle des 21. Jahrhunderts', Rede von Bundeskanzler Schröder vor der 35. Münchener Konferenz zur Sicherheitspolitik." 6 February 1999, in: Stichworte zur Sicherheitspolitik. February 1999. 25, 28.
[131] Economist, The. "Germany and Kosovo: The War Divides." April 22, 1999. http://www.economist.com/node/201137. Accessed on 28 November 2014.
[132] Schröder, Gerhard. War and Peace. http://gerhard-schroeder.de/en/war-peace/. Accessed on November 20, 2014.
[133] Clark, Wesley. "The Strength of an Alliance." September 17, 1999. From Buckley. 253.
[134] Clark, quoted in Buckley. 264. Also Talbot. 338. Clark told Talbot "If we start this thing, it will be a long haul."

Public Opinion and the Kosovo Intervention

There was little press coverage of the Kosovo issue before the Racak massacre in January, 1999, according to Holbrooke.[135] In September, 1998, for example, the Washington Post reported on the growing number of refugees in the region, noting that as many as 300,000 people had been displaced internally by Serb actions.[136] The American public was focused on the Monica Lewinsky scandal, and remained largely uninterested in the events in Kosovo, changing slightly after Racak. The Rambouillet conference and the lead up to the intervention in Serbia saw an uptick in U.S. support for operations. A Gallup Poll taken on February and March 19-21, 1998, showed a 3% increase in participants who supported military operations if no agreement was reached, from 43-46%.[137] Respondents increasingly conflated Kosovo with U.S. security, and between 19 February and 25 March, the number who thought that acting in Kosovo protected U.S. interests increased by 6%, from 37 to 43%.[138] A summary of these polls is seen below.

[135] Holbrooke interview with the author, April 7, 1999. Talentino. 256.
[136] *The Washington Post*. "Kosovo: The Jerusalem of Serbia," World Balkans Special Report, July 1999, http://www.washingtonpost.com/wp-srv/inatl/longterm/balkans/overview/kosovo.htm, from Phillips. 89.
[137] Redd, 2005. 136.
[138] The Gallup Poll. "Americans Hesitant, As Usual, About U.S. Military Action in Balkans." http://www.gallup.com/poll/3994/americans-hesitant-usual-about-us-military-action-balkans.aspx. Accessed on 10 November 2014.

Figure 4: Key polling data on Intervention in Kosovo, February-May 1999

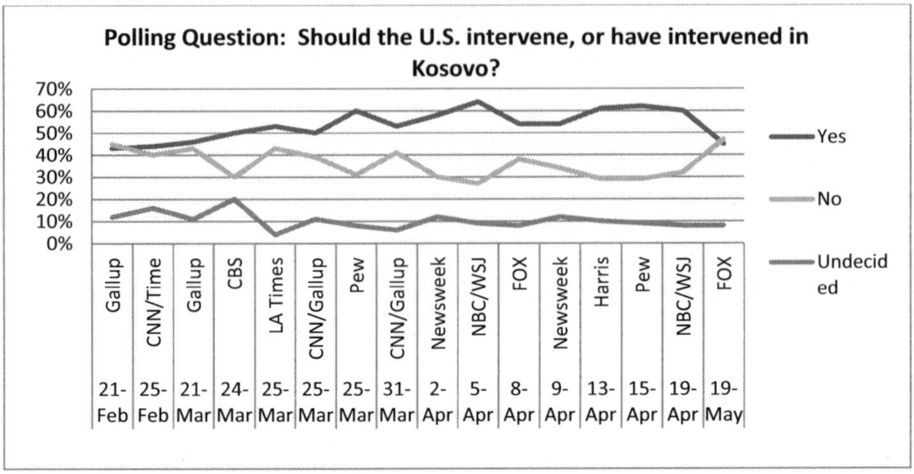

Source: Polling Report on Serbia and Yugoslavia[139]

What is most noteworthy about this collection of polling data is that support for intervention grew only slowly through the course of the Rambouillet peace talks, peaking only once intervention had actually begun on March 24, 1999. While Kosovo benefited from a lengthy period of framing, this did little to increase enthusiasm for the operation before it actually began.

The White House first commented on Kosovo in the context of the intervention crisis in March, 1998, but it did not emerge in presidential communications as a standalone issue until June, when Clinton specifically mentioned Milosevic during a joint statement he gave with Russian President Yeltsin. From September 1998 onwards, a series of communications began to clarify the situation and to frame the intervention, specifically naming Milosevic and his actions as the problem in the region.[140] By early March, as the negotiations

---

139 *Polling Report*. "Polling Report on Serbia and Yugoslavia, 1999." http://www.pollingreport.com/serb9905.htm. Accessed on 25 November 2014.

140 On October 12, Clinton famously said "Balkan Graveyards are filled with President Milosevic's broken promises," at a fundraiser for Senator Charles Schumer of New York. From Butler, Michael J. *Selling a 'Just' War: Framing, Legitimacy, and U.S. Military Intervention*. New York: Palgrave Macmillan, 2012. 146.

in France were failing, presidential statements increased in stridency and directly hinted at the air campaign which would follow if negotiations failed. Throughout, and throughout the actual bombing campaign, the messaging remained consistently focused on Milosevic personally and the need to correct his regime's "evil." Indeed, 45% of Administration speech acts on Kosovo were focused on the terminology "evil" and aimed at Congress and other government level decision makers, while 44% focused on justifying "intervention" and were aimed at the media and the public. [141]

One part of the framing effort for intervention was bitterly contested between supporters and detractors of the president's decision making and framing of the intervention. Clinton's announcement of the commencement of bombing attacks, on February 24, 1999, provided the context of the intervention to the American people, framing Milosevic's actions and explaining the increase in atrocities in Kosovo.[142] Clinton also made specific and repeated references to putting troops on the ground. With his clear statement, "I do not intend to put our troops on the ground in Kosovo to fight a war," Clinton sent very mixed signals to the Serb leadership, which military leaders credit with lengthening the conflict, since it gave them the impression that the administration was not serious in its intent.[143] Clinton's instinct domestically, however, appears to have been correct. In Fox News polls in May and June, 1999, specifically asking about sending ground troops into Kosovo, the results were nearly identical, with 27% in favor and 59-60% against.[144] Given the timing of the polls, this result seems to be a result of successful framing of the issue by the president. In any case, Clinton was adamant, and claimed throughout, and afterwards, that the introduction of ground force into

---

[141] Butler. 175.
[142] Clinton. 940.
[143] Halbertsam. 423.
[144] Fox News "Poll of June, 1999, with the question "Should the U.S. lead ground forces into combat against the Serbian Army in Kosovo?" From Wittkopf, Eugene. *The Domestic Sources of U.S. Foreign Policy*. Lanham, MD: Rowman and Littlefield Publishers, 2004. 103.

the conflict would ended up claiming more innocent lives than might have been saved.[145]

The dueling narratives of the planning effort turned out to be between the world-views of the two age groups represented in Clinton's cabinet. Like George H.W. Bush in the case of Saddam Hussein in 1990, Albright was quick to seize on the Munich analogy, conflating Slobodan Milosevic with Hitler, and strongly urging that he not be appeased over Bosnia and Kosovo as Hitler had been over the Sudetenland in 1938.[146] Either way, action was preferred to inaction, regardless of which imagery was used to appeal to which audience. Thus, the avoidance of a second Munich and the perceived appeasement of a new Hitler was the primary narrative coming from the Department of State, while avoidance of a Vietnam like quagmire was the mantra of other governmental departments and the large cadre of Vietnam veterans serving in the administration and Congress, such as John McCain, the powerful Republican member of the Foreign Relations and Armed Service Committees in the Senate.[147] This group also includes Defense Secretary Cohen and many of the senior uniformed military leaders, with the notable exception of Clark.

Models and the Kosovo Decision Process

The Kosovo intervention shows in clear focus the role of the powerful individual, or group of individuals, in the decision making process. Madeleine Albright was at the center of the process, to the point that the Kosovo conflict was often called "Madeleine's War" by her detractors. Holbrooke had a role as well, building on his central role as a Milosevic expert in the Dayton Peace Accords. Clark's role was highly significant, as in spite of the fact that he did not lead his

---

[145] Clinton. 941.
[146] Halberstam. 261-265.
[147] Ash, Timothy Garton. "The New Adolf Hitler." *Time*, 5 April 1999. http://www.cnn.com/ALLPOLITICS/time/1999/03/29/hitler.html. Accessed on 10 October 2014. Discussed in Schnabel and Thakur. 349-350.

organization, he was important enough of a player to have an independent, and important voice. President Clinton's main focus was on Congressional and public acceptance of the war.[148] Outside leaders, particularly Tony Blair, were also significant to the process, as was the key organizational player, NATO. Clinton would not have been pushed to agree to intervention without the U.S. trio of Albright, Holbrooke and Clark, with Blair thrown in from the outside.

With the exception of Clark's role, the Governmental Politics Model holds true for the decision making and framing processes for the Kosovo intervention. Since this intervention was not in response to a basic humanitarian need such as for food, shelter, or reconstruction, the agencies focused on those activities, such as OFDA and USAID had no role in the discussions. This was very much a Defense and Department of State show, with the intelligence agencies in a supporting role. As could be expected, with the interesting caveat on civilian versus military views on the use of force, the Department of Defense came down in general against involvement, while the Department of State came down in favor.

In terms of framing, this is the first case studied in which a planned framing effort leading to an intervention took place, indicating the decide/explain/act model in operation. Secretary of State Albright led a deliberate effort to frame the debate on Kosovo, even pre-empting official statements from the White House and her fellow cabinet leaders.[149] Immediately after the Racak massacre, Albright, then in Moscow, issued joint statement with Russian Foreign Minister Ivanov decrying the event.[150] This was one of a series of statements designed to ratchet up the pressure on all parties to act. However, there is little evidence that there was a government wide effort to frame to intervention to the public until immediately before the beginning of combat operations at the end of March. Efforts to influence the public

---

[148] Redd. 7.

[149] DiPrizio. 136. The Author terms it "Leading through Rhetoric" and notes that Albright was targeting all of her audiences, including allied governments, the public, and her own cabinet partners.

[150] Lippman, Thomas W. *Madeleine Albright and the New American Diplomacy*. Boulder, CO: Westview Press, 2000. 252

included use of Albright's former boss at the NSC, Zbigniew Brzezinski, who wrote for the Wall Street Journal supporting an intervention in the days before it began. His argument, specifically calling for a massive air assault on the Belgrade regime, echoed plans and orders that were already being circulated for implementation at the Pentagon and in Europe.[151] The themes Brzezinski and others laid out were consistent, and delivered at all levels, from the president down to staffers: Protect human rights, defuse the potential for war in the powder keg of Europe, and strengthen NATO.[152]

Tony Blair noted that there was "No direct U.S. interest, no public appetite for action, in Kosovo," other than that Europe should take care of the problem itself. [153] This begs the question of whether the intervention was a rational choice for the Clinton administration. The rationality of the Clinton decision to intervene was based not in the perception of a direct threat to the security of the United States, but from the need to preserve NATO and prevent strife in Europe.[154] An undercurrent from the various political memoirs examined is the need to prevent another Rwanda or Somalia, both for the political threat that an additional failure could cause, but also from some sense of moral outrage against such events in general. In this, Clinton was thinking of his legacy, oddly enough in a way similar to the way that George H.W. Bush was thinking of his own legacy when he intervened in Somalia in 1992.

Conclusion

According to former Czech President Vaclav Havel, the Kosovo intervention was the "first war that has not been waged in the name of 'national interest,' but rather in the name of principles and values."[155] David Gibbs

---

[151] Quoted in Buckley. 318.
[152] Brzezinski, Zbigniew. "In Kosovo, U.S. Cannot Stand Alone." *Wall Street Journal,* March 24, 1999. Printed in DiPrizio. 141.
[153] Blair. 252.
[154] Ibid.
[155] Talentino. 255.

counteracts this idea, claiming that the Kosovo intervention was an act of nearly pure national interest on behalf of the United States, which was intent on reaffirming its leadership over Europe and redeeming its military credibility after failures over the course of the decade.[156] Gibbs focused on the role of Holbrooke in what he calls false negotiations, noting in particular the final Holbrooke trip to Belgrade in March, which he calls simple coercion rather than diplomacy.[157] However, this seems unfair considering the events of the summer and fall, 1998, in which Holbrooke genuinely tried to negotiate, and the very real massing of Serbian forces for ethnic cleansing operations in Kosovo which have been related in this case study.

At first, the bombing campaign in Kosovo served to intensify Serbian atrocities in Kosovo, but as the air campaign intensified, Milosevic eventually surrendered to NATO and allowed NATO troops to enter Kosovo in June, 1999. As Blair related it, Clinton's increasing openness to the idea of a ground war after May 27th was mirrored in the "crumbling" of Milosevic's resolve, in that the more Milosevic appeared to weaken, the more open to ground troops Clinton became.[158] This led to confrontation with the Russians, who wished to further their own political in the region, but this was resolved diplomatically, and the whole affair was given legitimacy by the UN through UNSCR 1244.[159] While improving the situation in Kosovo, it also indefinitely delayed a permanent resolution to the problem, since Russia would be able to block any further changes in Kosovo's status through use of its veto in the Security Council, a situation which has changed little to the time of writing.

Kosovo, and its demonstration that major powers were willing to ignore the sovereignty of other nations in furtherance of humanitarian goals, ignited a major discussion on the future of such interventions. In response to a series of man-made

---

[156] Gibbs, David N. *First, Do No Harm: Humanitarian Intervention and the Destruction of Yugoslavia*. Nashville: Vanderbuilt University Press, 2009. 171.
[157] Clark. 148.
[158] Blair. 266.
[159] Talbot. 348.

humanitarian disasters after the end of the Cold War, the principal arose that the international community has a responsibility to protect the lives of citizens whose sovereign governments were unable or refused to do so. Kosovo joined Rwanda, Bosnia, and the ongoing Darfur crisis in inspiring the discussions.[160] A codification of the principal of humanitarian interventions came about as the result of the 2000 UN Millennium summit, and the subsequent International Commission on Intervention and State Sovereignty (ICISS) which officially coined the phrase "Responsibility to Protect" (R2P) in its final report of the same name. R2P was accepted by the UN General Assembly in 2005, with the implicit agreement that individual security stand equal to or above the long cherished Westphalian order, which was based on belief in the primacy of the state.[161] The UN Charter already provided foundations for R2P, including it's outlawing of war in Article 2 as well as its desire for the protection of human rights in its 1st, 55th, and 56th articles.[162] On the other hand, the charter's support for the sovereign rights of its member states in Article 2 created a tension between realist and utopian tendencies that R2P could potentially bridge.

R2P calls for UN members to intervene either to prevent serious suffering, stop genocide, war crimes, or crimes against humanity, or to rebuild societies which have been devastated as a result of such actions or failures.[163] In the case of Libya, prevention of serious suffering and war crimes are the most compelling of the reasons provided for R2P intervention. Under the terms of R2P, states which fail to offer adequate security to their citizens would forfeit the right of sovereign non-interference as set down in Article 2, and be subject to intervention by the international community. As previously mentioned, the ICISS report even went so

---

[160] Bellamy, Alex J. "The Responsibility to Protect," in *Security Studies: An Introduction*. New York: Routledge, 2008, 422-37. 423.
[161] Ibid. 424.
[162] Ibid. 424-425.
[163] Pape, Robert. "When Duty Calls: A Pragmatic Standard of Humanitarian Intervention." *International Security*, Summer, 2012: 41-80. 51. Further tenets for justifiable intervention were that the mission must be achievable, and be as small (tailored) as possible in its execution.

far as to place human security higher than that of the nation state.[164] This utopian desire, however, was not specifically endorsed by the UN Security Council, in part because of its implied "Responsibility to Prevent,"[165] abridgements of human security rather than simply reacting to their occurrence.[166] This move, as well as others, reflect an overarching problem for R2P; the lack of ability to agree on core definitions at any level of the discussion, from the definition of a major crisis to that of what an intervention seriously damaged the original, neo Kantian intent of the R2P proposal.[167] As R2P moved from proposal stage to a vote, it was significantly watered down, creating very high thresholds for action and with upholding the power of the Security Council to decide if a situation was serious enough to warrant intervention. Thus, the Security Council retains the right to authorize interventions, keeping them subject to the whims of the permanent/veto wielding members of the council.[168]

This case study focused on the decision making processes of the second term Clinton administration, specifically the case of the armed intervention in Kosovo from March-June 1999. It examined the context for intervention from a historical perspective in Yugoslavia, as well as a political perspective in Washington DC. It noted the influence of a small group of powerful leaders, namely Albright, Holbrooke, and Clark, who were in positions of influence, and, motivated to use that influence to drive decision making toward intervention. Furthermore, it discussed bi-lateral and multilateral relationships, with the UK and NATO, that impacted the operation and the decision making cycle significantly,

---

[164] The ICISS states that, after the host country, the Security Council has the primary responsibility to act. Sovereignty, International Convention on Intervention and State. The Responsibility to Protect. Final Report, Ottawa: Published by the International Development Research Centre, 2001.

[165] Responsibility to Prevent, although presented as a subset to R2P, actually goes beyond it, stating that the International Community can act against perceived humanitarian affronts, in other words, crimes which have not yet occurred.

[166] Bellamy. 426-427

[167] Pape. 51

[168] The ICISS report suggested that the permanent members agree in advance to forgo a veto in cases of R2P interventions, but this was never agreed to, nor was the proposal that R2P cases could be sent directly to the General Assembly in such cases. The Responsibility to Protect, Final Report. 2001.

and differently, than the UN had done in the previous cases. It addressed the role of a hostile great power, Russia, which also impacted the situation significantly, and in contrast to the way great power politics operated in the previous cases. Finally, it discussed the new thinking on state sovereignty, humanitarian interventions, and human security which resulted from the cumulative effects of the series of humanitarian interventions, armed and unarmed, which took place in the 1990s.

CHAPTER VI - Obama and U.S. Intervention in Libya, 2011

Spring 2011 will likely forever be known as the Arab Spring – a sequence of popular uprisings which overturned the established political order in several countries. Starting with an incident in Tunisia, the Arab Spring rapidly engulfed Egypt and spread to points east and west. While revolts were crushed in the gulf state of Bahrain, they flared in Syria. By February, 2011, Libya, which had undergone a remarkable, if cynical transformation from enemy to ally of the west in the early 2000's, was perched on the edge. As rebellion threatened in the eastern part of the country, Muhammar Gaddafi, ruling from Tripoli in western Libya, preached the status quo and commenced a policy of brutal retaliation.

The U.S. and the international community generally took a wait and see approach to the initial events of the Arab Spring. However, when the Libyan situation showed signs of disturbance, political elites in the region and Europe and the U.S. cried for intervention rather than support Gaddafi and the status quo. The U.S. and key European allies assembled a coalition for intervention, and were able to exert pressure on UN to act in favor of intervention. This was facilitated by the Arab League and the Gulf Cooperation Council, which were dominated by conservative Arab States which were simultaneously cracking down on protests in Bahrain. Thus, a coalition of members of both regional organizations and NATO launched what the U.S. called "Operation Odyssey Dawn" to enforce a no fly zone and later to provide air support to Libyan rebels. In March and April 2011, this amounted to some 100 cruise missile attacks and 1,900 aircraft sorties. From enforcing a no-fly zone, support grew into a full spectrum air offensive against pro Gaddafi Libyan forces, eventually enabling the rebel movement to expand its operations westward and overthrow the dictator, with an additional 24,000 sorties flown under NATO leadership through October 2011. In the end, Gaddafi was hunted and died during capture, and a largely Islamist and anti-western coalition has taken over the country.

Intervention in Libya was achieved through a variety of methods and channels, most innovative and notable of which was the invocation of the new UN doctrine of Responsibility to Protect (R2P). This chapter looks at the Libya intervention as a decision making process, both in terms of the deployment of forces, and in the framing effort in support of the operation and against Gadhafi. R2P features in the study as a framing device for encouraging the decision to intervene and in the justification of the intervention to relevant audiences. The study will review the history of the crisis in Libya as well as how that crisis fits into the overall world situation in 2011, continuing to examine the key players in the decision making process and the method by which the decision to intervene was made and framed to the American public. Research reveals that intervention was made possible through the pressure of a few key leaders in the Obama administration. Those leaders, most notably Ambassador to the UN Susan Rice and National Security Council staffer Samantha Power were both relatively junior in the positions they held in the administration, but their unique ties the president facilitated both access and influence. With the eventual turnaround in support by Secretary of State Hillary Clinton, they were able to encourage President Obama to decide in favor of intervention. Having decided on intervention, the government then rapidly launched a broad framing effort, including leaders who had been against the decision to intervene, in an effort to build support for the operation.

Libya and the Arab Spring 2010 – 2011 – Background to Intervention

Over the course of the early 2000s, Libya achieved a remarkable rapprochement with the west, largely undoing the enmity brought about by a series of confrontations with the U.S. in the 1980s, culminating with the Lockerbie bombing of Pan Am Airlines flight 103 in 1988.[1] Through destruction of extant stocks of weapons of mass destruction in 2003, and the foreswearing of efforts to obtain nuclear weapons, as well as the negotiation of a series of oil and other trade deals, Gaddafi achieved through diplomacy what aggression could not: A Libya that was seen as a lucrative trade partner and potential ally in northern Africa.[2] Libya's leader Gaddafi, always eccentric, was increasingly seen as a continental player in Africa through his efforts to influence the African Union coupled with Libya's immense reserves of oil (largest in Africa and the fifth largest in the world with 76.4 billion barrels in 2010) gave it a strong strategic and economic position.[3]

There was more to Libya than met the eye, however. Money tended to be concentrated in Gaddafi's home city of Sirte, and westwards in his capital, Tripoli.[4] Libya is a highly tribalized society, with government working as a function of deals the Gaddafi family made with the other tribes for various services. The growing interest and efforts of U.S. and European multinational corporations (beyond the obvious oil linkages) served to add a veneer of legitimacy to Gaddafi's rule, a reign which was becoming ever more authoritarian and removed from reality.[5] The disparity in economic wellbeing and religious beliefs between eastern and western Libya was stark. A clear cultural divide existed between east and west, with the traditional capital city of Tripoli dominating the largely pro Gaddafi west, while Benghazi, largest city in the east, and long considered to be anti-regime, was touted by the regime as a symbol of the improvements Gaddafi promised. But

---

[1] Chorin, Ethan. *Exit Gaddafi: The Hidden History of the Libyan Revolution.* London: Saqi Books, 2012. 5-6.
[2] Ibid. 182.
[3] Administration, U.S. Energy Information. Country: Libya. June 2012. http://www.eia.gov/countries/cab.cfm?fips=LY. Accessed April 15, 2013.
[4] Prashad, Vijay. Arab Spring, Libyan Winter. Baltimore: AK Press, 2012. 119.
[5] Chorin. 169-170.

infrastructure improvements could not change the fact that the most effective regime opponents were clustered in Benghazi and its hinterland. Eastern Libya was already known for the higher than average number of its young men who had gone to Iraq to take part in the resistance to the U.S. efforts there.[6] This was in part because of religious fervor and in part because of poverty and political disenfranchisement at home.

The first major blow to this reinvigoration of U.S./Libyan ties occurred as a result of the wiki leaks scandal, which broke in fall 2010. Many of the leaked documents were highly personal observations of Gaddafi and his family by embassy and other Department of State officials, describing the inner workings and inner peculiarities of the regime. This was seen as a shock and an insult by the U.S. to the Libyan leader and his family, to the point that U.S. diplomatic efforts and personnel were shut out and the Ambassador eventually withdrawn, just before what would prove to be a significant crisis for Libya and the whole region, the Arab Spring.[7]

The direct events leading to the Arab Spring began in December 2010, in Tunisia, with the protest suicide of a street merchant claiming to have been abused by the government. Fanned by new media and by the mainstream Al Jazeera network, the protests forced Tunisian leaders to flee the country by mid-January 2011. Egypt was next to experience unrest as a result of what was then seen as an Arab uprising, and by the end of January the Gaddafi regime was already censoring foreign media websites and trying to control as much of the information flow from outside as it could.[8] The U.S. intelligence community had been predicting political change in the Arab nations, but was caught by surprise by the scope and speed of the events of the Arab Spring in 2011.[9]

---

[6] Prashad. 119.
[7] Chorin. 171.
[8] Ibid. 190-191. Unlike its neighbors, internet and advanced cell phone communications were rather limited in Libya, particularly in the east, so that the traditional media bore the main load in informing the public and fanning the flames of revolution.
[9] Panetta, Leon. *Worthy Fights*. New York: Penguin Press, 2014. 277.

Egypt, the centerpiece of U.S. efforts to stabilize the Middle East since the Camp David Peace Accords brought peace with Israel in 1979, appeared to be tottering, potentially nullifying those thirty years of intense diplomatic and political labor, and exposing U.S. partner Israel to threat.[10] Furthermore, significant oil contracts between the U.S. and Libya, recently rekindled following Gaddafi's "About Face," were at stake.[11] Fears of the unrest cutting off a key supplier of oil to Europe led to negative expectations for further oil trade with Libya, another possible cause for intervention.[12] Thus, the three pillars of U.S. policy, oil, stability, and the protection of Israel, loomed large in the minds of leaders in Washington. There was more than one set of messages being transmitted, however, in what amounted to a series of dueling narratives. But on February 4, 2011, Iranian Ayatollah Ali Khamenei pronounced an "Islamic Awakening" across the entire Middle East, including Libya.[13] The U.S. and international response was characterized by what Maximilian Forte called the "ongoing militarization of U.S. foreign policy and the rise of the new military humanism."[14]

On February 14, 2011, the Arab Spring threatened the Arabian Peninsula for the first time, with the "Day of Rage" protests in Bahrain, and popular unrest growing in Yemen. With U.S. support, Saudi Arabian forces assisted the Bahraini government in a brutal crackdown which ended open dissent in the country. The Arab Spring was increasingly on the radars of the Gulf states, and they would lead the way in pushing for ever stronger responses to events in Libya.[15] On 15 February 2011, in an effort to diffuse protest, Gaddafi ordered wide scale arrests around the country. These arrests failed, however, and the net result was that significant

---

10 Prashad. 38-39.
11 Ibid. 45.
12 Copeland, Dale. "Economic Interdependence and War." *International Security*, 1996: 5-41. 39.
13 Prashad. 31.
14 Forte, Maximillian. *Slouching Towards Sirte: NATO's War on Libya and Africa.* Montreal: Baraka Books, 2012. 9. Also seen in President Obama's efforts to restrain Mubarak from attacks on Egyptians.
15 Gates, Robert M. *Duty, Memoirs of a Secretary at War.* New York: Alfred A. Knopf, 2014. 515.

protests broke out just two days later, on the 17th.[16] In a cascade of violence, Gaddafi ordered further crackdowns in response, culminating in the arrest of resistance leaders and their representatives including Fathi Terbil, a lawyer who had represented earlier victims of regime violence. Fathi's arrest turned out to be the catalyst which set Benghazi onto the path of rebellion.[17] By February 20th, events in Benghazi were spiraling out of control, and, following a poorly executed conciliatory speech by Gaddafi's son Saif, major demonstrations spread for the first time to Tripoli, and thus to the dictators very doorstep.[18] This was followed by one of the first international actions of the drama, when, on 21 February 2011, the UN representatives for Libya joined the rebels, declaring their support for them and entreating the military and other leaders of the government apparatus to do the same.[19]

Meanwhile, the Libyan government's threat to its citizens was growing. Unlike Egypt, whose army largely refused to fight its own civilians, the Libyan military, largely made up of foreign mercenaries who were loyal to the Gaddafi government first and foremost, had no qualms about employing violence.[20] By this time, over 75% of Libya's population center had already fallen away from government control.[21] In a February 22nd speech, Gaddafi himself promised to "cleanse Libya inch by inch", and began deploying significant military forces to the eastern part of the country.[22] This increase and threat of violence triggered the humanitarian crisis which would later be used to justify intervention. Libya had long relied on outside labor for many of its industries, including oil, and for its army, and now all of these people, as well as foreign government officials and

---

[16] Ibid. 510. According to Prashad, this was the so called "Days of Rage" protest. Prashad. 95.
[17] Chorin, 193.
[18] Ibid. 199.
[19] Ibid. 200.
[20] Clinton, Hillary R. *Hard Choices*. New York: Simon and Schuster, 2014. 364.
[21] Pape, Robert. "When Duty Calls: A Pragmatic Standard of Humanitarian Intervention." *International Security*, Summer, 2012: 41-80. 62.
[22] Chorin. 202. In Benghazi alone, this threatened over three quarters of a million lives.

Libyans fleeing persecution, were trying to leave at once.[23] On the same day, the UN retaliated by condemning the use of force against civilians, while the Arab League supported this action by suspending Libya's membership in it.[24]

The U.S. and the World in 2011 – Context for Intervention

Although the Arab Spring came to dominate the attention of the media and the Obama administration, there were a litany of other problems in late winter, 2011. Asia was the preferred focus area of the administration, and the decline of Japan coupled with the rising economic power of China and its tacit challenge to U.S. and allied power in the Pacific area were major concerns.[25] This coincided with calls among the Muslim population in China for a "Jasmine Revolution" of pro-democracy rallies modeled on the Arab Spring. Although there were assemblies in approximately a dozen Chinese cities, no popular uprising took place.

Japan was also a growing source of concern during this period. In late February, its credit rating was downgraded because of the increasing level of government debt. Then, on 11 March, a series of earthquakes hit northern Japan, culminating in a tsunami and which led the Fukushima nuclear reactor, located on the coast to flood and meltdown, instigating a massive U.S. military evacuation and assistance effort there. At $235 billion in damage, the Fukushima earthquake was the most expensive natural disaster in history, and further crippled Japanese efforts to re-assert itself economically and politically.[26]

As noted previously the wiki leaks scandal, which had broken in 2010, continued to cause embarrassment to the U.S., around the world, and to specifically

[23] Ibid. Chorin notes that 15,000 Chinese laborers were evacuated to Crete by boat, this is just one example of private individuals, to which must be added thousands of embassy and other government officials from around the world.
[24] Gates. 510.
[25] Fitzgerald, David and Ryan, David. *Obama, U.S. Foreign Policy and the Dilemmas of Intervention.* New York: Palgrave Macmillan, 2014. 88.
[26] Kim, Victoria. "Japan damage could reach $235 billion, World Bank estimates." *The Los Angeles Times*, 21 March 2011. Retrieved 10 October 2014.

impact U.S. perceptions in and of the situation in Libya. Over 250,000 documents, many of the classified Department of State cables, were periodically released over the period of January – May 2011. Wikileaks information on wide scale state of corruption in the Tunisian Government is credited by some with instigating the Arab Spring protests.[27] Protests in Tunisia eventually led to the overthrow of that country's President, Zine Ben Ali, in January 2011.

Elsewhere in the Middle East and Africa, spring 2011 saw a series of failed coups in Ivory Coast and the Democratic Republic of Congo, while an offensive against Al-Qaeda backed militants in Somalia resulted in hundreds of casualties. Two Iranian warships transited the Suez Canal into the Mediterranean Sea on February 22nd, the first time that this had occurred since the 1979 revolution which overthrew the Shah of Iran. On February 5th, Prime Minister David Cameron of the UK said that multiculturalism had failed and that the country needed to restore a strong national identity at a security conference in Munich. This same meeting sparked the ire of Palestinian leaders, since their call for statehood was not accepted by those present. Further tensions were fanned when the new Egyptian government decided to re-open crossings into the Gaza strip at Rafah. In East Africa, Somali piracy continued to be a major concern, with a series of incidents showing the growing response of the anti-piracy coalition. The U.S. was in negotiations with Iraq for what forces it would be allowed to keep in that country after its planned withdrawal in December, 2011. Operations in Afghanistan were still ongoing, with increasing concerns about the corruption of the government of Hamid Karzai. General David Petraeus, who had taken over command in the country from General Stanley McChrystal, was in the process of revamping counterinsurgency strategies there, as violence continued.[28]

[27] Dickinson, Elizabeth. "The First WikiLeaks Revolution?" *Foreign Policy*, January 13, 2011. http://foreignpolicy.com/2011/01/13/the-first-wikileaks-revolution/. Accessed on October 27, 2014.
[28] McChrystal was relieved following negative comments on administration key leaders in interviews provided to Rolling Stone Magazine in July, 2010.

In economics, German and French leaders met to try to save the European currency, the EURO, from a series of shocks, including the economic implosion of Greece and the ongoing impacts of the World Financial Crisis which had begun in 2007. The state of the world and U.S. economies was the only issue which came near to occupying public attention in the way that the Arab Spring in 2011. Gas prices reached their highest level in two years, in excess of 107 dollars per barrel, because of the uncertainty caused by the events in the Middle East. In domestic politics, increasingly bitter partisanship marked votes to limit collective bargaining and union power in Wisconsin and Indiana, and both became national news stories, with Republican leaders prevailing in both cases. A budget crisis and threatened government shutdown were averted at the last minute by what would become the sequestration process of deferred, but forced, budget cuts, particularly in the defense field, while the disestablishment of U.S. Joint Forces Command and the re-apportionment of that commands training and support duties was causing re-adjustment through the Department of Defense.

This case study differs from the others examined in one key way. Whereas each of the other crises, in Somalia, Rwanda, and Kosovo, took place along with or as background to more significant world events, in Spring 2011, the Arab Spring and the various protests and uprisings associated with it were they number one story and priority on the minds of decision makers. In the next section of the case study, those leaders and their decision making processes will be examined more fully.

The Obama Administration, Leadership, Processes, and Strong Voices

> "He (Obama) genuinely believes that he was elected to get America off its war footing that his legacy is to get the U.S. away from its over reliance on the military instrument."
>
> Julianne Smith, advisor to Vice President Joseph Biden.[29]

---

[29] Fitzgerald. 671.

Of the three men leading the U.S. in the armed humanitarian interventions covered in the case studies, Barack Obama was, on the face of it, significantly less qualified for a foreign policy role than either George H.W. Bush or Bill Clinton. This is based both on his academic background and his career before he assumed the presidency in 2009, and in spite of his claims that living and travelling abroad at various points in his life made up for this.[30] Upon winning a U.S. Senate seat in 2004, he set about remedying this lack with a reading plan on foreign policy issues and experts, and by contacting and learning from a series of experts, including Anthony Lake, Susan Rice, and Samantha Power, the latter two of who would be among his most trusted foreign policy advisors.[31] Obama's personal leadership style and decision making techniques were significantly different from the other leaders examined in the case studies. He is known to have limited his suit choices down to two types for his term in office so that he could focus more time on critical decisions than on minor ones.[32] Gates noted that that Obama was the "most deliberative president" that he had served, and "relished the exercise of his authority."[33] Moreover, he expected strong advice from his senior cabinet members, and when that was unavailable or perceived to be lacking, he was more than willing to ask second tier advisors for their advice, and to have the advocates for various responses to an issue argue out their stances in front of him, as would be seen in the Libya decision making process.[34] Obama did not seek an "honest broker" in his National Security Advisor, but often preferred to fill that role himself as a means of centralizing decision making power in himself, a process which often led to lengthy deliberations and long decision cycles.[35] In terms of what he sought

[30] Lizza, Ryan. "The Consequentialist: How the Arab Spring remade Barack Obama's foreign policy." *The New Yorker*, May 2, 2011. http://www.newyorker.com/magazine/2011/05/02/the-consequentialist. Accessed on 10 November 2014.
[31] Ibid, 2011.
[32] Staff, NPR. "Inside Obama's Decisions, from Libya to Lunch." NPR interview with Michael Lewis, Presidential Biographer. http://www.npr.org/2012/09/11/160898373/inside-obamas-decisions-from-libya-to-lunch. Accessed on 21 November 2014.
[33] Gates. 296.
[34] Pfiffner, James P. "Decision making in the Obama White House." Presidential Studies Quarterly 41, no. 2, 2011. 244-262. 247
[35] Ibid. 244, 247.

as goals for his White House, more Middle East time was not high on the list at the beginning. He believed that the U.S. had been over focused on the region since 9-11, and that a rebalancing would be necessary to rebuild America's reputation there.[36] In spite of this desire, it is said that the enemy always gets a vote, and the Middle East would not easily pass from center stage. Still, the desire to shift focus lead to some criticism, particularly after the White House failed to react to the political upheaval in Iran from 2009-2010 which had the potential to overthrow the hostile Ahmedinejad regime if care and attention had been given.[37] Obama thus personally entered the Arab Spring crisis stung and vulnerable to criticism, and potentially more willing to act than before.

According to the memoirs of then Secretary of State Hillary Clinton, President Obama sought to emulate President Abraham Lincoln, whose cabinet included serious political enemies, including his Secretary of State, William Seward, who became a close ally. This was the driving force behind the "Team of rivals" approach to development of the Obama cabinet.[38] Based on his own experience, and memory of the effectiveness of successful national security teams such as that of George H. W. Bush, Secretary of Defense Bill Gates recommended that Obama have a team that was a "complete package" of members who got along with each other. To that end, he pledged to Obama that he would, in spite of his different political leanings, never undertake a separate political agenda from the president.[39] In spite of that advice, the Obama team never came together in the way that was seen in the George H.W. Bush or second Clinton administrations.

In spite of Gates' recommendation, the team that President Obama actually assembled were not a "complete package" and in many cases did not know one another.[40] There were several reasons for this. One is that it had been eight years

---

[36] Lizza, 2011. Interviews with Thomas Donilon and Benjamin Rhodes, Deputy National Security Advisor.
[37] Lizza, 2011. 17-18.
[38] Clinton. 13.
[39] Gates. 272.
[40] Ibid. 275.

since the last Democrat administration, and there was somewhat of a passing of the torch in terms of age and experience. The senior statesmen such as Warren Christopher and Madeleine Albright of the Carter and Clinton years were gone, both because of simple aging and the considerable acrimony that existed between the Obama and Clinton camps, based on the bitterness of the struggle for the nomination of the party. With some exceptions, such as John Podesta (who headed the Obama transition team, but then stayed out of decision making until taking a position as Counselor to the President in 2013) and Leon Panetta (Who headed the CIA and then the Department of Defense after the departure of Gates in fall, 2011), senior Clinton leaders did not flock to Obama, nor were they welcome in the leadership, in spite of the appearance of a personal rapprochement between Obama and Hillary Clinton which culminated in her becoming Secretary of State.[41] Nevertheless, the gap between the members of the two teams remained an issue.

The President's immediate followers and advisors were also significantly different in personality than their predecessors. When briefing Gates, Podesta termed the incoming team "control freaks."[42] Gates described the political leadership team as "Smart and educated, but with no experience in governing.[43] Furthermore, they reflected a far more partisan era than that in which Gates had matured as a leader. For him, bipartisan approaches to foreign policy issues were central, whereas they had become anathema to the later generations of political and foreign policy leaders.[44] Foreign policy decision making was further complicated by the fact that there were many on the Obama staff who advised him directly on foreign policy issues, but independently of the associated senior cabinet members or the National Security Staff (NSS).[45] Rahm Emmanuel, the White House Chief

[41] Gates. 287.
[42] Ibid. 276.
[43] Ibid. 287. On Page 288, Gates describes his first situation room with the new set of advisors, in which nearly half of the attendees had their cell phones with them, and on, a major security violation and indicative of their lack of exposure to high level defense and foreign policy processes.
[44] Ibid. 288.
[45] The name was changed at the beginning of the administration to "National Security Staff" so as to incorporate the Homeland Security Staff and Council.

of Staff, Robert Gibbs, the spokesman, and special advisors Valerie Jarrett and David Axelrod, none of who held foreign policy portfolios, frequently offered their advice.[46] While Jim Jones was the first National Security Advisor, he estimated that at least six people had better contact with President Obama on national security issues than he did. His departure may have improved matters by 2011, since his successor, Thomas Donilon, was one of those who had regularly done end runs around him to the president.[47] Donilon had served as Chief of Staff to then Secretary of State Warren Christopher,[48] and he turned out to be a better fit than Jones had been, and had much better access to Obama, continuing the practice of having the NSC Principal's meet once a week to discuss issues for presentation to the president.[49] According to Lizza, Donilon explicitly sought to restore the Brent Scowcroft Model of how the NSC should run.[50]

Gates described Secretary of State Clinton as the only real independent center of power in the foreign policy decision making team, noting that she was "unfireable."[51] He and Clinton formed a power center together, at least until the Libya intervention, over which they came to disagree. However, all members of the cabinet who were not core Obama staffers had one attached, and Hillary was no exception. James Steinberg, who frequently disagreed with Clinton was appointed Deputy Secretary of State without her endorsement Clinton, and furthermore, was allowed seats both on the Principal's and Deputies Committees on the National Security Council.[52] With the departure of General Jim Jones from the position of National Security Council in fall, 2010, the national security team lost its only leader with significant military experience, although the factors mentioned above,

---

[46] Gates. 291. Clinton noted that Emmanuel had a "forceful personality and vivid language." 23.
[47] Gates. 291.
[48] Clinton. 24.
[49] Ibid. 18.
[50] Lizza, 2011.
[51] Gates. 288.
[52] Ibid. 289.

it is unlikely that this would have made a difference in the decision making for Libya.[53]

Gates himself might have suffered a similar fate, however, his role and approach were quite different. He was already known as someone who had been brought in by Bush to restore the Department of Defense after the perceived damage of the Rumsfeld years. His retention was recommended by many on both sides of the political spectrum, including senior Democrat party statesmen like former National Security Advisor Brzezinski.[54] Gates described his relationship with Obama as "…close, but always focused on business," noting that the new president was "…pragmatic and open to compromise," as he was to demonstrate during the Libya decision making process. On their first meeting, Gates noted that Obama was far more passionate about the prospect of the repeal of the military's "Don't Ask, Don't tell" policy on homosexuals in the military than he was about foreign policy concerns or the combat capacity of the armed forces.[55]

Vice President Joseph Biden followed the so called "Cheney" activist model for his role, in spite of advice proffered that a more supportive and less activist role might be more appropriate.[56] While Gates thought Biden incorrect on most of his major foreign policy ideas, Clinton noted that he had a "wealth of international experience."[57] Activism was further implied by the White House decision to appoint a series of special envoys to key regions of the world such as the Middle East, Pakistan/Afghanistan, and Sudan.[58] This may have been an effort to leverage administration stalwarts into key positions in Hillary Clinton's Department of State, although Richard Holbrooke's appointment to the Pakistan/Afghanistan position until his untimely death would seem to belie this. Holbrooke played an additional role that would be critical to the Libya decision making process. He had become a

---

[53] Ibid. 290.
[54] Gates. 259.
[55] Ibid. 298.
[56] Ibid. 288. This refers to the highly involved and operational role Vice President Cheney took in the administration of George W. Bush from 2001-2009.
[57] Gates. 288., Clinton. 22.
[58] Gates. 295.

mentor to journalist cum human rights advisor Samantha Power, and as a mutual friend smoothed over what had been a problematic relationship between her and Hillary Clinton.[59] The elevation of the post of Ambassador to the UN back into the cabinet also created friction, since Susan Rice, who had criticized Clinton openly during the campaign, would now both be Clinton's subordinate in the Department of State and her equal on the Principal's Committee.[60]

Samantha Power's career led her to be a hawk on humanitarian intervention in general and in the Libya operation in particular. Her work as a journalist covering the Yugoslav Civil War led to books both on that subject and on the failure to intervene in Rwanda, and the conclusion that "politicians shy away from humanitarian intervention because they see too much domestic political risk with little payoff for saving foreign lives."[61] After reading her book, then Senator Obama recruited her for his staff. She then served as a foreign policy advisor to the Obama campaign, famously attacking Hillary Clinton and her campaign, and marrying Obama confidante Cass Sunstein.[62] Returning once the election was over, Power served as Special Assistant to the President and Office of Multilateral Affairs and Human Rights Senior Director on the NSC. For Power, prevention of genocide was a U.S. strategic, if not national security interest, so it was no great leap for her to support the Libya intervention. In a later interview, She said that "failure to intervene in Libya would have been extremely chilly, deadly, and indeed a stain on our collective conscience.[63] Power also shared a strong conviction on the applicability of R2P to the situation in Libya, noting that it was becoming a popular

---

[59] Stolberg, Sheryl Gay. "Still Crusading, but Now on the Inside." *The New York Times*. March 29, 2011.
[60] Allen, Jonathan. "Susan Rice's Walk on the Mild Side." *Politico*, January 3, 2014. http://www.politico.com/story/2014/01/susan-rices-walk-on-the-mild-side-101705.html. Accessed on October 10, 2014.
[61] Talev, Margaret. "Samantha Power: The Voice behind Obama's Libya action." McClatchy Newspapers, March 25, 2011. http://www.mcclatchydc.com/2011/03/25/111084/human-rights-advocate-samantha.html. Accessed October 27, 2014.
[62] Stolberg, 2011.
[63] Klein, Edward. *The Amateur: Barack Obama in the White House*. Washington, D.C.: Regnery Publishing, 2013. 58.

and accepted international norm, especially in the European countries which were calling for intervention.[64]

With a career in national security going back to the 1990s, and her position as an assistant to Richard Clarke on the National Security Council and protégé of Secretary of State Albright, U.S. Ambassador to the UN Susan Rice had significant foreign policy experience as well as exceptional access to President Obama. She was heavily influenced by her time in the Clinton White House, specifically in the decision making process which led the U.S. to stay out of the crisis in Rwanda, in part at her urging, as noted in the Rwanda case study. After time at the Brookings institution during the first term of President George W. Bush, Rice became a senior foreign policy advisor to the John Kerry presidential campaign in 2004, and was one of the few senior policy leaders to sign on the Obama campaign in lieu of that of rival Hillary Clinton, a choice which gave her access to and clout with President Obama. Rice was a strong advocate of the concept and application of R2P, and carried with her memories of her stance on the Rwandan atrocities, as noted in the previous case study.[65] Her management style was gruff and notably off putting, as when she famously threw a particular insult at Richard Holbrooke during the Clinton administration, and she was known to be difficult to work with.[66]

Having led the agency himself, Secretary Gates was uniquely placed to offer comment on the incoming CIA director, Leon Panetta. Panetta was one of the few top tier Clinton era leaders who joined the administration, and although he had not served in the intelligence community in the past, Gates noted that this was not unusual, and that most directors had been appointed from the outside.[67] Panetta's skill as a manager, and the general proficiency and history of the CIA put him in stronger stead with Obama than his nominal superior, Dennis Blair, the Director of National Intelligence. Blair, like Jones, was a senior military commander who had significant difficulty adjusting to the world of politics and since he only associated

---

[64] Klein. 25.
[65] Ibid. 217.
[66] Allen. 2014.
[67] Gates. 292.

with Gates, Mullen, and Clinton of the other senior advisors, it was certain that Panetta would have more leverage with the Obama.[68] Panetta, who did not have a seat at the decision making table, did support the president's decision to intervene, calling the case for Libya "compelling" while noting that "Obama was torn about it, and did not desire another war in the Middle East."[69]

As the crisis in Libya unfolded, Obama utilized his team of rivals, but overall the inner core group that came into power with him had the most access, and influence, over his decision making. To the chagrin of outsiders such as Clinton, Gates, and Jones, this was the central fact of the Obama administration's decision making processes. This would become evident in the decision making process which led to the intervention in Libya.

Who Is Behind the Wheel? Drivers for Intervention

> "The world is watching the situation in Libya with alarm. We join the international community in strongly condemning the violence in Libya. Our thoughts and prayers are with those whose lives have been lost, and with their loved ones. The government of Libya has a responsibility to respect the universal rights of the people, including the right to free expression and assembly. Now is the time to stop this unacceptable bloodshed. We are working urgently with friends and partners around the world to convey this message to the Libyan government."
>
> Secretary of State Hillary Clinton, February 21, 2011.[70]

The decision to intervene in Libya has its roots in discussions of the situation in Egypt. On 28 January, the Principal's committee met to discuss the situation, with Clinton, Gates, Donilon, and Biden urging extreme caution over the response.[71] That day, Obama called for Hosni Mubarak, the President of Egypt, to

---

[68] Gates. 292.
[69] Panetta, Leon. *Worthy Fights*. New York: Penguin Press, 2014. 349.
[70] State, U.S. Department of. "Press Statement by Secretary of State Hillary Rodham Clinton." February 21, 2011. http://www.state.gov/secretary/20092013clinton/rm/2011/02/156836.htm. Accessed on October 15, 2014.
[71] Clinton. 339.

step down, sending Department of State Africa expert Frank Wisner as a special envoy to the opposition groups, but did not directly intervene there. The establishment and discussions of R2P encouraged the idea that force should be used to protect civilians from harm, even if the when and how remained in flux. These ideas would be tested by the Libyan crisis. However, it would take time for the world to decide exactly what the crisis was, and how to react. Following the basic principles of R2P, an intervention could have been utilized as the engine for the support of a protective action for eastern Libya not dissimilar from many other peacekeeping operations (albeit smaller in scale) in Africa and around the world. But the will and the plan to intervene would have to be constructed by powerful spokespersons. Based on the January 28th meeting, those spokespersons were not yet motivated. Through February, discussions continued as the situation in Libya continued to deteriorate. On February 17th, Libya was removed from the UN Human Rights Council at the urging of the U.S., and through the efforts of Clinton and Power.[72] On February 23rd, President Obama again spoke to the crisis, pledging U.S. support to the democratic aspirations of Libyans. This did not, however, lead to intervention.[73]

While the UN deliberated and U.S. leaders debated, others did not wait to provide humanitarian support, with France sending relief supplies to Benghazi as early as February 28th. France may have been compelled to act first because of the intimate ties the Sarkozy government had with Gaddafi, which made early repudiation of those ties crucial.[74] On the same day as the French acted, the U.S. stepped up the rhetoric, in the form of a call for Gaddafi to leave office by Secretary Clinton.[75] Other international organizations served as vehicles for discussion. Hillary Clinton used the Group of 8 (G-8) meeting on March 14th 2011 to discuss

---

[72] Lizza, 2011.

[73] Biden, Joseph R. "Obama on Rebellion in Libya." http://www.history.com/topics/joe-biden/speeches/obama-on-rebellion-in-libya. Accessed on 27 October 2014.

[74] Chorin. 220.

[75] Ibid. 222.

responses to the Libyan situation with key economic allies. At this time, French President Nicholas Sarkozy, whom Clinton believed was moved primarily by the suffering in Libya,[76] pushed the strongest for a military response before government forces could reach the town of Benghazi.

The French stance was based on several factors. Sarkozy was losing political popularity rapidly, and keen to continue his repeated practice of using foreign policy to buck up domestic poll numbers.[77] In the face of right wing opposition, he was keen to be seen taking a strong leadership role, particularly in a situation in which the U.S. did not appear willing to do so.[78] This stance was also aimed at convincing European partners, particularly Germany, that France still led Europe in terms of foreign and military policy.[79] Finally, the issue of Muslim immigration was of critical importance in France, being another tocsin waved by the opposition especially that of the right wing and the situation in Libya threatened to spiral into a flood of refugees across the Mediterranean.[80]

Clinton was unconvinced that intervention was needed.[81] Sanctions and an asset freeze by the UN Security Council were followed by the Arab League's suspension of voting rights for the Gaddafi regime.[82] As March began, Secretary of State Clinton noted that no decision had yet been made by the U.S.[83] Brutality and threat of brutality was not sufficient to warrant R2P invocation, with notable numbers of leaders on both sides of the American political spectrum coming out

---

[76] Clinton. 368.
[77] Stratfor. "France and the UK have different motives for intervening in Libya." March 29, 2011. http://www.forbes.com/sites/energysource/2011/03/29/france-u-k-have-differing-motives-for-intervening-in-libya/. Accessed on 18 November 2014.
[78] Kern, Soeren. "Why France was so keen to attack Libya?" *Gatestone Institute.org*, March 23, 2011. http://www.gatestoneinstitute.org/1983/france-libya-attack. Accessed on 26 November 2014.
[79] Stratfor, 2011.
[80] Davidson, Jason W. "France, Britain, and the intervention in Libya: an integrated analysis." *Cambridge Review of International Affairs*, May 30 2013, 310-329. 316.
[81] Clinton. 363.
[82] Daalder, Ivo and Stavridis, James. "NATO's Victory in Libya." *Foreign Affairs*, 2012. 2. http://www.foreignaffairs.com/articles/137073/ivo-h-daalder-and-james-g-stavridis/natos-victory-in-libya. Accessed on April 10, 2013.
[83] Chorin. 206.

against R2P and against intervention.[84] Secretary of Defense Gates' position was that intervention in Libya was not justified, since the American people were tired of what was then nine years of warfare, and that the still ongoing conflicts in Iraq and Afghanistan meant that the U.S. military was too overstretched for yet another operation.[85] The first suggestion for a U.S. action was a call for a U.S. enforced no-fly zone over Libya. Such calls began in February, but were deflected by Gates, who warned of the effort required, and the general futility of no fly zones in other cases, most notably over Iraq. Further, he pointed out that, unlike Iraq, significant preparation of the battle space would be required over Libya. These actions, including the suppression and destruction of the Libyan air defense apparatus, would be needed before air patrols could even begin, and such actions would be tantamount to war. In addition, experience in Iraq showed that a key ground attack and support asset, the attack helicopter, was very difficult to interdict with a no-fly zone, so that the utility of such a zone would be minimal even if it could be established.[86] A tit for tat exchange occurred on this issue in early March between the team of Gates/Mullen and Arizona Senator John McCain, most notably in a series of statements and press conferences on 1 March. General James Mattis, the general in command at U.S. Central Command, supported the Gates/Mullen point of view in testimony to the House Armed Services Committee the following day.[87]

Clinton noted that as late as March 9th, the Principal's committee had still not embraced direct U.S. intervention in Libya. The following day, she testified to a Congressional hearing that no action should be undertaken without international authorization, and that there should be no hurry to intervene.[88] The very next day,

---

[84] Friedman, Benjamin. "Intervention in Libya and Syria Isn't Humanitarian or Liberal." April 5, 2012. http://nationalinterest.org/blog/the-skeptics/intervention-libya-syria-isn%E2%80%99t-humanitarian-or-liberal-6739. Accessed on February 28, 2013. 1.

[85] Gates. 182.

[86] Gates, Robert M. "Statement on Libya by Robert Gates (House Armed Services Committee, March
2011," www.voltairenet.org http://www.voltairenet.org/article169227.html. Accessed October 27 2014.

[87] Gates, 2014. 518.

[88] Clinton. 367.

the authorization that Clinton needed began to take shape, with an Arab League request to the UN for humanitarian action.[89] On that day, General Wesley Clark, a Clinton ally, wrote in the Washington Post that Libya did not meet the criteria of threat to the U.S. required for action.[90] Although its own request did not mention military action, on March 12th the Arab League threw its support behind a UK request for a no fly zone over Libya to protect the population,[91] while Russia agreed to abstain from a Security Council vote on intervention.[92] The Gulf Cooperation Council (GCC), which saw its region threatened by the then still spreading Arab Spring, became a key player in the responding to it.[93] On March 12th, the GCC joined the Arab League in calling for intervention to "stop the bloodshed."[94] There was uncertainty about the reliability and motives of some of the Libyan rebels, considering the large numbers of them serving abroad with a range of terrorist organizations.

Further pressure to act came as thousands of guest workers, primarily from neighboring Tunisia and Egypt, attempted to leave the increasingly violent situation in Libya in February and March. Walking home was not an option due to the location of the workers and the harsh climate, and this, combined with continuing threats of violence, led to calls for an airlift to get them out of the country. Demands for an airlift merged into the growing calls for a no-fly zone and direct intervention, and brought some administration officials to switch sides in the debate. Biden and Donilon now pressed Gates to release aircraft for the purpose of an evacuation of the workers. Again, the Secretary of Defense pushed back, noting that with there were not enough aircraft or security forces available to do it at the scale requested. According to Gates, Biden tried to order him to act, to which Gates responded that

---

89 Clinton. 367.
90 Clark, Wesley. "Wesley Clark Says Libya Doesn't Meet the Test for U.S. Action." *The Washington Post*, March 11, 2011. http://www.washingtonpost.com/wp-dyn/content/article/2011/03/11/AR2011031103244.html. Accessed on July 30, 2014.
91 Prashad. 155.
92 Chorin. 224.
93 Prashad. 86.
94 Chorin. 225.

the vice president was not part of the chain of command, but that he would do whatever he was ordered to by the president.[95]

Decision recommendations to President Obama broke into two categories. Against intervention (this is perceived as intervention against the Libyan government, contrasted with Biden's desire to evacuate the foreign workers) were Vice President Biden, National Security Advisor Donilon, Chief of Staff William Daley, Joint Chiefs Chairman Mullen, and Counter Terrorism lead John Brennan. Biden had spoken in general favor of human rights interventions, but not specifically on Libya, in a speech in Israel on 24 February.[96] Donilon's opposition was based on the fact that an intervention in Libya would violate all three tenets of the "Obama Doctrine" which the president had promulgated during his campaign. The first tenet was that the U.S. would lead in humanitarian actions. The second was that there would be no foreign military actions that did not meet a specific challenge to U.S. national security. The third was that there would be no invasion of an Islamic country to overthrow an established government, even a dictatorship.[97] Obama's obvious effort to separate himself from the previous administrations actions in the Middle East was about to be turned on its head.

In favor of intervention were Susan Rice and NSC staffers Powers and Ben Rhodes. Rhodes' support is particularly noteworthy because of his role in strategic communication, messaging, and speech writing for the NSC, which would make him a key framer for any operation. Rice and Powers took the position that R2P provided adequate justification for U.S. action.[98] Gates noted that Hillary took a centrist position at first, but gradually moved to the side of the interventionists, specifically citing R2P language as one of the reasons for her eventual support of

---

[95] Gates, 2014. 514.
[96] *Foreign Policy.* http://thecable.foreignpolicy.com/posts/2011/02/25/biden_when_a_state_engages_in_atrocity_it_forfeits_its_sovereignty. Accessed on October 20, 2014. Biden said "When a State engages in atrocity, it forfeits its sovereignty."
[97] Klein. 213.
[98] Ibid. 216.

operations in Libya.[99] Gates describes the tone of the deliberations as "blunt and stubborn, but not insubordinate." As is the case in the Kosovo intervention, those pushing hardest for military intervention were those, particularly like Power, who were passionate about their issue, but had little knowledge of military operations.[100] The most significant non-administration player continued to be John McCain, who continued his attacks on the White House for its lack of action.

According to Clinton's memoirs, the use of the Libyan armed forces by Gaddafi to attack his own civilians is one of the factors that drove her to decide in favor of U.S. intervention. Her overall assessment was that Gaddafi had "Lost the legitimacy to govern."[101] In a speech to the UN Human Rights Council, she said that "The people of Libya have made themselves clear. It is time for Gaddafi to go, now."[102] In contrast to the Kosovo example, in which the Secretary of State was the prime mover for intervention, in Libya that push came from middling levels, meaning Power and Rice. But once Clinton was convinced, she swung her vote and her leadership skills toward intervention.

Hillary Clinton held the swing vote for intervention and took the lead in convincing President Obama to act.[103] Obama was convinced over a three day period to switch his personal effort toward intervention, thus hastening the passing of UN Security Council Resolution (UNSCR) 1973 within weeks, in contrast with similar efforts which took months to construct, such as the Gulf War coalition of 1990-1991.[104] The final decision to intervene in Libya took place on March 17th, 2011, and involved the Principals, key deputies mentioned, and the president.[105] The most noteworthy change in the previously noted lineup for and against the intervention was that Secretary of State Clinton, sensing the international support for the operation, had switched over from a neutral stance to a decidedly pro-

---

[99] Gates, 2014. 511.
[100] Gates, 2014. 512.
[101] Clinton. 364.
[102] Ibid.
[103] Ibid. 230-231.
[104] Jones, Bruce. "Libya and the Responsibilities of Power." *Survival*, May: 2011, 51-60. 53.
[105] Gates, 2014. 518.

intervention, R2P driven stance. She described her changeover as having taken on March 14th. On that day, the Arab League requested action, and Clinton met with, and was pressured by Sarkozy, UK Foreign Minister William Hague, and leading Libya expert Mahmoud Jibril to support intervention.[106] Clinton participated remotely in the March 17 meeting because she was still in the region at the time.[107] Gates recalls that President Obama made his decision after an hour and a half long meeting, and agreed to intervention with the caveat that no U.S. ground forces would take part in the operation, other than those needed for search and rescue operations in case of downed U.S. or allied aircraft.[108] Obama termed this decision a "51-49" vote, reflecting the strong opinions on both sides.[109] Edward Klein claims that some of Obama's resolve might have been fueled by allegations that his overall response to the Arab Spring had lacked firmness, and was therefore an effort to regain lost credibility.[110] Clinton noted that Obama's guidance was to participate "in a limited way" with the intervention, noting that it was "Unlikely to find a perfect George Washington waiting in the wings," and that the rebels would eventually become worthy partners for the U.S.[111] Having made the decision, with no dissent, follow on actions would need to be taken before intervention could begin. In keeping with the absolute need for international recognition for the intervention, Ambassador Rice set to pushing the relevant resolution through the UN, something that she called "A near miracle" of negotiation and tough talk.[112] In a press statement, Rice emphasized that the U.S. sought "actions that will effectively protect civilians and increase the pressure on the Gaddafi regime to halt

---

[106] Clinton. 383.
[107] Rogin, Josh. "How Obama turned on a dime toward war." Foreign Policy, March 18, 2011. http://foreignpolicy.com/2011/03/18/how-obama-turned-on-a-dime-toward-war/. Accessed on September 20, 2014.
[108]Gates, 2014. 518.
[109] Ibid.
[110] Klein. 215.
[111] Clinton. 369-370.
[112] Gates, 2014. 518.

the killing and to allow the Libyan people to express themselves in their aspirations for the future freely and peacefully." [113]

In Congress, the task was easier, as significant bipartisan support for the intervention existed in both houses so long as no ground forces were involved. The Senate unanimously called for a no fly zone in Libya on the 18th.[114] Congress had taken an early interest in Libya, although notably not in intervention, with 148 mentions of or events about Libya in the Senate and House of Representatives between January 1st and April 30th 2011, 89 of which were in the month of April, after the decision to intervene had been taken.[115] Reflecting popular opinion, (which will be discussed in the public opinion section of this case study) Congress supported the human rights of the Libyan people, while remaining skeptical of military support, ground intervention, and the potential to end the conflict in a timely manner.

The media blitz to build and ensure support for the operation began on the Sunday morning political talk shows on March 20th, with John McCain leading the way in supporting the intervention.[116] In this he was supported by Senator John Kerry, Democrat from Massachusetts, who acknowledged that the intervention was not in U.S. vital national interest but urged it anyway.[117] Former Secretaries of State Baker and Kissinger, and former National Security Advisor Brzezinski were notable in their support of the decision to intervene.[118] Brzezinski supported the

---

[113] *The Guardian.* "Libya Air Strikes urged by U.S. at UN." http://www.theguardian.com/world/2011/mar/17/libya-air-strikes-urged-us-un. Accessed on October 27, 2014.

[114] *Parrish, Karen. "Shift in Middle East Requires U.S. Engagement."* Armed Forces New Service, *March 2, 2011. http://www.defense.gov/news/newsarticle.aspx?id=62975. Accessed 15 October 2014.*

[115] Congressional Research Service. Congressional Record of the 112th Congress. http://thomas.loc.gov/cgi-bin/thomas2. Accessed on October, 21 2014.

[116] Gates, 2014. 519.

[117] Goodenough, Patrick. "Kerry in 2011: Military Intervention in Libya Not 'Vital' to U.S. Security Interests." CNS News. September 3, 2013. http://cnsnews.com/news/article/patrick-goodenough/kerry-2011-military-intervention-libya-not-vital-us-security. Accessed on 27 October 2014.

[118] Klein. 288.

effort particularly strongly in an interview on March 24th.[119] Joint Chiefs of Staff Chairman Admiral Michael Mullen and Secretary Gates also provided support both through media interviews and Congressional testimony explaining the relevance of the Libya mission to U.S. national security and emphasizing the coalition nature of the operations and their expected limited duration.[120]

Between March 17th and 19th, Rice and Clinton, working with France and the UK, and keeping Russian and China from using their Security Council vetos, negotiated and enacted UN Security Council Resolution 1973. The resolution is central to a discussion of the Libyan intervention and the role of R2P in it. As UN Secretary General Ki-Moon stated upon its enactment:

> "The Security Council today has taken an historic decision. Resolution 1973 affirms, clearly and unequivocally, the international community's determination to fulfill its responsibility to protect civilians from violence perpetrated upon them by their own government."[121]

The resolution, which had ten votes in favor and five abstentions, called for intervention to protect the people of Libya, in accordance with the principle of R2P, but did not mandate assistance to the rebels or general attacks on government forces.[122] The African Union (AU) promulgated a "Roadmap for Peace" on March 25th, but this was rejected, pushing the AU into an ambivalent stance toward the intervention thereafter.[123] UNSCR 1973 allowed for "No Fly Zones" to be established by whatever member states wished to intervene. But who would intervene? Clearly, the UN itself was not postured to do so.

---

[119] Reisner, Hiram. "Brzezinski - Libya action isn't war, but necessary intervention." *Newsmax*, March 24, 2011. http://www.newsmax.com/TheWire/Brzezinski-Libya-intervention-MorningJoe/2011/03/24/id/390587/. Accessed on September 30, 2014.
[120] *Mediaite.com*. "Admiral Mike Mullen – One of the outcomes of the operation could leave Gadaffi in power." http://www.mediaite.com/tv/adm-mike-mullen-one-of-the-outcomes-of-the-operation-could-leave-gaddafi-in-power/. Accessed on October 27, 2014 and Secretary Gates Testimony on March 31. http://www.voltairenet.org/article169227.html, accessed on October 20, 2014.
[121] Hehir, Aidan. *The Responsibility to Protect: Rhetoric, Reality, and the Future of Humanitarian Intervention.* New York: Palgrave Macmillan, 2012. 12.
[122] Prashad. 172.
[123] Responsibility to Protect. "The Crisis in Libya." *www.Responsibility to Protect.org*. 2013. http://www.responsibilitytoprotect.org/index.php/crises/crisis-in-libya (accessed March 1, 2013) 2.

Meanwhile the growing rebel movement (The Libyan National Transitional Council, or NTC) had no doubts what it wanted from the rest of the world. In meetings in mid-March 2011, rebel representatives requested specific airstrikes on military targets from French President Sarkozy and Hillary Clinton. Further, they requested openly that the west find a way to assassinate Gaddafi themselves.[124] The leaders of the growing coalition were to a certain extent open to such ideas. Naming Gaddafi as the opponent in the humanitarian effort help to complete a construction of the Libyan dictator as a murdering tyrant, a message that the U.S. in particular used to sell its operation at home as well as the coalition abroad.[125] While France did not want NATO to lead the military operation (NATO is not a regional arrangement empowered by the UN to act in its stead)[126], other NATO members insisted that it do so, even if, as in the case of Germany, they refrained from providing direct support.[127] Germany's abstention seemed to be tied more to its own domestic politics, since, on the surface, Berlin's insistence on a no fly zone and regional support prior to an intervention were met by the Arab league move.[128] In some ways, it was a case of the wrong organization being called upon, since Germany's preference was that the EU, rather than NATO, be the leading organization for the intervention.[129]

In spite of this, the Obama administration insisted that NATO be involved in order to provide command and control capabilities to what was expected to be a wide ranging coalition.[130] This strategy came to be called "Leading from behind," and ended up coordinating the efforts of fourteen NATO member states as well as

---

[124] McGreal, Chris. "Libyan Rebels Urge West to Assasinate Gaddafi as His Forces Near Benghazi", The Guardian, March 14, 2011. http://www.theguardian.com/world/2011/mar/14/libyan-rebel-leaders-gaddafi-benghazi. Accessed on April 10, 2013.

[125] Pape. 56.

[126] Abass, Ademola. "Assessing NATO's Involvement in Libya." New York: United Nations University. October 27, 2011. http://unu.edu/publications/articles/assessing-nato-s-involvement-in-libya.html. Accessed on March 30, 2013.

[127] Chorin. 224.

[128] Jones. 45.

[129] Gates, 2014. 515.

[130] Daalder and Stavridis. 1.

four partner countries, including the United Arab Emirates, in the coalition.[131] As the U.S. "led" from behind, the French and others took on the mantle of frontline leadership in the effort to enforce the UN mandated No Fly Zone enacted to protect civilians was under Arab League auspices, pursuant to Article 51 of the UN Charter. Even if it was mainly semantics, it was this taking on of authority by the Arab league which helped enable Russia and China to abstain on the 1973 vote, given their predilection toward support of regional organizations and against violations of national sovereignty.[132]

Military operations were scheduled to begin on March 21st (U.S. Operation Odyssey Dawn), but the French commenced strikes nearly two days early, which threw NATO planning and coordination efforts into disarray.[133] Every member of NATO, at that time 28 nations, voted for the military intervention in Libya. The real test of support was the material provision of assistance, however. Of the 28, half provided material support, with the lion's share of the command and control being provided by the United States.[134] Further complicating matters, military methodology took over the calculus of planning for the intervention. Air strikes require a series of preliminary attacks focused on the elimination of enemy radars and surface to air missiles, for example, and the preparatory strikes to achieve this end were an escalation which appears not to have been part of the intent of UNSCR 1973.

Public Opinion and the Libya Intervention

> "We're protecting innocent civilians in Libya…" to prevent "a humanitarian crisis…"
>
> President Barack Obama, March 28th, 2011.[135]

---

131 Clinton. 368.
132 Jones. 54.
133 Clinton. 373.
134 Gates, 2014. 521.
135 Obama, Barack Hussein. "Remarks By the President in Address to the Nation on Libya." Speeches and Remarks, White House.gov. Washington D.C.: www.whitehouse.gov, March 28, 2011.

From January to April, 2011, the U.S. economy and the Arab Spring dominated the American media. A Pew Research report noted that 34% of all mainstream media news coverage from 11 January to 6 March was on the Arab Spring, with an overwhelming focus after 15 February on events in Libya. By comparison, the economy, the second biggest issue, received 20% of coverage, and the threat of a federal government shutdown, the third most important, received 3%.[136] By the week of the U.S. intervention, Pew was reporting that 47% of news was focused on Libya, with the second issue, the Tsunami and nuclear meltdown in Fukushima, Japan, receiving 15%.[137]

By invoking human rights in his March 28 speech and the need to act decisively and powerfully in their defense, (although, notably, not R2P, an omission also notable in a joint declaration prepared by the leaders of the U.S., France, and the UK shortly thereafter) President Obama provided the moral imperative by which other intentions, even if driven by very realist power based motives, could be realized in terms of international protection and support for the Libyan people and the resistance movement.[138] Further statements by Ambassador Rice in the UN encourage this belief.[139] Even though R2P was not specifically mentioned, its basic tenets were in effect.

Arnold Wolfers posited that it was only by identifying national entities as the primary actors that a true study of international relations (IR) could occur.[140] IR realists would posit that the GCC and Arab League maneuvers regarding Libya were done in an attempt to gain their own control of the escalating Arab Spring, a

---

[136] Journalism.org. "News Coverage Index, February 29-March 6, 2011." http://www.journalism.org/2011/03/06/pej-news-coverage-index-february-28-march-6-2011/. Accessed on 27 October 2014.

[137] Journalism.org. "Libya Search." http://www.journalism.org/search/Libya/. Accessed on October 27, 2014.

[138] Pape. 62.

[139] Hehir. 13. Rice said: "we are interested in a broad range of actions that will effectively protect civilians and increase the pressure on the Gaddafi regime to halt the killing and to allow the Libyan people to express themselves in their aspirations for the future freely and peacefully." http://www.theguardian.com/world/2011/mar/17/libya-air-strikes-urged-us-un. Accessed 1 October 2014.

[140] Wolfers, Arnold. *Discord and Collaboration.* Baltimore: Johns Hopkins University Press, 1962. 9.

movement which was sweeping toward their own borders. This view would continue that ultra-conservative Arab interests were paired up with U.S. and European oil and security interests to bring about the intervention.[141] Secretary Gates confronted NATO Secretary General Anders Rasmussen about this, both in stating that a UN Security Council Resolution would be required for U.S. action in a NATO framework, and in directly asking why NATO countries were keen to intervene in Libya, and not elsewhere, unless oil were the cause.[142]

Secretary of State Clinton and Ambassador to the UN Rice bore the burden of selling R2P to the rest of the world as a justification for intervention.[143] The two were joined by National Security Council Directors Samantha Power and Gayle Smith. In spite of the nature of their directorates (multinational engagement and global development), they joined Rice and Clinton as the leading government hawks on intervention, convincing others to fall into line both by using R2P and by noting the benefits that intervention would provide to U.S. standing in the Arab World.[144] They were joined by Senator John McCain, although McCain's commentary was primarily focused on support of the NTC.[145] Of note is this contrast between those in less force oriented positions favoring intervention, while military leaders opposed the effort.

Public opinion of the crisis in Libya and the need for, and nature of, a U.S. response changed over the period from March - May 2011. The following graphics are based on key polls involving approximately 1000 respondents from across the political spectrum. The full list of polls examined can be found in the Appendix.

---

[141] Prashad. 160.
[142] Gates, 2014. 515.
[143] Prashad. 176.
[144] Chorin. 215 and 231. They became known as the "Warrior Women" as a result.
[145] CNN. "Sens. McCain, Lieberman critical of Obama over Libya." February 27, 2011. http://cnnpressroom.blogs.cnn.com/2011/02/27/sens-mccain-lieberman-critical-of-obama-over-libya/. Accessed April 1, 2013.

Figure 5: Polling Data on Intervention in Libya, March-May 2011, Part 1

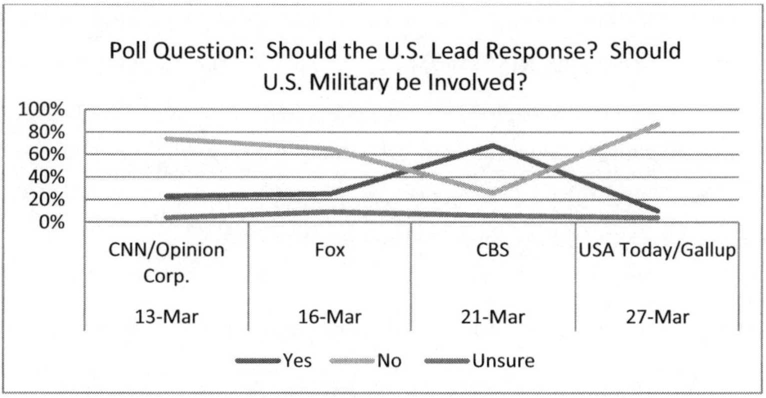

Source: Polling Report[146]

The polling data in Figure 5 above shows responses on the question of whether or not the U.S. should lead or be involved in a response. It reflects a spike in support for military operations, which began for the U.S. on 19 March. Support then begins to flag in the week after the 19th, but shows a slow drop off in the days before President Obama's speech explaining the intervention and justifying it on March 28th.

Figure 6: Polling Data on Intervention in Libya, March-May 2011, Part 2

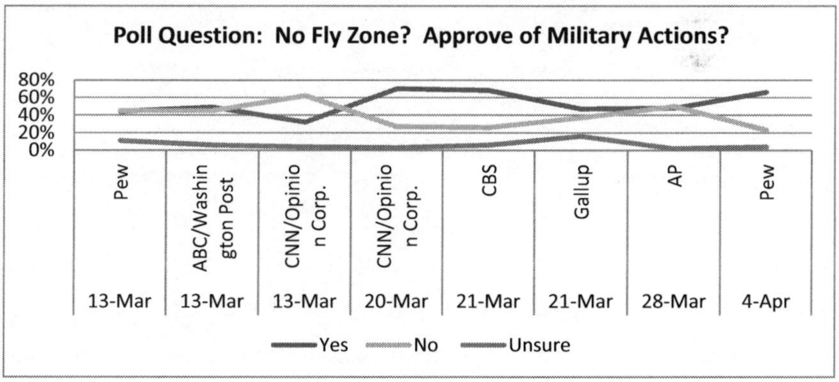

Source: Polling Report[147]

---

[146] Polling Report. Accesed on 27 October 2014.

[147] http://www.pollingreport.com/libya.htm. Accesed on 27 October 2014.

Figure 6 shows responses on the question of whether or not a no fly zone or any military action should be undertaken in regards to Libya. It shows a spike in support for operations which dropped off, but then surged again after President Obama's March 28th speech explaining the operation to the American people. After the speech, support began to drop off through April as the operation continued. U.S. forces moved from a leading role in operations into a reserve role on 4 April, which is why the polling sample ends on that day.

Figure 7: Polling Data on Intervention in Libya, March-May 2011, Part 3

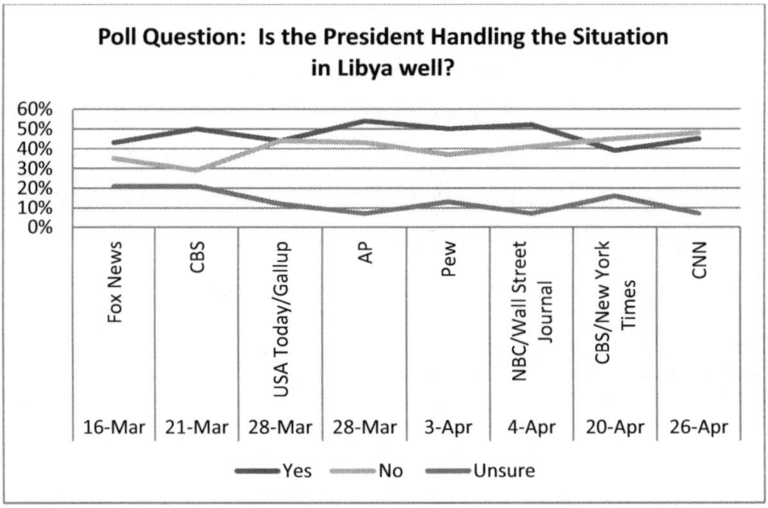

Source: Polling Report[148]

Figure 7, above, shows a presidential approval question, reflecting spikes in approval both when military action began on the 19th, and when President Obama addressed the nation on the 28th. Additional polls, taken on March 13th and 20th, and so covering the initiation of combat operations, showed a wide scale negativity toward the deployment of ground forces, with 80% of the respondents coming out against deployment on the 13th, dropping to 72% on the 20th, and staying there through April.

[148] http://www.pollingreport.com/libya.htm. Accesed on 27 October 2014.

Taken as a whole, the polling data shown reveals several things about the public mood in the U.S. surrounding the intervention. There is an uptick in support for the intervention once UNSCR 1973 went into effect, and when the air strikes began, supported by the aforementioned speech acts in Congress and by cabinet members and key advisors such as Mullen and Power. Furthermore, there was wide scale support for the no fly zone, but not for direct ground action in Libya. Finally, there was general, but not a majority, approval of President Obama's decisions and handling of the problem. Interestingly, this was true both before the decision to initiate military action (when the polls would indicate that the public were against military action) and after. While the initiation of combat saw an uptick in support, it quickly and predictably flagged. Obama's major address on the issue, on March 28th, improved opinion of the operations until the U.S. were pulled back from a leading role in combat operations.[149] In the same manner as the discussions and decisions on intervention were divided, support for the operation was bifurcated, with the same population supporting the protection of civilians, but opposing military action.[150] Of all of the acts of armed humanitarian intervention discussed in this book, the Libya intervention was the least popular, at 47%. By comparison, Kosovo had 51% and Somalia 65% popularity.[151]

Models and the Libya Decision Process

The decision to intervene in Libya shows evidence of two models. The Allison Governmental Process Model is exhibited in the stance of the Defense Department against intervention. This clearly reflected Secretary Gates acting as a

---

[149] The Polling Report. "U.S. Intervention in Libya." http://www.pollingreport.com/libya.htm. Accesed on 27 October 2014.
[150] *Talking Points Memo*. Poll – Plurality oppose Libyan intervention but support protecting civilians." http://talkingpointsmemo.com/dc/poll-plurality-oppose-libyan-intervention-but-support-protecting-civilians. Accessed on 23 October 2014.
[151] The Gallup Poll. "Americans Approve Military Action Against Libya." http://www.gallup.com/poll/146738/Americans-Approve-Military-Action-Against-Libya.aspx. Accessed on 27 October 2014.

representative of his cabinet agency. The same is true, at the beginning of the discussion of Secretary Clinton. Gates, as the owner of the intervening military assets, had significant coercive power in the debate over intervention. However, he never threatened insubordination or not to act. In this, he stayed within an organizational model as predicted by Allison. Gates noted that Obama himself had come a long way in his thoughts on intervention from the candidate who specifically said that "The president has no power in the U.S. Constitution to unilaterally authorize a military attack in a situation that does not involve stopping an action or an imminent threat to the nation."[152]

In terms of rationality, a threat to U.S. national security had to be constructed where it did not exist before, and this was the task of the key leaders who pushed for intervention. Libya also shows the power of the powerful or well-placed individual in bringing about decisions favorable to their wishes. Ambassador Rice and Samantha Power did not represent bureaucracies, but each brought their own personal histories to the decision making process, and this combined with their unique access to and influence on the president to enable them to push for action. Furthermore, while there is no evidence that Power or Rice personally convinced Secretary Clinton to change her stance on intervention, it is clear that the growing international pressure for, and acceptance of, intervention convinced Clinton that intervention was the best course of action. Thus her powerful swing vote came into play, and personal, rather than institutional prerogatives triumphed, and intervention took place.

The strategic communication process provides a useful angle through which to view the various messages coming from the diverse actors. For the U.S., the message was that Gaddafi was a bloody tyrant who was about to launch a massacre on a part of his population. At the UN, Libya's failure to protect its people was a failure of its sovereignty that could only be rectified by the international community. The French and the British used similar reasoning to the U.S., but with

---

[152] Gates, 2014. 528.

the added threat of mass immigration which might have occurred if the massacre had been allowed to take place. The Arabs and the Africans were public about the threat to stability posed by Gaddafi in general and how that could be exacerbated by ongoing violence. The Libyan rebels fed the U.S. argument, obscuring their ties to radical Islam and focusing on the tyranny of the dictator.

Strategic communication calls for synchronizing messages with deeds.[153] Although the various messages of the intervening or conceding states crossed a wide gamut, as shown above, (and even an internal gamut, as shown by the gulf between the statements of the White House and the Department of Defense as well as a bipartisan group in the NSC, the Senate and the House who spoke out against the intervention)[154] the deeds attached to them, the actions of protecting the people of Libya were consistent with the majority of statements made on the issue.[155] UNSCR 1973's appeals for a ceasefire and discussions to peacefully end the crisis before things got any worse. The resolution's specific mention of R2P was a critical measure of its importance and the future of humanitarian interventions.[156] In terms of framing, the primary evidence for framing the intervention to the media and the public came after the decision had been made to launch the operation, with the coordinated media "blitz" mentioned above, which included current and former cabinet members. Statements made before the decision to intervene seem to be primarily and overwhelming directed at the Gadhafi government, in an effort to coerce the dictator into reversing course, rather framing the intervention to U.S. audiences.

On the Libyan side, communications were used quite poorly. Given the recent past, in spite of superficial efforts at reform, it was difficult to undo the image

---

[153] Paul, Christopher. *Strategic Communication: Origins, Concepts, and Current Debates.* Santa Barbara, CA: Praeger, 2011. 8-9.
[154] Chorin. 215.
[155] Ibid. 210. Gates testified to Congress strongly against U.S. involvement in Libya, citing the "nonessential nature" of U.S. interests there.
[156] Claes, Jonas. "Libya and the "Responsibility to Protect." Washington, D.C.: U.S. Institute of Peace, March 1, 2011. http://www.usip.org/publications/libya-and-the-responsibility-protect. Accessed March 11, 2013. 2.

of Gaddafi as a terrorist and a tyrant. Tripoli's efforts to paint the rebellion as a threat to stability to rival Iraq failed to draw their targets, the west, into the right conclusion, that the regime needed support to crush the rebellion. Instead, that message was used as a justification for the argument that the people of Libya needed to be protected, from outside, against an ineffective regime. In her 2 March speech, Secretary Clinton noted her concern of "...Libya descending into chaos and becoming another Somalia."[157]

For the Arab League and the GCC, the deal was simple. In return for supporting the Libya intervention, the GCC got carte blanche to operate against a threat far more dear to it, Bahrain. GCC countries were enabled to crackdown on the Shiite Bahraini's with impunity, and prevent the spread of the Arab Spring, which had caused unrest in Bahrain, Oman, Iran, and Yemen by that point.[158] The African Union also worked in favor of the intervention, although President Obama had to intervene personally in a meeting with South African President Zuma to help sway the vote.[159]

The intervention in Libya was a successful example of R2P, in the sense that the human security of the people of Libya was successfully used as a justification for a military intervention. However, since Libya lay outside NATO and the EU, the primary intervening agencies, it cannot in that sense be called an act of collective security. According to constructivist theory, social structures are generated through understood definitions and knowledge.[160] Based on its use in rhetoric and in the UN resolutions, R2P has been constructed into an institutional norm, and one that has been used to undermine the importance of state sovereignty, a core tenet of structural realism as a philosophy, as well as the principles of the Westphalian state system. The Libyan intervention was undertaken with raw power, in a manner consistent with UN authorities and powers embedded in its

---

[157] Chorin. 217.
[158] Prashad. 186.
[159] Ibid. 188.
[160] Wendt, Alexander. "Constructing International Politics." *International Security,* Summer 1995: 71-81. 73.

charter, far predating the relatively recent discussion of R2P.[161] Nevertheless, the invocation of R2P as a lever or justification for actions which might otherwise not have been taken is a significant step toward a constructivist or institutionalist theory for international politics. The Libya vote and intervention was a crucial test for and affirmation of the strength of international norms, of which R2P is a part.[162] This is notwithstanding the Obama administrations additional increased desire for regime change in Libya.[163]

In a contrasting realist model, the U.S. and Europe acted to protect their dwindling stake in Africa, both politically and economically, and the real enemy was not Gaddafi, but China and the BRICs. Negative feelings on Libyan oil, fostered by interdependence in oil, particularly with Europe, furthered the desire by the UK, and France, among others to secure the vital material.[164] This model has the French, British, and Italians removing Gaddafi because of his influence in the Pan African movement, while securing the oil for themselves.[165] In this case, the fact that Obama invoked human rights was not relevant because he also cited the threat to "Interests and values" in his primary Libya speech.[166] By doing so, he was able to successfully frame a melding of idealism and realism, the two sides of U.S. foreign policy thought for over a century.[167]

Conclusion

> "NATO's operation in Libya has rightly been hailed as a model intervention. The alliance responded rapidly to a deteriorating situation that threatened hundreds of thousands of civilians rebelling against an oppressive regime. It succeeded in protecting those

---

[161] Hehir. 14.
[162] Jones. 59.
[163] Stewart, Patrick. "A New Lease on Life for Humanitarianism." *Foreign Affairs*, March 2011: 1. 1.
[164] Davidson. 319. Stratfor noted that the UK needed an oil "win" after the disastrous British Petroleum Gulf Oil Spill in 2010.
[165] Forte. 204-205.
[166] Hehir. 16.
[167] Atlas, Pierre. "U.S. Foreign Policy and the Arab Spring: Balancing Values and Interests." *Digest of Middle East Studies*, Spring: 2012, 354.

civilians and, ultimately, in providing the time and space necessary for local forces to overthrow Muammar al-Qaddafi. And it did so by involving partners in the region and sharing the burden among the alliance's members."

Admiral James Stavridis, Commander, U.S. European Command, 2012.[168]

For some months after the end of the intervention in Libya, it was deemed a success, as noted in the quotation above. Little treasure in terms of financial cost or loss of military personnel for what appeared to be significant gain. The people appeared to have been protected from the dictator. Viewed in light of the events which followed it, however, a far dimmer appreciation of events is apparent. President Obama would eventually call Libya one of the biggest mistakes of his term in office.[169] What should be said is that, after months of back and forth struggle through the summer of 2011, stalemate seemed to set in. However, as the rebels streamlined their leadership as a result of the deaths of some of their key leaders, and airstrikes ramped up, the tide turned decisively against Gaddafi.[170] On October 20th, as the result of disruption caused by a NATO airstrike, the dictator was killed, execution style, as a result of a combined attack between NATO air forces and Libyan rebels on the convoy in which he had been travelling near his hometown of Sirte. Although some of his family remains at large, the Islamist rebel movement NTC claimed victory.

The purpose of this research was to assess how the coalition for armed humanitarian intervention in Libya was built. Without perfect vision of future outcomes, we cannot be certain whether or not R2P in Libya prevented a massacre, and without that crystal ball, Libya joins the list of armed humanitarian interventions of the post-Cold War era, potentially adding to what Robert Pape calls

---

[168] Daalder and Stavridis. 1.

[169] Friedman, Thomas L. "Obama on the World: President Obama talks about Iraq, Putin, and Israel." *The New York Times*, August 8, 2014. http://www.nytimes.com/2014/08/09/opinion/president-obama-thomas-l-friedman-iraq-and-world-affairs.html. Accessed on 28 November 2014. Obama said that he did not regret the act of intervention, but rather the lack of follow up and management after the fall of Gaddafi.

[170] Chorin. 247-249.

"modest" progress in the field.[171] While oil, commercial interests, internal politics among the interveners, or a simple loathing of the dictator Gaddafi may have been the cause for intervention, it appears that R2P and the humanitarian crisis Gaddafi started were the primary factors which lead the U.S. to advocate military intervention and to see it through even when it looked as though stalemate might be the result. For this reason, R2P can be seen as an influential factor for intervention. Hence, the construction of a new vision of sovereignty and the responsibility of nation states to their citizens, as well as the use of institutions such as the UN both to enshrine that vision as an operating procedure, indicate that the realist fundament of raw power politics can at least be mitigated by both.

This chapter reviewed the U.S. decision to intervene in Libya. It examined the historical buildup to the Arab Spring and the Libyan crackdown, and how the pressure for intervention built in the international community, which in turn enabled key leaders in the U.S. foreign policy decision making process to push for intervention. Further, it examined the process by which the decision to intervene was framed to the media and the American people, and that those efforts only marginally improved support for the intervention. The Libya intervention had significant consequences for U.S. foreign policy. Like the Somalia intervention, its aftermath soured the U.S. to further interventions, which would have repercussions for other hot spots in the Arab Spring and worldwide, most notably with the U.S. decision not to intervene in Syria from 2011 – Fall 2014, and the decision not to intervene in the growing humanitarian and military crisis in Eastern Ukraine in Spring 2014.

---

[171] Pape. 42.

CHAPTER VII - FINDINGS

The purpose of this section of the study is to synthesize the lessons of the case studies in the preceding chapters into useable conclusions on the decision making and framing processes. Careful consideration will be given to the role of powerful individuals in shaping decisions and framing efforts in the armed humanitarian interventions and non-interventions discussed. The findings for this study are organized in such a manner as to shed light on a series of critical questions. In each case, broad historical similarities and differences will be examined to see if there are general situational themes surrounding humanitarian interventions. Next, the leadership teams of the four administrations involved in the case studies will be reviewed for similarity or difference in order to explain how that organization and those changes might have impacted decision making and framing. Then, the actual process of the decision making will be examined with an eye toward the validation of the models of decision making and framing as set forth in chapter two above. Finally, framing will be examined as a separate factor, with the process and differences in framing for each case discussed and compared. Since these interventions took place in chronological sequence, the impact of each decision on follow on interventions is an important factor which will also be discussed.

Following an examination of the factors mentioned above, the applicability of the findings to a post-Libya case study, the Syria crisis of 2013, will be examined in chapter eight. The purpose of this mini case-examination is to see if the findings can provide a sound explanation for why the U.S. chose not to intervene in Syria in August, 2013, after having intervened in Libya and tacitly agreed to repression in Bahrain in 2011. A summary of this mini-study is that a combination of different geographic and geo-political factors, the strong ability of the targeted state, Syria, to counter-frame an intervention using powerful propaganda and social media tools, and the lack of a powerful individual in the Obama administration with the motivation to push for intervention meant that the U.S. failed to do so after the August 2013 gas attacks in Syria. Since the result of the failure was significant embarrassment to an administration that already had a growing list of foreign policy problems, understanding how the events unfolded may help current and future leaders from avoiding the mistakes that were made by President Obama and his national security team, as well as congressional players such as Senator John McCain.

Armed Humanitarian Interventions

In each of the cases examined, the definition established by the literature review (Appendix II below) was met. To repeat, an armed humanitarian intervention is "A coercive action by one or more states, in the legitimate context of an international organization, involving the use of armed force in another state without the consent of its authorities, and with the purpose of preventing widespread suffering or death among the inhabitants."[1] In Somalia, military forces engaged in combat-like operations for the purpose of providing humanitarian assistance to a starving population. This involved coercive action to deliver that assistance, and was envisioned as such during the decision making process. Had the intervention taken place, Rwanda would have entailed the rapid deployment of armed peace-keepers to literally stand between the Tutsis and the Hutus to

---

[1] Pape, Robert A. "When Duty Calls: A Pragmatic Standard of Humanitarian Intervention." *International Security* 37, no. 1 (2012): 41-80. 44.

physically prevent slaughter before it was too late. Kosovo saw the use of air strikes to coerce the government in Belgrade from perpetuating genocide, or at least a brutal repression, on a minority population, as was also the case in Libya, at least in the early part of the intervention there.

In all of these cases, there was either no central government to welcome or resist U.S. involvement (Somalia), or the host government resisted or refused to work with the international community to alleviate the crisis (Kosovo, Libya) or denied offers of assistance and intervention (Rwanda). In all of them, there was the legitimating context of the support of an international organization. In the cases of Somalia and Libya, the UN was the lead international actor, with NATO, the Arab League, and the Gulf Cooperation Council as strong supporting actors. In the case of Kosovo, the UN was a player, but a secondary one to the primary regional actor, NATO. In the case of Rwanda, the specific lack of a UN or other mandate helped lead to the decision not to intervene. In fact, the direct resistance of interested regional powers such as France and Belgium helped to ensure that there would be no stomach in the U.S. for an intervention.

In each case, a humanitarian crisis was at the root of the problem and the intervention. For Somalia, the core purpose was to ease starvation, with attempting a political settlement as supporting reason which ended up taking on primary importance after the Bush administration left office. Rwanda would have been direct prevention of genocide, literally standing physically between murderers and victims. Kosovo and Libya were both efforts to stop the mechanisms of genocide by use of air power, both to cause such pain to the existing government that it would no longer see the value in its oppressive acts, and in physically destroying the capabilities of the aggressive governments to perpetrate those acts.

Comparing Contexts for Intervention, and Each Intervention's Impact on Others

Each of the interventions in the case studies took place in a unique time and place, and was discussed and implemented by a unique and changing group of decision makers and external change agents. However, there are some similarities between them. This section will discuss the political and historical contexts for intervention, or non-intervention, and note those similarities and dissimilarities where they appear.

One of the four case studies, Somalia, took place in a one term presidency. Three of them, including Somalia, Rwanda, and Libya, took place in the first term of a presidency, leaving Kosovo as the only one of the four that took place in a second term. The importance of this is seen in the process of decision making, the power of the president and the national security advisor as the leaders and coordinators of the decision making process (respectively), and the role allowed powerful leaders outside of the presidency, both in terms of shaping policy and in framing the intervention efforts which followed. This is a question of coherency in decision making. The Bush administration, for reasons discussed, was the most cohesive and effective decision making body of the three administrations examined. They had, in effect, been governing together at least since 1980, and in some cases back as far as the Nixon administration. They had ended the Cold War together, and also planned and implemented operations in Panama and Iraq. These were people who knew each other well, many were close personal friends, and were all comfortable with working with one another while backing President Bush implicitly. Bush was at the center, he was the key and most powerful decision maker, and it was he alone who needed to be persuaded to act in Somalia. Once he did, the administration fell into lock step behind his decision, and moved into an implementation mindset. It is this unusual, and potentially unrepeatable level of cohesion which actually gives Somalia more in common with Clinton's Kosovo intervention than with Rwanda or Libya.

Another factor in common between Somalia and Kosovo is that in both cases, the presidents were keen to accomplish something big. For Bush, it was a closeout to his administration and an effort to lock the newly elected Clinton team into a path of positive, but seemingly painless, foreign policy action. For Clinton, it was an effort to cleanse his legacy of the failure in Rwanda internationally, and for the Monica Lewinsky scandal specifically, with a nearly risk free military option that would also preserve unity of and U.S. dominance of European defense matters through strengthening NATO.[2] Although Clinton was on his second, and in some cases third set of cabinet officers, by 1998, they had, for the most part, worked together in one or another capacity for six years, and had achieved some of the familiarity and coherency that the Bush team enjoyed.

In contrast, the Clinton team which made the choice not to intervene in Rwanda actually has more in common with the Obama administration which decided to intervene in Libya in 2011. New in office, that team had been thrust immediately into crises in Yugoslavia and Somalia. The senior leaders of the administration were either Clinton loyalists, or had been brought in from the last Democrat administration, that of Carter, twelve years before. Many did not know each other, or know how to best work together or with their boss, who was distinctly averse to foreign policy, preferring to deal with domestic economic crises.[3] Similarly, the Obama team also had two foreign wars to deal with, in Iraq and Afghanistan. The events of the Arab Spring took place further into the administration's tenure than that of Clinton (Rwanda began in earnest about one year after the inauguration, while the Arab Spring was two years after Obama's inauguration), however, and Obama's cabinet was significantly different in structure. Unlike Clinton, Obama did not take a significant number of senior leaders from the previous Democrat administration, and those that he did take all had a deputy or senior subordinate who was an Obama stalwart, and who often had better access to the president than his or her appointed lead.[4] This created a deep divide in the team, with further issues such as the retention of cabinet members such as Gates from the Bush administration. Returning to the comparison, both the Clinton and Obama teams were divided, neither president wanted foreign policy to

---

[2] Gellman, Barton. ''Allies Facing the Limits of Air Power.'' *The Washington Post*, March 28, 1999. 1A.

[3] Hyland, William. *Clinton's World: Remaking American Foreign Policy*. London: Praeger Books, 1999. 8.

[4] Gates, Robert M. *Duty, Memoirs of a Secretary at War. New York*: Alfred A. Knopf, 2014. 291.

be a leading issue, and neither wanted the specific events, Rwanda and Libya, to take on a central role. Differences between the two events include that Rwanda began just as another intervention, that in Somalia, was failing, whereas the events in Libya took place in a post Rwanda world with key leaders such as Samantha Power, who were specifically working with its memory in mind. Furthermore, the Libya crisis was just one of many that made the Arab Spring impossible for the White House to ignore. The bottom line was that no notable cabinet or sub cabinet officials wanted to intervene in Rwanda, whereas key empowered individuals, namely Power, Rice, and, later, Clinton, pushed for and achieved the intervention in Libya.

As has been noted, U.S. policy toward interventions changed as a result of the perception of failure of the Somalia intervention, with a significant reduction recommended for future interventions.[5] Since the major negative act of the Somalia intervention, the attempt to intervene in Somali politics which ended with the battle of Mogadishu and the "Blackhawk Down" debacle took place after the installation of Clinton as President, it would be under his administration that the lessons of the intervention would be learned and implemented. Unfortunately, those final events happened so close in time to the early rumblings of trouble in Rwanda that they overshadowed an objective discussion on that crisis, and directly impacted the decision not to intervene there. The lessons of Somalia, then, appeared to be clear. In summary, the U.S. government, from Congress to the White House to the cabinet agencies lost its ardor for large scale use of ground forces for humanitarian interventions, an opinion which has not changed since 1994.[6] The price in money, lives, and embarrassment was more than any in government were willing to repeatedly bear. For the Defense Department, the Powell Doctrine was vindicated, and the idea of sending in a large force with what became increasingly poorly defined mission and goals should not be repeated. The idea of being neutral in a

---

[5] Clarke, Walter and Herbst, Jeffrey. "Somalia and the Future of Humanitarian Intervention." *Foreign Affairs,* March/April 1996, (1996): 70-85. 70.
[6] Ibid. 70.

humanitarian crisis also left the debate as the last U.S. troops came home from Somalia. Future armed interventions would clearly support, or protect, a victimized side against the government, and those actions would be part of the initial mandate of the intervention.[7] As noted previously, OFDA proposed that the U.S. international aid community and the Department of State develop an early warning system for humanitarian crisis which might allow for pre-emption, but this failed to materialize in a way that brought about further interventions, and played no role in Rwanda, Kosovo, or Libya.

Rwanda would clearly suffer both for the failure in Somalia and for the newness of the Clinton team and his lack of interest at that time in foreign policy. The genocide in Rwanda, which began soon after the end of the Somalia mission, would redefine the terms of western armed humanitarian intervention and shape future discussions of state sovereignty, failed states, and human security.[8] The Rwanda case study, on the decision not to intervene, noted the different decision making dynamic of the first Clinton administration and the impact of a perceived failure in the Somalia intervention on the possibility of involvement in the Rwandan Civil War and genocides. The failure to respond to genocide in Rwanda generated a discussion on human security and the meaning of state sovereignty when human rights and security were endangered which would both encourage the Kosovo intervention. The demonstration there that major powers were willing to ignore the sovereignty of other nations in furtherance of humanitarian goals fueled the development of the concept of Responsibility to Protect, which in turn eventually lead key members of the Obama administration to support the Libyan intervention of 2011.

Many players in the administration changed between the first and second Clinton terms, but two were most important. The first was the replacement of

---

[7] Clarke and Herbst. 82.

[8] United Nations. "Report of the Independent Inquiry into the actions of the United Nations during the 1994 Genocide in Rwanda." December 15, 1999. www.un.org/news/ossg/rwanda_report.htm. Accessed on September 15, 2014. This and other reports were not available at the time of the decision making in 1994. 1.

Warren Christopher with Madeleine Albright, who would turn out to be the prime activist for intervention. The second was the replacement of Anthony Lake with Sandy Berger as National Security Advisor. Like Obama would do later on with Tom Donilon, Clinton had placed Berger, his own man, as deputy to Lake. While their relationship was not as acrimonious as that described by many of the Obama cabinet secretaries towards their Obama loyalist subordinates, there is no question that Berger was more in tune with Clinton's preferences and desires than Lake had been, and better able to translate to requests of the other interested parties in the foreign policy realm into actionable items for the president.[9] Because of these factors, Berger stands with Brent Scowcroft as the two most effective of the four national security advisors examined in the case studies. Each had a keen knowledge of the interests and desires of their boss, they were also close friends with that boss, had shared life experiences, and also understood the need for a smoothly functioning cabinet. It is important to mention though, that the comparison has its limits. Scowcroft did not make decisions for Bush, or speak in his name, both of which Berger frequently did.[10] Berger, furthermore, actively envisioned his role as a very public one, in which he would be a primary salesman for foreign policy decisions, position in stark contrast to that of Scowcroft. It is possible to argue that Albright's job was not to convince Clinton, but Berger, of the need to intervene in Kosovo.[11]

The similarities between Scowcroft and Berger are not meant to pair Anthony Lake with James Jones or Thomas Donilon, the two Obama era National Security Advisors examined. Lake was close to the president, but as a career diplomat tended to operationalize his role in events rather than serve as arbiter for the president. His focus on Russia in 1994, for example, while very justified,

---

[9] Rodman, Peter. *Presidential Command: Power, Leadership, and the Making of Foreign Policy from Nixon to George W. Bush*. New York: Alfred A Knopf, 2009. 207.

[10] Daalder, Ivo, and Destler, I.M. In the Shadow of the Oval Office: Profiles of the National Security Advisors and the Presidents They Served - from JFK to George W. Bush. New York: Simon and Schuster, 2009. 248

[11] Albright, Madeleine. *Madam Secretary, a Memoir*. New York: Harper Collins, 2013. 386.

helped to blind him and the cabinet to events in Rwanda.[12] Jones' number one problem was that he was not an Obama insider, and never became one. As a hierarchically trained military leader at the highest level of the armed forces, he was unable to adapt to the Obama leadership circle, which was non-hierarchical and saw numerous information streams go to the president, many of them outside of Jones' knowledge or control.[13] Donilon also suffered from this issue, but he was new in his role at the time of the Libya decision, and in any case more entrenched players, Power, Rice, and Clinton all carried more clout when the moment came to decide.

Comparing the Key Players Across Administrations – Seeking the "Powerful" Actor

In terms of seeking the dominant actor for the foreign policy decision making and framing processes, the first case study examined, Somalia, turns out to be an outlier for the discussion, for several reasons. The UN and the Secretary General had a greater impact on U.S. decision making for Somalia than for any of the other cases except for the negative role in Rwanda. It is the one study in which U.S. players outside of the normal cabinet structure had influence. Herman Cohen and Frank Wisner at the Department of State fit this bill, as did ODFA lead James Kunder and USAID leader Andrew Natsios. Congress also took on a much greater role in pushing for intervention in Somalia than in any other case, notwithstanding the individual role that John McCain took in pushing for intervention in the Arab Spring events, most particularly in Libya in 2011. In spite of significant actions by these lower tier actors, more than in any of the other interventions, there is no question in the histories of memoirs that the Somalia decision was solely in the hands of President Bush, and that he made his decision to intervene with advice

[12] Power, Samantha "Bystanders to Genocide." Atlantic Monthly September, 2001. http://www.theatlantic.com/magazine/archive/2001/09/bystanders-to-genocide/304571/ Accessed on April 20, 2014.
[13] Gates. 291.

from senior cabinet officers, but not from a cabinet vote or other collective decision making means, as was the case in other interventions, such as the Obama cabinet's Libya debate and vote for intervention.[14] Bush, then is the "powerful actor" sought by the model, who had the conviction and influence to dominate the decision making process for intervention. Again, Bush is unique among the presidents examined for two reasons. The first was his deep background in decision making at the highest levels of government. This was a man who was comfortable in his role, and unafraid to exercise command. The second reason, touched on repeatedly, was the unique nature of the George H.W. Bush cabinet. These were men who were not only friends, but had served together in government for decades, with players sitting in different seats, sometimes superior, sometimes subordinate to one another. This is clearly seen in the manner in which the DOD turned on a dime in its approach to Somalia. Bush and Cheney had worked with each other on and off since the Nixon Administration, as had Colin Powell. Each understood the hierarchy and their role in it, and once the boss decided, the discussions ended.

Bush's motivations for decision are not dissimilar in kind from those of other leaders examined, particularly in the case of Clinton and Kosovo. To restate, Bush was motivated by: African experience prior to his presidency; by the need to take decisive action as the Republican National Convention and the reelection loomed (but in an area that seemed easier to "win" than the growing quagmire in Yugoslavia); by media reporting and the reports of subordinates, most notably the U.S. Ambassador to Kenya, and congressional leaders on the horrors occurring in Somalia;[15] and then after the election by the simultaneous needs to secure his political legacy and to lock the incoming president into what was thought were salutary actions on the world stage.

---

[14] Clarke, Walter and Herbst, Jeffrey. *Learning from Somalia*. Boulder, Colorado: Westview Press, 1997. 9.

[15] Brent Scowcroft, as interviewed by Western, Jon. "Sources of Humanitarian Intervention: Beliefs, Information, and Advocacy in the U.S. Decisions on Somalia and Bosnia." International Security 26, no. 4 (2002): 112-142. 125.

The Rwanda mini case study is the other outlier in terms of the quest for decisive leadership in decision making. There simply was no decisive stance on Rwanda at any level of government. In the wake of the Battle of Mogadishu, there was no interest in another entanglement, this time in a remote, hard to reach part of the world, and one to which the American people and government leaders were already inured to accept large casualties and brutality on a regular basis. Unlike the case in Somalia, President Clinton was not interested, which meant that powerful leadership would have to rise up from lower levels of the cabinet. Since the issue in Rwanda was not one of reconstruction or food aid, but primarily political, the actors one would expect to push for intervention, USAID, OFDA, and the foreign assistance NGO's were largely silent. Political officers in the relevant sections of the Department of State, such as the Africa Bureau, were motivated, but as mentioned above were inured to accept significant death and mayhem before they realized the true gravity of the massacres.[16] By that point they largely switched over from benign disinterest to being stunned by the enormity of the atrocities. At the next level of government higher, the cabinet level, the only motivated actor seemed to be U.S. Ambassador to the UN Albright, and even she noted that while she was concerned, there was so much else going on in the world that the gravity of the situation was simply not evident.[17]

Similarly, NSC staffers, such as Susan Rice, were clearly more concerned about the political fallout from Somalia, and about the potential impact of more negative news on the upcoming mid-term elections.[18] She was right to be so concerned, since the Republican landslide of that year did change the political landscape, and was in part due to foreign policy failures by the administration. The DOD remained against potential operations in Rwanda from the beginning, and there was no significant effort to sway DOD from that stance. One rung even higher up the food chain saw even more disinterest on behalf of the two leaders most likely

[16] Power, 2001.
[17] Albright. 149.
[18] Rice quoted in Power, 2001.

to be able to sway the president and the DOD, since National Security Advisor Lake was focused on Russian politics, and Secretary of State Christopher could not even find Rwanda on a map.[19] It would be simplistic to say that intervention will only take place when there is a powerful individual interested, as in the case of Rwanda it is one of a plethora of reasons why action did not take place. But that lack is a significant cause for inaction and a key finding of this study.

The Kosovo intervention and that in Libya both feature the intervention of powerful individuals who had the power to shape the decision making process to secure their desired end state, presidential approval for action. As noted above, the administrations of Clinton and Obama were in different places developmentally at the time of intervention, and the personalities of the two leaders were quite different. The Obama administration had a tendency to micromanage foreign policy, whereas Clinton was far more likely to let Berger make choices, at least when things were going well.[20] Furthermore, Clinton was strongly distracted by domestic politics, in particular the Lewinsky scandal. While the Obama administration had no desire to be sucked further into the Middle East, the Arab Spring joined the World Economic Crisis to dominate the news and the administrations attention in 2011. As mentioned above, the Clinton cabinet had nearly all been with the president since the beginning, and their time together eased some of the decision making process, certainly the Kosovo intervention was decided on much more readily than that in Libya. The main new player was outside of the central governing sphere, in the form of General Wesley Clark, whose own political acumen and ease of working with the real insiders in the Clinton administration gave him clout beyond the normal role of a combatant commander.[21]

Whereas in the Somalia case study, the Department of Defense actively resisted intervention until it was ordered otherwise, and Rwanda, where it successfully resisted intervention, Kosovo represented a notable victory for the

---

[19] Power, 2001.
[20] Daalder. 254.
[21] Halbertsam, David. *War in a Time of Peace*. New York: Scribner, 2001. 433.

Department of State against DOD. Madeleine Albright, with Richard Holbrooke and Wesley Clark in support, waged a multi month long struggle to motivate the rest of the cabinet, in particular Berger and Secretary of Defense Cohen, to support intervention. Clinton himself came around when the domestic challenges to his attention were resolved in winter, 1999, and when atrocities and violation of agreements by Serbia became too blatant to ignore. His motivations were in part driven by guilt over failure to act in Rwanda, and a need to complete the still ongoing Yugoslav crisis in response to criticism over the failure of the Dayton accords. Clinton was legitimately concerned about the suffering of Kosovar Albanians, and was able to be convinced by Albright, through Berger, that intervention was necessary. He was so desirous of intervention that, in lieu of significant UN support, he turned to NATO as the international legitimator of action.

For the Libya intervention, the roles of three players in convincing President Obama to act are well known. Power, Rice, and Clinton directly convinced Obama to act in a discussion and vote. Although the discussions took place over a two to three-week period in March, 2011, the actual decision happened quickly, and in the most egalitarian decision making environment seen in the three case studies. What is interesting about the Libya decisions is that, unlike the other interventions, they were decisively influenced by the actions of second and third tier agents, meaning Rice and Power, respectively. It was they who stood nearly coequal to a first tier advisor, Clinton, who in turn helped the other two overcome cabinet opposition and pushed the president toward intervention. While Kunder, Natsios, Herman Cohen, and Wisner all had their roles to play in the Somalia decision making process, there is no evidence that any of them were allowed into the inner decision making circle in the way that Rice and Power were for Obama. This was because of the close and special nature of the relationship that each of them had with the president, relationships that predated the administration and allowed them to circumvent the usual channels for cabinet decision making.

Intervening Factors: Geography, Great Power Hostility or Support, International Affirmation, Domestic Politics, and National Interest

Five intervening factors in decision making emerged from the research. Each played a major role in the decision making and framing process for armed humanitarian interventions. The first is geography, meaning the ease of access by military forces into the area in which intervention is to take place. While the U.S. has an impressive array of land, sea, and air power, it prefers to utilize that power in certain ways. The preference is for interventions which can be reached by sea, since sea lift is a major U.S. military strength, and much larger logistical loads can be moved more effectively by ship than by air.[22] Furthermore, the U.S. Navy is unrivaled in its medium, and control of sea lanes where desired by U.S. forces is generally assumed, particularly in an era when the U.S. has less access to forward land bases than during the Cold War.[23] An additional geographic consideration is nearness to friendly airfields. While U.S. aircraft can strike anywhere in the world, for logistical and pilot rest reasons, the preference is that aircraft not be forced to refuel in the air or launch their missions from CONUS.[24] Finally, the U.S. Marine Corps, the military body most specifically tailored for sudden militarized boots on the ground intervention, is sea based, and each region of the world has Marine forces afloat which can respond nearly instantly to crises within range of its embarked helicopters and amphibious vehicles.[25]

How is this borne out in the case studies? Somalia was easy to reach amphibiously and by air from friendly locations. Marines could exercise their sea borne supply option, and aircraft carriers could have provided rapid support if

---

[22] Mullenbach, M. J. and Matthews, G. P. "Deciding to intervene: An analysis of international and domestic influences on United States interventions in intrastate disputes." *International Interactions*, 34, 2008, 25-52. 30.
[23] Ignatieff, Michael. "The Challenges of American Imperial Power." Naval War College Review 56, No. 2. Spring, 2003: 9-18. 13.
[24] A notable exception to this is the use of Strategic bombers, most particularly the B2, which the U.S. does not normally base outside its borders for security reasons.
[25] U.S. Marine Corps 26th Marine Expeditionary Unit. "About the 26th MEU." http://www.26thmeu.marines.mil/About/MEU.aspx. Accessed on November 1, 2014.

needed. In the case of Kosovo, nearby Italy served as the base for the majority of U.S. airstrikes, along with aircraft carriers in the nearby Adriatic and Mediterranean Seas. Ground forces could have been introduced from the forces already located in neighboring Macedonia, Bosnia, or readily deployed by helicopter or medium lift aircraft such as the C-130 from Italy or from ships at sea. Libya was the easiest of all in this regard. There was never a question of ground forces in Libya, but since the overwhelming majority of targets were coastal towns, deploying them by helicopter or amphibious assault would have been easy. Airstrikes were launched from nearby aircraft carriers and from the European mainland. Since NATO countries such as Italy, the UK, and France were involved in the airstrikes, access to nearby bases for U.S. forces was not in question.

Rwanda forms the outlier for geography, and it's remoteness was touted at the time as a reason not to intervene. Landlocked, Rwanda was nowhere near the normal sources of U.S. maritime power. None of Rwanda's neighbors were U.S. allies, so there was no way to get U.S. forces close enough to stage into the country, or in which to base U.S. tactical and logistical aircraft.[26] Any U.S. military effort would have had to be staged in by aircraft, which would have generated their own requirements for escorts, ground support security forces, and supplies. This assessment is in no way meant to judge the decision not to intervene, but reflect part of the Pentagon's reasoning in resisting intervention.[27]

The second and third external variables in determining intervention involve the international community and the establishment of legitimacy for militarized interventions which would violate state sovereignty. As a proponent of international law and the concept of state sovereignty, the U.S. seeks to act within the legitimization of an international mandate, as evidenced in its seeking of such legitimization in each of the case studies. For Somalia, this was the U.N., and is

---

[26] Albright. 153.

[27] National Security Council of the United States. "Memorandum for Deputy Assistant to the President for National Security Affairs." National Security Council. May 5, 1994. From Ferroggiaro, William, "The U.S. And Rwanda, 1994, Evidence of Inaction", George Washington University http://www2.gwu.edu/~nsarchiv/NSAEBB/NSAEBB53. Accessed October 14 2014.

evidenced by President Bush working directly with Boutros Boutros Gali to encourage passage of UN Security Council Resolution 1973, specifically tailored for what would become the U.S. led coalition. Interestingly, the withdrawal of U.S. forces in the wake of the battle of Mogadishu was not mandated or forced by the UN, but was a choice of the Clinton administration. In the contrasting case of Rwanda, the international community was working specifically against intervention from the start, as the UN pulled more and more of its own peacekeepers out of the country. This proved to be yet another factor which led to the non-intervention there. In Libya, as well, pushing through a UN resolution, and rallying other international bodies such as the Arab League, the GCC, and NATO were all central both in the justification of the intervention and framing that justification to the American people.

Kosovo provides a more interesting case, in that the legitimacy which would be provided by UN support for intervention was distinctly lacking, in part due to Russian doubts about the operation, forcing the administration to rely on NATO as an admittedly lesser international legitimating body. That said, the Clinton administration saw both the strengthening of NATO and its support in the operation as vitally important, along with mollifying Russia so that it would not actively oppose the intervention in the UN Security Council.[28] Further, the future of NATO itself as a cohesive alliance seemed to be at stake, a factor which helped frame the intervention.

As a third factor, the role of foreign actors turned out to be a critical factor in decision making for and against interventions. For Somalia, this influence was primarily provided by pressure from the UN and its Secretary General, Boutros-Gali. For Rwanda, French support of the Tutsis, and French and Belgian actions in the UN helped to influence the U.S. against intervention. Russian resistance would have doomed an effort to intervene in Kosovo, since Moscow viewed Serbia as a client state. By the same token, initial German reluctance to intervene was

[28] Talbot, Strobe. *The Russia Hand: A Memoir of Presidential Diplomacy*. New York: Random House, 2003. 348.

significant, just as British support for intervention was a strong motivating factor for the U.S. Similarly, for the Libya intervention, France and the UK strongly influenced the U.S. intervention, even providing the "ahead" as the U.S. led from "behind."

U.S. domestic politics form an additional, if coincidental, external factor which was revealed through examination of the case studies. The imminence of presidential or mid-term congressional elections seemed to be a factor in all but one of the case studies, although the impact of those elections on the interventions is not consistent and may be minimal or irrelevant. Presidential elections, however, were much more obviously a factor. In 1992, the presidential election cycle was a major consideration. The challenger, Clinton, turned lack of action in Somalia into a campaign issue which influenced Bush's decision making, leading to the approval of the airlift in August, timed to provide a bump in approval before the Republican National Convention. Further, during the main electioneering season, from September to early November, the administration was completely absorbed in the campaign.[29]

1994 was a midterm election year for the Clinton administration's first term, and this directly impacted the decision making on the Rwanda intervention, as specifically mentioned by then NSC staffer Susan Rice.[30] Coming on the heels, as it did, of the failed peacemaking effort in Somalia, the election was a significant factor in explaining the inaction of the administration and the lack of congressional pressure for an intervention that might have proven to be as unpopular as Somalia had become. Elections also bore on the decision to intervene in Kosovo, with Clinton purposefully insisting on a discrete mission that would be over with before the 2000 election cycle got fully underway, so as not to saddle his chosen successor, Al Gore with the burden of a potentially uncomfortable conflict.[31] Like Bush

[29] Redd, Stephen B. "The Influence of Advisors and Decision Strategies on Foreign Policy Choices: President Clinton's Decision to Use Force in Kosovo." *International Studies Perspectives*, Volume 6, 2005. 137.
[30] Power. 2001.
[31] Redd. 137.

during the election cycle, Clinton was also badly distracted by domestic scandals, most notably the Monica Lewinsky affair and subsequent impeachment.

Each of the four factors above combine with economics and history to suggest a fifth, national interest. U.S. national interest varies by region and subject, with the traditional conflict between moralistic and realist actions seen in each. At its core, national interest, as described by Alexander George, is more than "minimum objectives" which he states as survival, economic well-being, and liberty.[32] In the post-Cold War era, the U.S. was more willing to take realist, i.e. militarized action, in regions of the world where it had been directly attacked, where vital resources were at stake, where one of its allies or alliances was directly threatened, and where it had historically had a role. National interest ultimately kept the U.S. out of Rwanda, but into the other examples, and it was the role of the dominant actor in each decision making process to make the case that U.S. interests were at stake. For Somalia, George H.W. Bush wished to lock his replacement, Clinton, into a series of policies that did not include intervention in Bosnia. For Clinton, years later, intervention in Kosovo was couched in terms of avoiding war in Europe, and in strengthening the NATO alliance. Over a decade later, goals in Libya were similar, to back the play of allies in the region and prevent the spread of instability.

Decision Making Models

This research sought to evaluate and validate several models of decision making. The first two are Graham Allison's Rational Actor Model (RAM) of government politics, decision making, and group dynamics, while the second, influenced by the first, is the Governmental Politics Model.[33] To restate, the RAM's core concepts include: The ranking of objectives, discussion of

---

[32] George, Alexander. Presidential Decision Making in Foreign Policy: The Effective Use of Information and Advice. Boulder, Colorado: Westview Press, 1980. 227.

[33] Allison, Graham and Zelikow, Philip. *Essence of Decision: Explaining the Cuban Missile Crisis. Vol. 2.* New York: Longman, 1999. 13-16.

alternatives, attachment of consequences to the alternatives, and a rational selection of the alternatives to act upon based on required goal completion.[34] Further assumptions include the primacy of unitary states as actors, and the perception of the international environment as a self-help anarchic world with no higher authority to moderate state action.[35] In each of the four case studies, the RAM is evident in the decision making process, from the deputies level up through the president. For Somalia, that process brought about the August airlift, and led to the decision to intervene, but under strict guidelines that left out regime change or political involvement. For Rwanda, the discussion never got above the deputies, the same types of discussions took place, and the situation was deemed not worth of intervention. In Kosovo, a wide range of pressures were tried, including attempting to work diplomatically both with Serbia directly and through Serbian sponsor Russia, with intervention occurring when those efforts were seen to dramatically fail. For Libya, the decision to intervene was taken under some time duress, nevertheless, the compromise solutions presented by Gates, Biden, and others, were considered before intervention was selected as the course of action. Seeking international legitimacy for armed humanitarian interventions also falls within the realm of rationality, as an effort to mitigate the effects of the anarchical system.

The Government Politics Model (GPM), is less positively present through the case studies. In this model, these decisions are viewed as "outputs of large organizations functioning according to standards of behavior."[36] Outcomes will be influenced by organizational, not individual, dynamics and cultures.[37] The various bureaucracies which make up the decision making process serve themselves first, then their higher authorities, which can cause the creation of gaps between the choices of leaders and the implementation capabilities and priorities of subordinate organizations.[38] In the cases in which more junior leaders decidedly impact

---

[34] Allison and Zelikow. 13-16.
[35] Ibid. 15-16.
[36] Ibid. 143.
[37] Ibid. 255.
[38] Ibid. 257.

decision making, such as Libya, it is difficult to see the GPM, and its assertions of hierarchy in play.[39] Under this model even a paramount leader, such as the president, must seek consensus with his subordinates, if for no other reason than to prevent misunderstandings, and even presidential power may be curtailed by powerful subordinate bureaucracies.[40]

Looking at events through the prism of the GPM, it is seen to be partially relevant to the case studies. Regarding Somalia, each of the cabinet and interagency players stuck to their own institutional lines of interest. DOD resisted intervention, as contrary to its existing doctrine, until it perceived and acted on the president's desires. Humanitarian aid-focused agencies argued for intervention from their own points of view. Where the GPM breaks down, however, in the case of Somalia, is in the nature of the final decision to intervene. There is no evidence that Bush was influenced in any way by the organizational resistance of the DOD toward intervention. Given his long career as a foreign policy practitioner, he did not need to be told of what and why the military resisted intervention. He also did not have to cut deals with any agency or player in order to give force to his directives. When he decided on intervention, the government acted. Because of this decisive and unchecked action, the GPM cannot be credited with well explaining the Somalia decision making process. This is not to deny the power of the presidency in all of the cases, however, the central role that Bush played in the process is unique among the cases.

Rwanda may be the purest example of the GPM in action of the case studies, however, this is not helpful since a successful GPM would then appear to mean that the U.S. will not ever engage in armed humanitarian operations. The Rwanda example remains relevant, however, since it demonstrates one outcome that can occur when no dominant actor makes the case the president for intervention. Since the issue of Rwanda was never seriously discussed at the highest levels, we must

---

[39] Bendor, Jonathan and Hammond, Thomas H. "Rethinking Allison's Models." The American Political Science Review 86, no. 2 (1992, June): 301-322. 306. The term they use is "Single Time Period" organization.
[40] Woll, Peter. *American Bureacracy.* New York: Norton, 1977. 206-207.

examine what did happen, which was interagency discussions at the deputies level and below. In these, the GPM is seen to function, with each agency making its arguments from its own bureaucratic point of view, and none being able to overcome an overall reluctance to act. Since none of the major bureaucracies was motivated sufficiently to intervene, no recommendation to sway a president, who was not focused on the issue, to take place.

The Kosovo intervention saw the GPM in action, with each of the key players arguing for or against intervention from an institutional point of view, with National Security Advisor Berger at the pinnacle of the decision making process. Given the nature of the humanitarian crisis in Kosovo, the interagency community focused on food and medical aid was not a major player. The intelligence community did not play an advocacy role, but served its customary function of providing information, leaving the Departments of State and Defense as the two key players. As in the Somalia case, however, we see the GPM as only a partial solution, for several reasons. One is that there is no evidence that President Clinton had to bargain in order to implement his decisions. Once he decided, the key players, in this case Holbrooke at State and Clark at DOD acted. Furthermore, while the Department of State acted as a relatively unified body in the decision making process, the Department of Defense was significantly divided, with an institutional bias against intervention on the one hand, and a powerful player on the ground in Europe, Wesley Clark, who was convinced of the need for intervention and did not hesitate to make that known outside of his chain of command, or to work with those in other agencies outside of his own bureaucracy, in this case the Department of State, to push for and implement intervention.[41]

Of the three case studies which observed actual interventions, the Libya case study comes closest to an intervention which took place as the GPM would have predicted, with the caveat that U.S. allies, most notably in France and the GCC, provided powerful external catalysts for armed intervention. The players all

---

[41] Halbertsam. 433.

spoke from their institutional points of view. While Rice, as an Ambassador, technically worked for Hillary Clinton in her role as Secretary of State, the reality is that the Ambassador to the UN has often served as a personal delegate and confidante of the president, particularly in Democrat administrations, and this places Rice as her own power center. The institutions which are customarily against intervention, most notably DOD, were against it in this case, while those whose mandate covered humanitarian issues were in favor. The negotiations which took place saw bargaining, particularly on the issue of whether or not ground forces would be used in the operation. There is no memoir to suggest that Obama was personally against this, as Clinton openly was throughout the Kosovo Crisis. Based on polling data and Congressional statements, it appears that ground forces were not bargained away to please the DOD, but rather as an assessment of the prevailing public opinion on the matter. Therefore, one key piece of the GPM, bargaining from the top, does not appear to be present.

Noteworthy criticism of the GPM focuses on whether goals of leaders at the cabinet level are actually so disparate, and both whether and why a president would have to bargain with his own appointees.[42] They posit that a president would try to avoid bargaining if possible, and that he would normally be in a paramount position to do so. In all three of the cases where intervention took place, presidential decision making was final once the orders to intervene were given. Therefore, looking at the case studies through the lens of the GPM is an inadequate vision of how the decision making for the examined interventions actually took place.

A third model, the Theory of Government Politics Model (TGM), posits that key leaders acted as "pied pipers" and brought others along with them through persuasive power, particularly if the outlook of and relationships among the group members were similar and strong.[43] Given that this model was built around the first Bush administration and their actions in the first Gulf War, it is unsurprising that

---

[42] Bradford, Jeffrey P. "Political Aspects of Strategic Decision Making in British Defence Policy." Cranfield University, 1999. 18.

[43] Yetiv, Steve A. *Explaining Foreign Policy: U.S. Decision Making and the Gulf War*. Baltimore: Johns Hopkins University Press, 2004. 120.

the model works well in describing the actions which led to the Somalia intervention. Again, Bush himself was the chief engine for decision making who provided the central guidance which got DOD on board for intervention and made the actions of December 1992 possible. The similar outlook and close relations among the key leaders involved facilitated this, as it had done in the Gulf War. The TGM is also sadly predictive of the non-intervention in Rwanda, if only, once again, in an unsatisfactory way, since the lack of a strong spokesperson meant that the de facto mindset, against intervention, could take hold and prevent action.

The model turned out to be partially useful for explaining the interventions in Kosovo and Libya, in which powerful actors, although not always in paramount roles, formulated their positions and drug other key leaders along. In the case of Kosovo, and for reasons previously discussed, the Clinton team, which had a term and a half of working together under its belt, and which had a president who had become very comfortable in his role as international decision maker, comes close to the Bush model, and the TGM is useful in predicting the outcome that Madeleine Albright would be able to pull the decision making apparatus along to her point of view. If one takes Wesley Clark, not Defense Secretary Cohen, as the leading player for the Defense Department, then the TGM fits the process even better. Indeed, it seems that the main competitor for Albright's attention on the issue of Kosovo was not international, but rather Clinton's absorption by the events of the Monica Lewinsky case and his impeachment. When those two issues were resolved, decisions on Kosovo came quickly, and Albright's voice found its full audience and impact.

The TGM is very evident in the Libya case study, in which Rice and Power, neither of whom were in traditionally dominant influential positions, exercised the pied piper role. Aided by pressure from the international community, actions by France and other allies, and growing personal concern about reports of violence and genocide, Hillary Clinton came to support intervention.[44] The three then convinced

---

[44] Clinton, Hillary R. *Hard Choices*. New York: Simon and Schuster, 2014. 364.

President Obama to act, in spite of significant pressure against intervention by other powerful players. In contrast to the TGM, however this took place in an environment in which the key players had nowhere near the comfort level working with each other, and little commonality of vision or understanding of authority compared to the Bush administration. So Libya gives the result, but without what it predicts would be the necessary factors. Finally, Libya suffers somewhat from the same problem that critics such as Bradford raise with Allison, which is that he covered his subject too recently after its occurrence, and before key evidence was available in terms of memoirs and classified documents.[45] The world is a much more partisan place now than it was in the 1960s, or even 1990s, and the events in Libya are still central to a heated political debate which will likely continue as long as any of the players involved seek to run for elected office. The critical memoirs of Rice, Power, and President Obama himself are not yet available. Based on what is known about the Libya decision making process, the author does not expect significant changes to take place in the story of the decision to intervent, but would be remiss in failing to note the possibility.

In summary, for decision making processes, the case studies bear out some of the predictions made in the introduction and methodology sections of this book. The RAM turned out to be useful and more or less predictive, if overly general. The GPM was the least useful of the models, affirming criticisms of its assumption on the constraints organizations impose upon individuals.[46] The TGM proved to be the most predictive in the three cases, although, again, it works best when the specific factors it needs to function are in place. Sadly, and unsatisfactorily, all of the models, in one way or another, are useful in predicting the lack of intervention in Rwanda in 1994.

---

[45] Bradford. 20.
[46] Bendor and Hammond. 309.

Framing and Intervention

According to Entman, the purpose of a frame is "to generate support or opposition to a political actor or policy."[47] This is what he calls the "Cascading Network Association Theory".[48] Since the government remains the primary source for information, this creates a system of asymmetric interdependence, but this can only be taken advantage of if there is unanimity in the message. Castells drew upon and added to this concept in *Communication Power*, positing that Network Power is the power to modify, change, or create networks.[49] To Castells, power lies within networked systems. According to Entman, the government is generally successful in framing when it can call on shared themes fitting the national mood and ideals and get its themes in "early and often."[50]

In all of the cases examined framing played some role in the decision making process and in the justification of intervention to key audiences, generally the media and the American people, but also sometimes to allied nations and other audiences. In all cases, the government was the organization with the power and interest to establish, maintain, and capitalize on the power of communication networks in order to frame the debate on armed humanitarian interventions, and to persuade stakeholders of the need to intervene. Where the cases vary is the extent of framing, and on the ability of highly placed, powerful individual actors who create the frames used to encourage intervention. Conflicting frames also exist in each case, provided not only by the media, but by the party out of power. Counter framing was also occasionally provided by the government of the opposing power, meaning the country being intervened in. As stated in the methodology, a model drawing off the work of Entman and Castells would expect to see a concerted, planned effort by senior decision makers to set the terms of public discourse on a

---

[47] Entman, Robert M. *Projections of Power: Framing News, Public Opinion, and U.S. Foreign Policy*. Chicago: University of Chicago Press, 2004. 47.
[48] Ibid. 17-21.
[49] Castells, Manuel. *Communication Power*. Oxford: Oxford University Press, 2009. 45.
[50] Entman. 10.

given issue, and to capitalize on the government's unique position as a single source for definitive information on key foreign policy and defense issues. Influencers outside of the foreign policy decision making process would be counteracted and refuted in order to maintain information primacy. Narratives would attempt to draw simple parallels to historical examples, not always contextually relevant, but well known and inflammatory at times. Control or influence on information networks would be established and increased so that messaging could be enhanced.

Entman's theory is validated in the way in which the media were influenced by government information, and later, in the impact that media reporting had back up the information chain to President Bush during the Somalia decision making process. As noted, some of the key second tier players such as USAID and OFDA leaders used the media to facilitate their own efforts to force decisions on key issues, such as the airlift.[51] But there is no evidence that framing by the government was undertaken in a systematic way, or that such decisions were an implicit part of the decision making cycle for the decision to intervene. Instead, the framing that took place was a byproduct of the primacy of the government as an information holder and broker, and because of the unique nature, and high danger, of the situation on the ground, which put the government in the position of having a monopoly on the information needed by the media to generate accurate reporting.[52]

For Rwanda, public and congressional opinion was stacked heavily against another intervention on the African continent. The frame of the failure in Somalia was dominant, along with an even grimmer frame that accepted a certain amount of death, mayhem and destruction in Africa as the norm. That frame deadened government officials to the crisis, officials who, had the same level of mayhem occurred elsewhere, would have been forced into action. Finally, and along with the Somalia frame, Yugoslavia, another crisis altogether, successfully dominated the national security establishment of the U.S. Rwanda showed no framing, except

---

[51] Livingston, Stephen and Eachus, Todd. "Humanitarian Crisis and U.S. Foreign Policy: Somalia and the CNN Effect Reconsidered." *Political Communication* 12, 1995, 413-429. 424.
[52] Ibid. 415.

in a negative way, in an active attempt by the U.S. government to avoid use of the term genocide so that intervention could be avoided.[53]

In terms of the Kosovo intervention, the American public were, when focused on government policy at all, most interested in the scandals which surrounded the Clinton administration, as well as his ongoing struggles with Congress, which culminated in impeachment proceedings shortly before the intervention began. As a result of these factors, the White House was on the defense in terms of messaging and framing, slowing both the U.S. response and the effort to justify that response through framing. Outside public and congressional pressure to intervene was minimal. As discussed, the construction of Slobodan Milosevic as the central villain of the Kosovo crisis began some months earlier, in fall 1998.[54] The failure of the Rambouillet conference is the event that generated modest support for operations, as discussed in the case study.[55] At this time, presidential statements increased in stridency and directly hinted at the air campaign which would follow if negotiations failed. A central part of the framing effort was to reassure the American people and allies and other great powers that the U.S. would not place troops on the ground as part of the intervention. The result of these efforts was that by the commencement of hostilities, nearly half of the American public saw Kosovo as a security issue of vital interest to the U.S.[56]

The Libya intervention shows different framing challenges, in part because of changes in the media, but it also presents conflicting frames, in particular Gadaffi's efforts to refute the U.S. frame, and the Iranian effort to frame the entire Arab Spring to its benefit. Furthermore, unlike the previous case studies, the Arab Spring dominated the media in spring 2011, coming to eclipse even the ongoing economic crisis. This meant that the American people did not have to be familiarized with information on the crisis, and that the U.S. government had no

---

[53] Power, 2001.

[54] Butler, Michael J. *Selling a 'Just' War: Framing, Legitimacy, and U.S. Military Intervention.* Chippenham and Eastbourne: Palgrave Macmillan, 2012. 146.

[55] Redd. 136.

[56] Ibid.

monopoly on information, which was plentiful and readily available. The rise of social media, even if not used much in Libya itself, meant that a much broader discussion took place among stakeholders than had ever been the case before. Framing the intervention in Libya began in the second week of March, 2011, culminating with the decision to intervene a week later, and the ultimate speech act, the Obama speech to the American people, the week after that. In spite of efforts by President Obama and the senior leaders of his cabinet to provide the moral imperative for the intervention, public support for the operation stayed relatively flat, and barely crossed over into the approval side of the ledger, and even that only occurred because of a strict adherence to a policy of keeping ground forces out of Libya. Correspondingly, Congressional support for the operation also hinged on a basic promise to avoid a ground invasion of Libya.

The Combined Decide/Frame Model

Based on the hypothesis that armed humanitarian interventions occur when a powerful leader or small group of leaders dominates the decision making and framing apparatus to force and explain such an intervention, it is necessary to construct a theory that explains the concurrence or nexus of the decision making and framing processes. Based on the literature review and a thorough examination of the Allison, Yetiv, Entman, and Castell's models, it could be suggested that when the foreign policy decision making process is dominated by powerful individuals with a motivation toward intervention, and the framing process is dominated by the same or similarly minded individuals, armed humanitarian interventions take place driven by this alignment. Such individuals become dominant actors due to a combination of their holding of a senior cabinet position, a personal connection to the president, and the personal quality of willpower to motivate and explain decision making.

As noted in the methodology, this model would expect to see the decision making process dominated by key stakeholders with powerful interests in a given issue formed by their own experiences and pressures on them formed through their own participation in events, both in forcing a decision on a given issue (in this case, armed humanitarian interventions) and in framing that process and the associated decisions to the various stakeholders (in this case, the public, through the media).

Once again following the framework of taking each case study individually, the Decide/Frame Model seems least relevant to the Somalia intervention. Framing, where it took place, was spasmodic, and centered around key events. One example of this is the airlift of August, 1992. The decision was made so quickly that the only public information available was the announcement of the action. Similarly, the actual intervention in December was not preceded by a major framing effort by the government, even in the intervening weeks between the Thanksgiving decision and the landing of the Marines two weeks later.[57] This is not to say that there was no awareness or support on behalf of the American people, however, basic awareness of the situation came from the media. While the case study demonstrated that the media got most of its information from government sources, there is no evidence that the information given was developed in such a way as to be anything more than informational, in other words, information provided was not done so in order to frame an intervention, but rather to increase awareness.

The model's application to the Rwanda intervention is, as with many facets of that tragedy, non-satisfying, but that perversely helps to prove the point of the research. There was no order from the top ordering the non-intervention. Instead, the conversation remained at the Deputies level and lower, and focused more on how to justify the non-intervention than any other factor. Careful and assiduous avoidance of the term "Genocide" was the centerpiece of the framing effort, and inasmuch as there was no intervention, this can be seen as a clear, if unhappy, success.

The Kosovo intervention showed perhaps the most systematic example of a conscious effort to frame an intervention through the decision making process and

---

[57] Klarevas, Louis J. "The Polls-Trends: The United States Peace Operation in Somalia." Public Opinion Quarterly 64, (2000): 523-540. 524-525.

to the decision to intervene and the actual intervention of U.S. forces. Statements made by Albright, Holbrooke, Clark, and others in the summer and fall of 1998 were not successful at creating public motivation for intervention, but set the stage for convincing Cohen, Berger, and ultimately President Clinton of the need for intervention, particularly after the end of the Lewinsky affair as a public factor and increasingly violent atrocities in Kosovo itself in January and February 1999. By February, the administration was concurrently negotiating between the Serbs and Kosovar Albanians, planning to intervene, and actively running a media campaign designed to frame Milosevic and the Serbs as genocidal, a national security issue, and needful of a U.S. and western response. That effort continued through the end of the intervention, morphing to fit the changing needs of the frame. This is seen in the change from adamant refusal to consider ground forces to open threats of their use as the Serbian will seemed to crack from April 1999 onwards.

The Libya intervention falls somewhere in between Somalia and Kosovo in terms of combined decision making and framing. The crisis had a much shorter lead up than any of the others except for Rwanda. Events in Egypt and Tunisia had only been going on for weeks when Libya exploded, and U.S. intervention began about one month after the first major atrocities had taken place there. That said, the Arab Spring was a number one news event from nearly the moment that it started, so a long term effort to frame potential intervention may not have been necessary.[58] In terms of the decision making cycle, the main cabinet member to support intervention, Hillary Clinton, had to be convinced that intervention was necessary by a combination of the pressure of growing evidence of atrocities in Libya, a growing sense that the administration was taking the blame for mismanagement of the crisis, and the pressure of advocates such as Rice and Power. That trio, supported by an outside, but important actor, Senator McCain, then

[58] Journalism.org. "News Coverage Index, February 29-March 6, 2011." http://www.journalism.org/2011/03/06/pej-news-coverage-index-february-28-march-6-2011/. Accessed on October 27, 2014.

brought about the pressure which led President Obama to decide on intervention.[59] The week following that decision saw a media blitz by the foreign policy decision making leadership to justify the intervention that was coming, and to explain it after it began.

The premise of this research is that that by unifying the two key processes (deciding and framing) into a single model, and incorporating the role of the powerful individual in the decision making and framing processes, the weaknesses of all of the models can be overcome. This also helps to account for the impact of external variables on as well as the experience of past interventions on current and future intervention decision making, since the decision and framing cycles do not end, and constantly feed each other in accordance with Entman's theory. The research performed on the case studies led to several conclusions on the validity of such a model, affirming its utility.

One major revelation of the research is that the decision cycle for interventions is significantly shorter than had been envisioned at the outset of the research. For Somalia, while discussions had been ongoing for months, the decision cycle Bush to make choice to intervene took place over approximately two weeks, the time from the electoral defeat to Thanksgiving in 1992. The time from the decision to intervene to the actual landing of troops was another two weeks. For Rwanda, the time frame for an intervention decision was similar, as intervention would have been most effective from mid-March to mid-April, or a one month period after which the impact would have been minimal since most of the killing had been completed by that time. Kosovo, as noted, had the longest lead up, with nearly a year of discussion and active framing before the intervention. Even the immediate decision cycle was longer, over about two months from January to March, than that for Somalia. Finally, the Libya intervention decision cycle took place over a three week period from late February to early March, 2011, with the broader Arab Spring crisis extending back another month.

---

59 Talev, Margaret. Samantha Power: The Voice behind Obama's Libya action. *McClatchy Newspapers*, March 25, 2011.

The brevity of the decision cycles revealed limited government opportunities for framing intervention. It cannot be said that any of the interventions were bolts out of the blue, and there was public awareness of all of the events considered, with the exception of Rwanda. But in most of the cases, time to build support for operations was limited, and this is reflected in the relatively low public approval ratings of the interventions, particularly the last two, Kosovo and Libya. This is in spite of the long lead up for the Kosovo intervention.

The role of the powerful individual is clearly seen in all of the interventions, as well as being negatively demonstrated by the Rwanda example. In each case of successful intervention, a powerful leader, who was not, in all cases, the president, made the case for intervention both in the decision making cycle, and to the public. This is best demonstrated in the Kosovo and Libya cases. In both cases, it was the Secretary of State who played the key role, with significant support. For Kosovo, that support came from Holbrooke and Clark, for Libya, from Rice and Power. But, in both examples, it was ultimately the Secretary of State who compelled the president to agree to intervention. Where there was no strong individual, there was no intervention, as was seen with the Rwanda example.

None of the models presented in the research provide a total, satisfying result when applied to the case studies, however, each provides a useful piece of the puzzle. Rationality is an important foundation for all decision making. Bureaucracies matter in decision making, and sometimes the inertia created by them must be overcome in order for action to take place. There is some give and take in negotiating among decision makers. Powerful, motivated individuals are a key factor in interventions and framing. Useful parts of each model have been shaped to attempt to provide a more encompassing model that covers both decision making and framing. Considering the timelines of intervention, the decision cycle, and the role of the dominant actor in decision making and framing, the primary conclusion of the study is that a Decide/Frame model based on the influence of a dominant actor is a useful answer to the question of how foreign policy decisions are made in terms of explaining U.S. armed humanitarian interventions in the post-

Cold War period. In the presence of a powerful, motivated individual who sought armed intervention, such interventions took place, and were framed to the American people. In the absence of such leadership, such interventions did not take place.

CHAPTER VIII - Models in Action: The Decision not to Intervene in Syria, August, 2013

> "We cannot accept a world where women and children and innocent civilians are gassed on a terrible scale."
>
> Statement by President Obama, August 30, 2013.[1]

> "August 31st, 2013 - Obama says he had authorized the use of military force to punish Syria, with military assets to carry out a strike in place and ready to move on his order, but he would first seek authorization from Congress."
>
> Reuters. 2013. Timeline of U.S. Syrian Crisis. [2]

This chapter, essentially the second part of the findings, will look briefly at a more recent intervention decision process to see if the findings of the research are valid, or if they represented non repeatable events. As each event of the Arab Spring unfolded, the next seemed to be even more violent, culminating, for now at least, with the Syrian rising against the Bashir Assad regime and the civil war which followed, and is still ongoing. The following section will examine Syria by the same process as the case studies. To date, there has been no armed humanitarian intervention in Syria, however, discussions of intervention followed a significantly different path than was the case in Rwanda, the other non-intervention examined.

---

[1] Reuters. 2013. Timeline of U.S. Syrian Crisis. August 31, 2013.
http://www.reuters.com/article/2013/08/31/us-syria-crisis-timeline-idUSBRE97U0D820130831.
Accessed November 14, 2013

[2] Ibid.

The time period deals specifically with the period ending in August, 2013, with the decision not to intervene in Syria following a series of atrocities committed there involving the use of chemical weapons.

In Brief: The Syrian Civil War 2011 – 2013

In terms of general background, the Syrian Civil War was an outgrowth of the Arab Spring, as described in the Libya case study. The introductory events of the Syrian Civil War were concurrent with the Libya intervention and its aftermath, as well as the ongoing world economic crisis, which included the U.S. government sequestration crisis of spring, 2013. Syria, however, was a very different case than other notable Arab Spring events, for several reasons. Ambassador Stephen Ford, the U.S. envoy to Syria and a noted Arabist in the Department of State, was one of a faction who predicted that the Assad regime would respond positively to the Arab Spring, and not react violently, as Gaddafi had done.[3] That turned out to be nearly the opposite of what actually happened. Initially, a careful silence in Syria contrasted significantly from each other and from other trends in U.S. Middle East policy.[4] The administration dealt with each country in the Arab Spring on a case by case basis, with strategic interests and oil, not morality, as the key factors for policy making, and each case increasing in threat and violence.[5] In March, 2011, while the administration was deciding to intervene in Libya, the first major Arab Spring protests were taking place in Syria, fueled by a release of political prisoners by the Assad government.[6]

Syria's connections with terror groups such as Hezbollah and Hamas, and its meddling in Lebanon, as well as its enmity with Israel, are further factors which made it difficult to isolate the regime or push forward an intervention, and

---

[3] Gates. 523.

[4] Pinto, Maria Do Ceu De Pinho Ferreira. "Mapping the Obama administration's response to the Arab Spring." *Review of Brasilian International Politics*, 2012, 109-130. 109.

[5] Ibid., 110.

[6] Panetta, Leon. *Worthy Fights*. New York: Penguin Press, 2014. 410.

Washington's response to the outbreak of rebellion was primarily rhetorical, in calls for regime change in the country.[7] As early as April, 2011, the U.S. involved itself in Syria, with sanctions imposed as a result on the Assad regime's attempts to quell the Arab Spring uprising.[8] By the summer, President Obama and other western leaders were calling for the regime to relinquish power.[9] Syria, of course, did not involve oil, but it did involve Russia and Iran, making intervention a difficult issue to justify and frame, particularly in concert with the demonstrated capability of the regime to resist efforts by social media-augmented rebels to discredit the regime, a factor which had been central to the other revolutions.[10]

In July 2012, Syria upped the ante in the conflict by announcing that it had chemical weapons with which to defend itself from aggression. This led to the infamous "Red Line" statement against their use by President Obama in August.[11] His statement indicated that the "calculus" would change toward intervention if those weapons should be used or deployed. Further warnings in December did not prevent the use of the weapons near Aleppo in March, or the follow on attack on 21 August 2013, in which 1500 Syrians died, and which generated the intervention crisis which ended with the decision not to intervene in September of that year. There was considerable discussion, and indications that the White House was willing to consider military strikes on Syria, with significant support from Senator John McCain. There was little coordination between Syrian rebel groups, in contrast with the cases of Libya and Kosovo, this made it unclear who was actually to be supported in the Syrian Civil War, and accordingly difficult to frame an intervention. [12] In June, 2013, President Obama increased aid to the Free Syrian Army, however, knowing which groups to favor with support and which to ignore was problematic, and has become even more so since the rise of the Islamic State

---

[7] Panetta. 120.
[8] Reuters. 2013. Timeline of U.S. Syrian Crisis.
[9] Ibid.
[10] Lindgren, Simon. 2013. "The Potential and Limitations of Twitter Activism: Mapping the 2011 Libyan Uprising." *Triple C,* 2011, 207-220. 207.
[11] Reuters. 2013. Timeline of U.S. Syrian Crisis.
[12] Panetta. 410.

2013.[13] The Islamic state, also known as the Islamic State in Iraq and the Levant (ISIL) or by its Arabic name Daesh, had its origins in the Al Qaeda in Iraq organization of Abu Musab al-Zarqawi, and was a major player in the region from 2013 to its near defeat by U.S. backed regional forces in 2017. By the time key U.S. allies, the very allies who had pushed the U.S. into intervention in Libya, began to defect in late August, the frame for intervention in Syria was in shambles, and the president turned the matter over to Congress for approval, which was tantamount to backing down.[14] In the end, resistance to intervention proved to be too great and the status quo was selected over the attack option.

The Obama Second Term: Some New Faces, Some Battered Egos

The Obama administration underwent some significant changes in between 2011 and 2013, most notably in the changeover of the Secretaries of Defense and State. Gates gave way to Leon Panetta, a strong Hillary Clinton supporter, but also a prominent Democrat who was far more in line with the administration's goals than his predecessor. Panetta's term lasted into the Syrian crisis, with his successor, former Republican Senator Chuck Hagel, assuming control of the Pentagon in February 2013. Hagel had originally taken a stand against the Libya intervention, but later changed that position during his confirmation hearings.[15] Hagel's appointment represented an effort by the administration to bring in a moderate Republican who would have cache with the armed forces while shaping the department along lines dictated by the White House.[16]

---

[13] Clinton. 465.
[14] Reuters. 2013. Timeline of U.S. Syrian Crisis.
[15] Pollack, Joel B. "Hagel 2011: Obama wrong on Gadhafi, Libya was a mistake." *Brietbart*, February 22, 2013. http://www.breitbart.com/Big-Peace/2013/02/22/Hagel-2011-Obama-Wrong-on-Gadhafi-Libya-Was-a-Mistake. Accessed on November 28, 2014.
[16] Walt, Stehpen. "Top five reasons Obama should pick Chuck Hagel for SecDef." *Foreign Policy*, 13 December 2012. http://www.foreignpolicy.com/posts/2012/12/13/top_five_reasons_obama_should_pick_chuck_hagel_for_secdef. Accessed on 20 November 2014.

The most significant change in the leadership was the transition of leadership of the Department of State from Hillary Clinton to former Massachusetts Democrat Senator John Kerry in February, 2013. Clinton came to express her regret over the events in Benghazi, although not the overall intervention in Libya.[17] The transfer of office took place after Susan Rice, the former Ambassador to the UN, withdrew her nomination for the position following sharp criticism for her role in providing false explanations for the causes for the Benghazi riots and attacks which led to the death of four Americans, including Ambassador Chris Stephens, on September 11, 2012. Rice would go on to become National Security Advisor after the departure of Donilon on 5 June 2013. Denis McDonough, in turn, moved from the Deputy NSC position to that of White House Chief of Staff. Samantha Power, in turn, replaced Rice at the UN on 2 August, 2013, shortly before the chemical attack crisis in Syria later that month. Given that Rice and Power were already administration leaders, and that John Kerry had been Senate Foreign Relations Committee Chairman before he became Secretary of State, Hagel was the only person truly new to the foreign policy team. However, President Obama's role in decision making has also changed, in part because of the relentless partisanship of the political environment in Washington DC. Obama maintained a preference to hear the direct opinions of interagency leaders, to hear the why and wherefore of disagreements, in detail, and then make his decisions, a process which drew significant criticism as being slow and non-committal.[18]

In terms of politics, 2012 saw Obama's reelection, so that the Syria events of 2013 fall within his second term. Given that fact, and the relative cohesion of his cabinet, as well as the fact that they had agreed to intervene in Libya, one might expect that Obama would have gone for intervention in Syria, in a manner similar

[17] Riley, Mollie. "Hillary Clinton: 'My Biggest Regret Is What Happened In Benghazi'." *The Huffington Post*, January 27, 2014. http://www.huffingtonpost.com/2014/01/27/hillary-clinton-benghazi_n_4674529.html. Accessed on November 20, 2014.

[18] Lizza, Ryan. "The Consequentialist: How the Arab Spring remade Barack Obama's foreign policy." *The New Yorker*, May 2, 2011. http://www.newyorker.com/magazine/2011/05/02/the-consequentialist. Accessed on 10 November 2014.

to that which drove Clinton to intervene in Kosovo. However, with some reservations, the Rwanda intervention provides a better model for what actually occurred, since several pre-existing frames competed against a frame for intervening in Syria. The major difference between the two is that, unlike Rwanda, Syria was an issue for discussion by the Principal's Committee and the president, so that there was a conscious decision not to intervene at the highest levels.

Deciding, Framing, and Public Opinion in the Syria Non-Intervention

> "all hell broke loose on social media… it was ordinary citizens who reported all of these horrors".
>
> Secretary of State John Kerry on the Syrian chemical attacks, August 22nd, 2013.[19]

In spite of flare ups of interest in events in Syria, usually tied to high casualty incidents in its civil war, it never became the central media event that Egypt and Libya. But, by the time events in Syria truly rose to prominence in 2013, it had none of the influence on U.S. policy makers that Egypt or Libya had previously, and the primary international influence on the revolution was coming from Iran and Islamist groups. This different international dynamic is one key to understanding why there has been to date no intervention.[20] Unfortunately, the effort to frame the intervention in 2013 was not based on human rights per se, but specifically on the use of chemical weapons. It cannot be said with certainty, but the tepid U.S. and international response may indicate the weakness of chemical weapons as a framing tool.

Of note is this contrast between those in less combative or force oriented positions favoring intervention, while military leaders opposed the effort. This is in keeping with past models of armed interventions, such as in Kosovo and Libya,

---

[19] Hirsh, Michael. "How Social Media Could Help Obama Make his Case on Syria." *The Atlantic Monthly*, August 30, 2013: 1-2. 2.

[20] Akder, Derya Gocer. "Theories of Revolutions and Arab Uprisings: The Lessons from the Middle East." Istanbul: *Ortadogu Etutleri*, 2013, 85-110. 100.

in which diplomats urged action while military leaders urged restraint. In contrast, Syria had no regional influence and did not threaten the Europeans directly, as Libya had done. Therefore, it proved to be impossible to form a valid coalition against them either within the U.S. government or outside of it, as was seen in the summer of 2013 when the U.S.'s most reliable ally, the UK, publicly voted against intervention and against the stated will of its Prime Minister.[21]

The level of domestic resistance to the intervention in Libya meant that the frame it supported may have been weak. Obama's "Lead from behind" strategy in Libya and the great emphasis on the small size of the U.S. involvement reflected this.[22] Competing frames in Syria were also too hard to overcome. War weariness, for example, particularly in the Middle East, was a heavily mitigating factor.[23] The successful efforts of the Syrian regime and its allies to disrupt rebel and U.S. framing efforts was another factor.[24] Domestic dissatisfaction with other administration policies was also a major consideration, as seen in the bitter partisan debate over the rival news story of the August, 2013, the impending implementation of the Affordable Care Act, which joined a list of other issues, including Benghazi and other scandals to fuel Republican resistance to what seemed to be all White House initiatives.[25] In terms of foreign policy, the administration was facing an increasingly strident Russia, while still attempting to implement its so called "Pivot to Asia." The efforts of Congressional Republicans to keep alive the Benghazi attacks, which were blamed on these specific policies, were another factor. Other

---

[21] British Broadcasting Corporation. "Syria crisis: Cameron loses Commons vote on Syria action." http://www.bbc.com/news/uk-politics-23892783. August 30, 2013. Accessed on October 10, 2013.

[22] Wilson, Scott. "On Libya, Obama willing to let allies take the Lead. The Washington, Post. www.washingtonpost.com. 9 March, 2011. Accessed on 1 April 2013.

[23] Ose, Erik. "War Weary Public Rejects Attacking Syria." *The Huffington Post.* 12 September 2013. www.huffingtonpost.com. Accessed on November 10, 2014.

[24] Zennie, Michael. 2012. "Obama campaign website taken down by Syrian Electronic Army - the latest target of pro-Assad hackers." *Mail Online*. October 27, 2012. www.dailymail.co.uk/news/article-2478094/Obama-campaign-website-taken-Syrian-electronic-army--latest-target-pro-assad-hackers.html. Accessed October 24, 2013

[25] People-press.org . "Public Opinion Runs Against Syrian Air Strikes." September 3, 2013. Accessed on November 20, 2014. In the third week of August, 39% of respondents to the polling focused on Syria as the top issue, with 23% focused on the impending healthcare regulations.

than the indefatigable John McCain, there was limited bipartisan Congressional support for intervention in Syria at any point between 2011 and 2013.[26]

R2P was never invoked in the case of Syria, and this could be a result of its discrediting in Libya. Just as the Rwanda crisis suffered in its timing following the perceived failure in Somalia the year before, any further intervention in the Arab Spring, particularly after the events in Benghazi in 2012, would be viewed in light of what is increasingly perceived as a failure there. Other frames of perceivably failed military operations plagued efforts to build a frame for Syria. In particular, Obama and the new Secretary of State, John Kerry had to fight an older frame, that of the justifications for Operation Iraqi Freedom in 2003.[27] The Bush administration's perceived folly in false intelligence reporting on Iraqi weapons of mass destruction development overshadowed the Obama team's efforts to frame the Syrian regime's use of nerve gas and chemical agents on its own population. Government statements, such as discussing "multiple streams of intelligence" could not help but sound a lot like the testimony that Colin Powell gave to the U.N. concerning Iraq's elusive chemical weapons.[28]

Unlike the case in Egypt and Libya, the international media has had very little access to Syria, with a ban in place the beginning of the conflict in 2011.[29] Without outsiders, and with the success of the regime in counter-framing, a so called "unreliable narrative" has helped to mitigate against building a coalition for intervention as had been done in Libya.[30] The nature of a post Assad regime and its potential Islamist character is unsettling, particularly considering the course that

---

[26] Parker, Peter. "Obama seeks approval by Congress for Strike in Syria." *The New York Times*, August 31, 2013. http://www.nytimes.com/2013/09/01/world/middleeast/syria.html?_r=0. Accessed on November 1, 2014.
[27] Hirsh. 1.
[28] Ibid.
[29] Parker, Emily. "Why Don't We Care About Syria." *Slate*, February 14, 2012. http://www.slate.com/articles/technology/future_tense/2012/02/syria_uprising_twitter_and_social_media_revolution_fatigue_.html
[30] Ibid.

the Egyptian uprising took before that countries army restored order in the summer of 2013.[31]

Another difference between Libya and Syria, but also dealing with the media, was the question of social media. This is an issue of how a new technology can directly impact framing in a way not seen or planned for previously. With a dearth of social media usage, the Libyan intervention was achieved through a variety of methods and channels, most innovative and notable of which was the invocation of the UN doctrine of R2P and the subsequent framing of the Libyan intervention in humanitarian terms. At the same time, Syrian threats and use of chemical weapons failed to generate enough interest in an armed humanitarian intervention there. While U.S. and international leaders made successful use of R2P as a framing tool to create an overwhelming need to violate Libya's sovereignty to protect its citizens, they did not do so in the case of Syria. [32]

Social media was not a major factor in the Libyan revolution, primarily because of the backward state of technology in the country. Telephones, texts, and radio served as the primary ways to move information. In contrast, social media in Syria has served as an important source for information and intelligence to the outside world, and this is in line with conventional wisdom on social media utilization in other conflicts, particularly in Egypt, with citizen posted reports far outstripping conventional news coverage, especially early in a conflict.[33] However, there are several reasons why the various social media platforms did not have the same impact in the Syrian Civil War that they did in Egypt. One is that the Syrian government has had a well-developed sense of how to control and manipulate the media in general and social media in particular. That regime is, in effect, a

[31] Keiswetter, Allen. "An Arab Spring Primer." *Foreign Service Journal*, 2012. 15-18. 18.
[32] Realists would posit that the Libyan intervention was undertaken in pursuit of power interests by the great powers. This could include control of Libya's oil, its strategic position, or other, national level means power sources and would have nothing to do with its mode of leadership or the status of its citizens.
[33] Nanabhey. 575.

"Neopatrimonial state,"[34] in which it is profoundly difficult to organize any sort of protest or revolt, since discontent must spread to a very large group of society in order to gain momentum and protect itself from retaliation.[35] This has allowed the Syrian government to successfully dispute frames while establishing its own.

Facebook was banned in Syria almost from its inception in 2004, and although those who were very determined could find a way around the blockage, the government's ability to interdict social media was and remains formidable. Assisted by tracking equipment supplied by Iran, this process continues to the present, with a new twist.[36] The Assad regime has come to understand the value of social media for its own information operations, and currently allows Facebook to remain open as a tool for its own outreach, while countering and blocking opposition sites when and where it can. In theoretical terms, this amounts to a Syrian counter network powerful enough to disrupt U.S. efforts at the consolidation of networking and framing power. In cases where it cannot specifically target its enemies, or where volume is too high to controvert, the regime will still resort to simply pulling the plug on Facebook until interest dies down.

The "Syrian Electronic Army" may be the most well-known of the counter-revolutionary elements who explicitly use social media tools for their political ends. Most famously, they hacked President Obama's campaign website during the summer of 2012, however, their activities have been pervasive since they came into the spotlight during the Arab Spring.[37] The "Army" claims to be made up of informed and cyber savvy citizens who support the regime, but their independence or lack thereof from the regime is uncertain. What is certain is their usage of the full range of social media manipulation to cast doubts on the veracity both of the rebel cause and their messaging.[38]

---

[34] Comunello, 454. Such a state is defined by Comunello as being based on the systematic expansion of the power of an authoritarian leader or 'Sultan' who is able to control the fate of a country for a long period of time but who does this at the expense of formal institutions.
[35] Ibid. 455.
[36] Ibid.
[37] Zennie, 2012.
[38] Ibid.

According to Information Wars:

> "Every serious political or militant actor with a stake in what is happening in Syria has a presence on social media through some combination of officially hosted websites and blogs, as well as Facebook, Twitter, Tumblr, YouTube, Flickr, online chat room forums, short message service platforms, and other venues"[39]

That said, the density of usage is not the same as it was in Egypt. Both Libya and Syria had far fewer tweets per day in the revolutionary period than did Egypt. The quoted report reinforces the view that social media has allowed the various rebel groups to perform at a somewhat more leveled playing field, but that the prowess of the regime in the social media field has prevented successes such as those in Egypt. Social media is, in effect, a tool that anyone can use, making anyone a potential journalist, or framer.[40] This fact has come to increasingly dominate all discussion of the information environment and its role in international relations and armed conflict.

Given the Assad regime's lockdown on all types of media, including traditional news outlets, the ever harried social media users within the country proved to be the most effective at getting the word on events out to the international community. Thus, social media outlets and vetting services, such as Storyful were used to break the central event of the conflict, the August 21st chemical attack which killed over 1400 people. In the end, reports of missiles raining "chemical death" were reported by over a dozen separate locations on a variety of social media.[41] Platforms such as You Tube and other video sharing services were central in a self-

---

[39] Zambelis, Chris. 2012. "Information Wars: Assessing the Social Media Battlefield in Syria." *Combating Terrorism Center at West Point,* July 24, 2012, 1-3. 1. https://www.ctc.usma.edu/posts/information-wars-assessing-the-social-media-battlefield-in-syria. Accessed on June 10, 2013.

[40] Ibid. 1.

[41] Panetta. 410.

journalism role which helped to get vital information and images to the west, and this proved to be true both in Egypt and in Syria.[42]

In the U.S., however, social media has come to heavily impact every sector of public discourse, including national security decision making and the ways in which the government attempts to frame its intentions and actions to its stakeholders.

In summary, there was no strong support within the Obama administration for an intervention in Syria between 2011 and spring, 2014.[43] In fact, the only factor which, over a year later, finally drove the U.S. to intervene in Syria in a solely military way is the emergence of the ISIL in Syria and Iraq, and the threat that group posed to the world oil markets and overall stability in the region. With the group owning much of Syria and threatening Baghdad, Obama could no longer deny the threat, and was forced to take action.

Models and the Syria Non-Intervention

Why did the U.S. avoid intervention in Syria in 2013? In accordance with the Decide/Explain model, there was no powerful actor in the foreign policy decision making apparatus with enough interest in the Syrian Civil War to force either the decision making process or to frame the intervention in terms which might lead to action. Of course there are other factors to consider, as discussed earlier in the findings section of the study. According to Joseph Nye, geography can play a greater than expected role in the use of the cyber domain and internet based social media. This is true both in terms of physical control of network systems, but also in the political control of the internet within national or geographic borders.[44] This would be borne out in the great disparities in reaction

---

[42] Nanabhey, Mohammed. "From Spectacle to Spectacular: How Physical Space, Social Media and Mainstream Broadcast Amplified the Public Sphere in Egypt's 'Revolution'." The Journal of North African Studies, (2011): 573-603. 574.
[43] Panetta. 410.
[44] Nye, Joseph. *The Future of Power*. New York, Public Affairs, 2011. 134.

and framing between the Syrian and Libyan cases, given Syrian adeptness at manipulating opinion through social media usage.

The direct influence of Iran in Syria, the lack of oil, and Russian interests joined those above to defeat efforts to frame a Syrian intervention in the same way as succeeded in Libya.[45] Pierre Atlas noted the dissonance in U.S. goals and framing efforts in *U.S. Foreign Policy and the Arab Spring: Balancing Values and Interests* for the Digest of Middle East Studies. He points out that the inclusion of an idealistic strain into U.S. dealings with the Middle East is the incongruity, and represents an ideational change in U.S. policy toward the region. The struggle has been particularly apparent in the comparison of the Libyan response, which had a realist undertone (oil) but no security threats, and could therefore take on a moral character, and that in Syria, which had no oil, many regional threats, and an impossible moral dilemma to solve, that of who to support and what the result would be.

Other important factors precluding an early intervention in Syria were its location and the presence of chemical weapons. Syria is not a primarily coastal country, as Libya was, and its location and terrain made the prospect of operations there problematic.[46] It was estimated that a ground force of 75-90,000 troops would be necessary to effect a humanitarian intervention in the country.[47] Most importantly, however, is the impact chemical weapons and their use and potential use had on the efforts to frame the events. By September, 2013, with the failure of the British government to gain approval for intervention, Obama was backed into a corner, claiming that he authorized attacks, but turning to Congress for permission to attack which would never come.[48] In the end, the Russians intervened politically in order to secure the destruction of Syria's chemical weapons, and the rise of the Islamic State has rekindled interest in Syria, at least in terms of interdicting supplies

---

[45] Pinto. 118.
[46] Panetta. 410.
[47] Ibid.
[48] Reuters. 2013. Timeline of U.S. Syrian Crisis.

and troops moving from ISIL bases in Syria into neighboring Iraq.[49] There is still no signaled intent to place U.S. ground forces in Syria as of the time of this study.

A key factor, and difference, between the various revolutions, can be found in the diversity of those engaging in them. For Libya, it was eastern and western ethnic groups struggling, for Egypt, a mélange of Socialists, Islamists, capitalists, and reactionary conservatives.[50] In Syria, the makeup of the rebels is quite different, and includes pro-Iranian, Shiite, and Al Qaeda supported elements. Unlike the others, the Syrian leadership come from a minority group, the Allawaite Christians, but are far more entrenched and capable, through the mechanism of the Ba'ath political party of centralized resistance to rebellion than in other cases.

Conclusion

A brief look at the decision not to intervene in Syria in 2013 has been provided as a further check on the theoretical models and to assess the validity of the proposed Decide/Frame Model and the findings of the case studies of this research project. There was no strong support within the Obama administration for an intervention in Syria between 2011 and spring, 2014.[51] In fact, the only factor which, over a year later, has finally driven the U.S. to intervene in Syria in a solely military way is the emergence of the fundamentalist Islamic State in Iraq in Syria, and the threat that group posed to the world oil markets and Iraqi government through its invasion of that country.

Like Rwanda, there was no intervention, and so the results are not satisfactory in that there has been no alleviation of the ongoing humanitarian crisis in Syria. However, the study does validate many of the models examined in the

---

[49] Gordon, Michael. "U.S. and Russia Reach Deal to Destroy Syria's Chemical Arms." *The New York Times,* September 15, 2013. http://www.nytimes.com/2013/09/15/world/middleeast/syria-talks.html?pagewanted=all&_r=0. Accessed on November 20, 2013.
[50] Auroagh, Miryiam. 2012. "Social Media, Mediation, and the Arab Revolutions." *TripleC Cognition, Communication, Cooperation*, 2012, 518-536. 529. http://www.triple-c.at/index.php/tripleC/article/view/416. Accessed on September 30, 2013.
[51] Panetta. 410.

other case studies. Like other studies, one finds a sense of the Rational Actor Model, in play. The RAM stands, in this case, as one reason why no convincing argument has generated an intervention, at least until the eruption of the Islamic State in Iraq and Syria became such a threat to Iraq in summer, 2014, that military intervention in Syria could be reframed in national security terms. The GPM and TGP models are both seen to be in play, with the various parts of the foreign policy apparatus, most notably, the departments of Defense and State, taking positions reflective of their bureaucratic stances. Interestingly, as noted in the discussion of the Libyan intervention, those stances were not what one might expect, with the State Department advocating intervention and the Defense Department, which would have to actually perform the intervention, resisting doing so until and unless ordered by the President.

In terms of framing, too many competing frames, combined with the lack of a U.S. spokesperson interested enough and decisive enough to overcome them, have defeated frames linked to the desirability of armed humanitarian intervention, and certainly did so in the Syrian case. Memories of what had come to be seen as a failed intervention in Libya (particularly after the amateurish execution of Gaddafi and the September 11, 2012 attack on Benghazi which ended with the death of the American Ambassador) soured the public and policy makers against interventions in the Middle East. Extremely effective use of social media by the Assad regime to justify its own actions and discredit those of its opponents is a noted cause of this failure, but geography, the lack of an oil-threat narrative, such as existed in Libya, and the direct sponsorship and intervention of a great power, in this case Russia, also help explain the failure of effective framing. As a result of these factors, no cabal of leaders emerged with the clout and cohesiveness of the Bush or Clinton teams, or the persuasiveness and connectedness of the Obama team which generated the Libya intervention in terms of pushing the administration to intervene. As a result, those leaders such as Kerry who appeared to want intervention did not have the political clout to be able to frame Syria in as favorable light in terms of the need to intervene. Put simply, there was no Hillary Clinton with the clout and the desire to intervene.

The graphic below summarizes the cases and the general explanatory power of the various models used. Weak is the lowest rating, while Strong is the highest.

Figure 8: Utility of Models in Explaining Decisions on Armed Humanitarian Intervention and Framing

Intervention/Model	RAM	GPM	TGP	Decide/Frame Model	Powerful Actor
Somalia 1992	Partial	Weak	Strong	Weak	President
Rwanda 1994	Strong	Strong	Strong	Strong	None
Kosovo 1999	Partial	Weak	Partial	Strong	Secretary of State
Libya 2011	Partial	Strong	Strong	Strong	Secretary of State/Junior Cabinet Officers
Syria 2013	Strong	Strong	Strong	Weak	None

The decision to send U.S. troops into harm's way is not an easy one. It is also not easy to frame such a decision to the American people. The findings of this study are important because they show the power of individual leaders in convincing a given American President of the need to act in cases where U.S. national interest is not necessarily clear. The power of the Secretary of State, when used to persuade, is evident in many of the studies, and came as somewhat of a surprise given the professional experience of the author, and the dominance of that experience by the DOD. In retrospect, the three cases and two mini cases examined were enlightening and useful since each showed the criticality of decisiveness both in the president and his key advisors. Of course a president cannot be decisively engaged on every issue at all times, but must become so and be supported adequately in cases where U.S. armed force is to be utilized. But the cases used and the lessons learned apply across senior government decision making, whether it be foreign policy, domestic, economic, or other policies. While the cabinet position of the dominant actor will change based on the issue area, the need for one, both to channel internal and external support, will remain.

CHAPTER IX - CONCLUSION

Armed humanitarian interventions have formed a significant part of the military and diplomatic history of the post-Cold War world. If it had not been for the 9-11 attacks and the U.S. military response to the, Somalia, Kosovo, and Libya might have been the main military actions of the decades since the Persian Gulf War in 1991. As such, these interventions provide a useful tool for examining the foreign policy decision making process, the framing process, and the role of the individual decision maker in those processes. This book set out to explore those interventions in order to see exactly what role each of these processes had in the interventions, and to see if it was possible to use lessons learned from such a study to make predictions on when and how future interventions might take place.

The fundamental finding of the research is that interventions took place when a dominant actor in the decision making apparatus, usually from either the Department of State or the National Security Council, becomes interested enough in an intervention both to use his or her influence to convince others of the need to intervene, and to be able to frame that intervention to the public. This is not to detract from the ultimate decision making power of the presidency in decision making, but to rather to describe how the president is convinced of the need to act by well placed, eloquent, powerful thinkers. Someone must make and sustain an argument that the need for intervention can be conflated to some national security threat to the United States or its allies, or that the U.S. is the only country capable of required actions to alleviate suffering. There is no attempt here to deny the power of the President of the United States in decision making. Indeed, that power is clearly seen in the case studies. The Somalia intervention is the most glaring example of presidential power, with Bush notably making the decision to send U.S. forces there after being briefed by his cabinet, but without the particular influence of any particular member.

Presupposing that armed humanitarian interventions are a good and useful thing, what factors can lead to them happening, at least in terms of U.S. foreign policy decision making? A unified national security cabinet is not critical, but does help. This is evidenced in primarily in the Bush cabinet and to a lesser extent in that of Clinton. The cabinet of George H.W. Bush is well known as one of the smoothest functioning and synchronized in American history. Bill Clinton's second term cabinet, while not as cohesive, was still seasoned both to each other and to Clinton's governing style by the time of the Kosovo intervention. Barack Obama's cabinet was sharply divided, by the rigors of the electoral campaign and the rancor between the Obama team and the adherents of the presidential challenger cum Secretary of State, Hillary Clinton.[1] That said, Clinton's power, and her lock step, to that point, with Robert Gates, who was against intervention, was such that she had to be brought into the fold for the final decision for intervention to be made. Thus was the cohesiveness of the earlier foreign policy teams reached.

Another important lesson is that the Department of State must be on board for an intervention to occur. Why State? The answer to this lies in governmental politics. The Department of Defense was not in favor of a single one of the armed humanitarian interventions mentioned, indeed, in each case, it was ordered to act against its recommendation. In two of the three cases, however, it was the specific initial or converted support of the Department of State which proved to be the decisive influence toward intervention. The major non-intervention covered, in

[1] Gates, Robert M. *Duty, Memoirs of a Secretary at War*. New York: Alfred A. Knopf, 2014. 287.

Rwanda, never got raised to the level of Secretary of State, and as a consequence was never a serious discussion point for the president.[2]

International support is another critical factor, demonstrated by the case studies to be absolutely critical to an armed humanitarian intervention taking place. Usually, this support comes in the form of a UN resolution, and this was the case in Somalia and Libya. Where UN support is not unified, such as in the case of Kosovo, other bodies, such as NATO, can provide the international top cover for an intervention to take place. This was even more important when NATO itself seemed to be at risk of a major loss of credibility, as was perceived to be about to occur because of Serbian intransigence over the issue of Kosovo independence and the ongoing atrocities against Kosovar Albanians, particularly from 1998 onwards.[3] In the period studied, the United States did not launch an armed humanitarian intervention without the implied authority of the international community. Although there are other reasons, this stands as one leading cause for the failure to intervene in Rwanda.

Concurrent with the issue of international support is that there must be a lack of major international resistance to armed humanitarian intervention. Russia, therefore, became a key player in the Kosovo intervention, since its historical patronage of Serbia and its role as a great power seemed to be at stake with the NATO intervention. In addition to international support, Russia had to be given assurances on Serb regime survival and its own national reputation in order to prevent its resistance to the intervention. In each of the other cases, there was little or no great power resistance to U.S. and coalition actions. In Somalia, no great power significantly resisted the push to armed intervention, and in Libya, as in Kosovo, Russia and China were satisfied enough that their interests would be met that they did not exercise veto rights in the UN Security Council. Notably, in the case of Rwanda, there was significant resistance to intervention by key U.S. partners, notably France. This is not to assume that the U.S. was ever significantly

---

[2] Albright, Madeleine. *Madam Secretary, a Memoir*. New York: Harper Collins, 2013. 152.
[3] Blair, Tony. *A Journey: My Political Life*. London: Knopf, 2010. 252.

motivated to intervene there, but even if it had been, the international community was not.

Domestic politics also play a key role in the question of whether or not to intervene. The 1992 election cycle both deferred U.S. intervention in Somalia, but perversely, may have made intervention more likely after Bush was defeated. The Lewinsky affair certainly delayed significant action in Kosovo. Conversely, the domestic backlash against the perceived defeat in Somalia in 1993 virtually guaranteed that there would be no intervention in Rwanda. War weariness based on U.S. involvement in Afghanistan and Iraq did not eliminate the chance for an effort in Libya, but did ensure that the U.S. role would be limited to air support, and that even that effort would be lessened over the course of the air campaign and eventually turned over to NATO leadership.

The findings of this research should be useful in predicting when and where the U.S. will engage in future armed humanitarian interventions. When powerful leaders, most often in the Department of State, can be convinced, and convince the president that intervention is necessary, and when there is international and domestic support for such an intervention, it will occur. When those factors do not exist, an intervention will not take place. An informed, cohesive foreign policy decision making establishment is important, but even more critical is an informed president with an understanding of and commitment to action in foreign policy.

An example of these principals in action provided by looking at the discussion on armed humanitarian intervention in Syria in August, 2013. The Obama team which generated the Libya intervention in terms of pushing the administration to intervene, and, more importantly, those leaders such as Kerry who have made the push were not able to frame Syria in as favorable light in terms of the need to intervene. None of the leaders who were so adamant about Libya and the concept of R2P were public activists for an intervention in Syria, and neither was the Secretary of State himself, so that, in combination with significant domestic turmoil, war weariness, and international resistance from Russia and China, meant that there would be no intervention.

Other cases also demonstrate how important it is for the intervention of powerful leaders and the alignment of the external variables examined in the study for an intervention to occur. The most notable of current humanitarian disasters to suffer in this way is the continuing crisis in Darfur. Darfur, a largely Christian region in north- west Sudan, has been subject to drought, famine, and government sponsored oppression since 2003, however, there has been no boots on the ground U.S. intervention there, in spite of the fact that the death toll rivals that of the Rwanda genocide.[4] No senior U.S. official has taken on Darfur in the way that was seen in Libya and Kosovo. Significant international resistance to intervention exists, not only from great powers such as China, but also from neighboring countries. There is no oil in geographically remote Darfur, and western interest in the plight of the population seems to fall victim to the same acceptance of a robust African death toll that was seen during the Rwandan genocide.

Framing of armed humanitarian interventions by the foreign policy establishment is another significant focus of the study, and the case studies demonstrate that it is tied into the decision making process, but only in those cases where a fairly lengthy decision cycle, measured in weeks and months, rather than days and weeks, are available for decision making and planning. In general the case studies showed that the U.S. public is averse to lengthy involvement in combat operations for humanitarian purposes. Only in Kosovo was a lengthy time period available to frame the intervention. In that case, too, one must look farther back than the immediate time frame of intervention to realize that by 1999, Slobodan Milosevic had been an international villain for nearly a decade.[5] Similarly, in spite of his rapprochement with the west in the 1990s and 2000s, Muammar Gaddafi had multi decade history as a supporter of terrorism and specifically as an enemy of the

---

[4] Tisdal, Simon. "Sudan fears US military intervention over Darfur." *The Guardian Online*, January 15, 2009. http://www.theguardian.com/world/2009/jan/15/sudan-unamid-obama. Accessed on 20 November 2014. There has, however, been delivery of supplies to the region, but no armed intervention.

[5] Independent International Commission on Kosovo Report. Oxford, Oxford University Press, 2000. 38-39.

U.S. In spite of this "free framing" in both cases, support numbers for the interventions against the two dictators rarely topped 50%, and ticked up slightly only when operations were actively underway. The point of this finding may well be that framing is not that important to the implementation of armed humanitarian interventions. Only one of the interventions studies, Somalia, ended because of a drastic change in public opinion, and that was tied directly to what was perceived as the defeat in Mogadishu. None of the other interventions studied ended simply because of public opinion. In all cases they continued until either the mission was accomplished, UN mandate ended or changed, or the enemy gave in.

Having noted the results of the research, the question must be asked if the Decide/Explain model can be useful for other foreign policy activities. This is a significant question, which begs a weighter greater than "yes, if someone wants to." Clearly going to war, even in a limited way, is a task not to be undertaken lightly, if at all, and any model that predicts when and how a country might go to war would be welcomed by academics and policy makers alike. History provides us with several examples of powerful leaders who had a goal and a voice. The most famous of these is probably Marcus Porcius Cato the Elder, who famously uttered the phrase "Cartago Delendam Est", in or out of context, during Roman Senatorial debates over a period of years between the second and third Punic Wars, until finally Rome did attack and destroy Carthage in 146 BC, ending a major threat to its domination of the Mediterranean.[6] This simple and powerful framing shows how, over a period of time, an argument for intervention can be made at multiple levels. A further example of this is the year and a half long period after the September 11 attacks, which saw a steady framing campaign against Saddam Hussein which culminated in the invasion of Iraq and the overthrow of the dictator in spring, 2003. In that case, a small group of committed and powerful leaders convinced a reasonably cohesive foreign policy team, and the president, that there was a national security threat, and that intervention was necessary. President Bush

[6] Carthage must be destroyed.

was already predisposed toward an armed intervention in Iraq by the history of his father's presidency.[7] Even in the absence of a direct attack on the U.S., by Iraq, the fact that the U.S. had been attacked made it easier to frame the invasion as well as other interventions which make up the Global War on Terrorism. Even in this example, however, the U.S. attempted to operate within an international mandate provided by the UN, and to go out if its way to frame the operation as a response to a national security threat.[8]

Armed humanitarian interventions stand out in a review of modern warfare for two reasons. The first is that they are limited operations, usually not using combined arms, and have limited objectives. The second is that they are not framed in terms of occupation of conquest, but rather as human security operations, establishing a principal of human rather than national sovereignty as a paramount concern. While it was possible to argue both that Kosovo was a threat to the U.S., and that the U.S. must lead a response, there was very limited call for armed intervention in Georgia in 2008, when Russian troops invaded and occupied part of the country. This is also true of the Russian occupation of Crimea in 2013, or China's occupation of Tibet in 1950. Here the size of the potential military and political resistance and the likely lack of international support would predict that the U.S. will not intervene, and not perceive the actions taken as direct threats to its own national security. Kosovo, however, should serve as a warning to Moscow that the U.S. does take NATO seriously as an alliance and an international body, and will react strongly to any direct threats to it.

Two questions remain to be discussed. First, whither armed humanitarianism? Following the Libya intervention, the idea of R2P has faded from the forefront of political discussion. This begs the question of whether the

---

[7] Haass, Richard N. *War of Necessity, War of Choice: A Memoir of Two Iraq Wars.* New York, Simon and Schuster, 2009. 198. Haas discusses the urging of Paul Wolfowitz to consider action against Iraq immediately after the September 11 attacks, urgings which grew into the decision to invade by 2003.

[8] United Nations General Assembly Session 57 *Verbatim Report 2.* A/57/PV.2 page 6. Transcript of George W. Bush speech from September 2, 2002. http://www.un.org/ga/search/view_doc.asp?symbol=A/57/PV.2. Retrieved 10 November 2014.

whole idea of armed humanitarians a product of a combination of UN triumphalism and U.S. uni-polarity after the Cold War? 2011 and the Libya intervention marked a watershed for several reasons. The turn of the Arab Spring into a victory for non-democratic Islamic fundamentalists, combined with the rise of China, the resurgence of Russia, and the acknowledged failure of the last great intervention, in Libya, to secure its goals of protecting the people of Libya could mean the end of the phenomena. The transnational threat posed by criminal and extremist elements, such as ISIS in Iraq and Syria, may trigger a military or humanitarian response such as was seen in Libya, or Somalia, if divisions on what to do in response can be overcome in the national security cabinet by a dominant actor who can influence the president decisively. Beyond the U.S., it may be that China, Russia, or other great powers may see such armed humanitarian interventions as a valid course of action should they choose to take on a greater burden in international security leadership. In either case, the findings of this research on how armed humanitarian interventions are decided on, framed to the public, and implemented will be of direct use.

Finally, what does this study mean for framing and decision making? A series of models were discussed, with a proposal to combine the models in order to better explain the nexus between decision making and framing, as well as the role of key individuals in each. A clear result of the study is that the key leaders in the decision making and framing processes must be motivated by an issue in order for armed humanitarian interventions to take place. As wars of choice, these operations must be carefully explained to the American people, something that works best with a long lead time for deciding on and framing intervention. Although many of the sources consulted for this study did not specifically discuss how they planned their framing efforts in each case, they all noted that such efforts did occur. In addition, the key deciders in each case were also the key framers, implying strong linkages between the two. Since armed humanitarian interventions were merely a prism through which to review the decision making and framing processes, and the role of key individuals in them, the critical lesson of the study, one which applies across the various decision making realms of the U.S. government, is that powerful leaders must be motivated to support decisions and frames which are not inherently popular or obviously vital to the U.S. public. Without a powerful leader to counteract the entrenched interests and bureaucracies behind every government decision, inertia will be the result, with potentially embarrassing, or even disastrous consequences.

BIBLIOGRAPHY

Abass, Ademola. "Assessing NATO's Involvement in Libya " *United Nations University* (October 27, 2011). [accessed March 30, 2013].

U.S. Energy Information Administration. "Country: Libya" http://www.eia.gov/countries/cab.cfm?fips=LY.

Akder, Derya Gocer. "Theories of Revolutions and Arab Uprisings: The Lessons from the Middle East." *Ortadogu Etutleri*: 85-110.

Albright, Madeleine. *Madam Secretary, a Memoir* Perennial. New York: Harper Collins, 2013.

Allen, Jonathan. "Susan Rice's Walk on the Mild Side." *Politico* January 3, 2014, (2014).

Allison, Graham. *Essence of Decision: Explaining the Cuban Missile Crisis*. Vol. 2. New York: Longman, 1999.

Alvarado, Jaime. "New Multilateralism in Action for Peace: A Case Study of the U.S. Lead Operation Unified Assistance for the Asian Tsunami Disaster." *Global Economic Review* 36, no. 2 (2007): 183-192.

Aouragh, Miryiam. "Social Media, Mediation, and the Arab Revolutions." *Triple C Cognition, Communication, Cooperation*, (2012): 518-536.

Ash, Timothy Garton. "The New Adolf Hitler." CNN, 1999.

Atlas, Pierre M. "U.S. Foreign Policy and the Arab Spring: Balancing Values and Interests." *Digest of Middle East Studies*, (2012): 353-385.

Auerswald, Donald P. "Integrated Decision Model of Nato Policy in Kosovo." *International Studies Quarterly* 2004, no. 28: 631-664.

Avant, Deborah. "Conflicting Indicators of "Crisis" in American Civil Military Relations." *Armed Forces and Society* 24, no. 3 (1998): 375-388.

Bahador, Babak. "The CNN Effect on Western Policy before the Kosovo Intervention: A Book." *ISA Conference, Montreal, Canada* 2004, (2004).

Barnett, Michael, and Weiss, Thomas. *Humanitarianism in Question: Politics, Power, and Ethics*. Ithaca, NY: Cornell University Press, 2008.

Baumann, Rainer, and Hellmann, Gunther. "Germany and the Use of Military Force: 'Total War', the 'Culture of Restraint' and the Quest for Normality " *German Politics* 10, no. 1 (2001): 61-82.

Bell, Peter. "The Tragedy in Somalia Can't Wait for Clinton." *The New York Times*, no. November 5, 1992 (1992).

Bellamy, Alex J. "The Responsibility to Protect." In *Security Studies: An Introduction*, edited by Paul D. Williams, 422-437. New York: Routledge, 2008.

Bellamy, Alex J. *Global Politics and the Responsibility to Protect*. New York: Routledge, 2011.

Bendor, Jonathan and Hammond, Thomas H. "Rethinking Allison's Models." *The American Political Science Review* 86, no. 2 (1992, June): 301-322.

Bennett, Lance, and Entman, Robert. *Mediated Politics: Communication in the Future of Democracy*. Cambridge: Cambridge University Press, 2001.

Berinsky, Adam J. and Kinder, Donald R. "Making Sense of the Issues through Media Frames: Understanding the Kosovo Crisis." *The Journal of Politics* 68, no. 3 (2006): 640-656.

Biden, Joseph, R., "Biden-When a State Engages in Atrocity, It Forfeits Its Sovereignty." http://thecable.foreignpolicy.com/posts/2011/02/25/biden_when_a_state_engages_in_atrocity_it_forfeits_its_sovereignty (accessed October 20 2014).

Biden, Joseph R. "Obama on Rebellion in Libya", http://www.history.com http://www.history.com/topics/joe-biden/speeches/obama-on-rebellion-in-libya (accessed October 27, 2014 2014).

Blair, Tony, "Address by Tony Blair to the United Nations General Assembly, 21 September 1998", United Nations General Assembly http://news.bbc.co.uk/2/hi/events/clinton_under_fire/latest_news/169395.stm.

Blair, Tony. *A Journey: My Political Life*. London: Knopf, 2010.

Blumenthal, Sydney. *The Clinton Wars*. New York: Farrar, Strauss and Giroux, 2003.

Bonner, Kaymond, "Buy up the Somali's Guns", The New York Times http://www.nytimes.com/1992/12/02/opinion/buy-up-the-somalis-guns.html (accessed August 20 2014).

Boutros-Gali, Boutros, "Agenda for Peace", United Nations http://www.cfr.org/peacekeeping/report-un-secretary-general-agenda-peace/p23439 (accessed October 10 2014).

Boutros-Gali, Boutros. "Remarks in the Un Security Council." *Facts on File* 52, no. 2700 (July 23, 1992).

Bradford, Jeffrey P. "Political Aspects of Strategic Decision Making in British Defence Policy." Cranfield University, 1999.

British Broadcasting Corporation. "How the Genocide Happened." 2004.

British Broadcasting Corporation, "Syria Crisis: Cameron Loses Commons Vote on Syria Action" http://www.bbc.com/news/uk-politics-23892783 (accessed October 10 2014).

Brook, Douglas A. "Budgeting for National Security: A Whole of Government Perspective." *Journal of Public Budgeting, Accounting, and Financial Management*, (2012): 32-57.

Brooks, Stephen G., and Wohlforth, William C. "American Primacy in Perspective." *Foreign Affairs* 81, no. 4 (2002): 20-33.

Brooks, Stephen G. and Wolhforth, William C. "International Relations Theory and the Case against Unilateralism." *Perspectives on Politics* 3, no. 3 (2005, September): 509-524.

Brzezinski, Zbigniew. *Power and Principle: Memoirs of the National Security Adviser 1977-1981*. New York: Farrar, Strauss, and Giroux, 1983.

Buckley, William Joseph. *Kosovo: Contending Voices on Balkan Interventions*. Grand Rapids, MI: William B. Eerdmans Publishing Company, 2000.

Burke, John P. "The Neutral/Honest Broker Role in Foreign Policy Decision Making: A Reassessment." *Presidential Studies Quarterly* 35, no. 2 (2005): 229-258.

Burke, John P. *The National Security Advisor and Presidential Decision Making*. College Station, TX: Texas A and M University Press, 2009.

Bush, George H.W. *All the Best: My Life in Letters and Other Writings*. New York: Scribner, 1999.

Bush, George H.W. and Scowcroft, Brent. *A World Transformed*. New York: Vintage Books, a Division of Random House, 2011.

Butler, Michael J. *Selling a 'Just' War: Framing, Legitimacy, and U.S. Military Intervention*. Chippenham and Eastbourne: Palgrave Macmillan, 2012.

Byman, Daniel L. and Pollack, Kenneth M. "Let Us Now Praise Great Men: Bringing the Statesman Back In." *International Security* 25, no. 4 (2001): 107-146.

The Cable. "Biden - When a State Engages in Atrocity It Forfeits Its Sovereignty." *Foreign Policy*, (2011).

Cable News Network. 2011. "Sens. McCain, Lieberman Critical of Obama over Libya," http://cnnpressroom.blogs.cnn.com/2011/02/27/sens-mccain-lieberman-critical-of-obama-over-libya/ (accessed April 1, 2013).

Castells, Manuel. *Communication Power*. New York: Oxford University Press, 2009.

CBS Evening News, "Text of Clinton's Rwanda Speech, March 25, 1998" CBSnews.com (accessed October 20 2014).

Cheney, Richard. *In My Time: A Personal and Political Memoir*. New York: Simon and Schuster, 2011.

Chiwis, Christopher. *Toppling Qaddafi: Libya and the Limits of Liberal Intervention*. New York: Cambridge University Press, the Rand Corporation, 2014.

Chollet, Derek, and Power, Samantha. *The Unquiet American: Richard Holbrooke in the World*. New York: Public Affairs, 2012.

Chorin, Ethan. *Exit Gaddafi: The Hidden History of the Libyan Revolution*. London: Saqi Books, 2012.

Claes, Jonas, "Libya and the "Responsibility to Protect"" http://www.usip.org/publications/libya-and-the-responsibility-protect (accessed March 13 2013).

Clark, Wesley. "Wesley Clark Says Libya Doesn't Meet the Test for U.S. Action." *Washington Post*, March 11, 2011 2011.

Clark, Wesley. *Waging Modern War*. New York: Public Affairs, 2012.

Clarke, Paul. "Reevaluating the National Security Policy Process." *49th Annual Convention of the International Studies Association*, (2008): 1-19.

Clarke, Walter and Herbst, Jeffrey. "Somalia and the Future of Humanitarian Intervention." *Foreign Affairs* March/April 1996, (1996): 70-85.

Clarke, Walter and Herbst, Jeffrey. *Learning from Somalia*. Boulder, Colorado: Westview Press, 1997.

Clinton, Hillary R. "Clinton: U.S. Worried About Libya Becoming 'Giant Somalia'", Deutsche Press-Agentur http://en.trend.az/regions/met/arabicr/1839151.html (accessed March 20 2013).

Clinton, Hillary R. "Clinton's Remarks at the International Conference on Libya, March 2011", Council on Foreign Relations http://www.cfr.org/libya/clintons-remarks-international-conference-libya-march-2011/p24542 (accessed March 10, 2013 2013).

Clinton, Hillary R. "Clinton's Remarks on Unsc Resolution 1973 Regarding Libya", Council on Foreign Relations http://www.cfr.org/libya/clintons-remarks-unsc-resolution-1973-regarding-libya-march-2011/p24437. (accessed February 18, 2013 2013).

Clinton, Hillary R. "Press Statement by Secretary of State Hillary Rodham Clinton", U.S. Department of State http://www.state.gov/secretary/20092013clinton/rm/2011/02/156836.htm (accessed October 15 2014).

Clinton, Hillary R. *Hard Choices*. New York: Simon and Schuster, 2014.

Clinton, Press Statement by Secretary of State Hillary Rodham, http://www.state.gov/secretary/20092013clinton/rm/2011/02/156836.htm (accessed October 15 2014).

Clinton, William J. "Excerpt from Transcript of the President's Address at the University of Virginia" http://millercenter.org.scripps/archive/speeches/detail/3932. (accessed October 14, 2014 2014).

Clinton, William J. *My Life*. New York: Knopf, 2004.

Cohen, Herman. *Intervening in Africa: Superpower Peacemaking in a Troubled Continent*. New York: St. Martin's Press, 2000.

Cohen, Jared. *100 Days of Silence: America and the Rwandan Genocide*. Lanham, Maryland: Rowan and Littlefield Publishers, 2007.

Coll, Alberto R. *The Problems of Doing Good: Somalia as a Case Study in Humanitarian Intervention* Pew Case Studies in International Affairs.

Washington, D.C.: Insitute for Study of Diplomacy Publications, Georgetown University, 1997.

Comunello, Francesca. "Will the Revolution Be Tweeted? A Conceptual Framework for Understanding the Social Media and the Arab Spring." *Islam and Christian-Muslim Relations*, (2012): 453-470.

Congressional Research Service, "Congressional Record " http://thomas.loc.gov/cgi-bin/thomas2 (accessed October 9 2014).

Congressional Research Service, "Congressional Record of the 102nd Congress" http://thomas.loc.gov/cgi-bin/thomas2 (accessed October 9 2014).

Congressional Research Service, "Congressional Record of the 112th Congress" http://thomas.loc.gov/cgi-bin/thomas2 (accessed October 21 2014).

Copeland, Dale. "Economic Interdependence and War." *International Security*, (1996): 5-41.

Craig, Gordon. *The Diplomats, 1939-1979*. Princeton: Princeton University Press, 1994.

Cresswell, John W. *Research Design: Qualitative and Quantitative Approaches*. London: Sage Publications, 1994.

Daalder. Ivo, and Destler, I.M. *In the Shadow of the Oval Office: Profiles of the National Security Advisors and the Presidents They Served - from Jfk to George W. Bush*. New York: Simon and Schuster, 2009.

Davidson, Jason W. "France, Britain, and the Intervention in Libya: An Integrated Analysis." *Cambridge Review of International Affairs*, (2013): 310-329.

Deutsch, John. "Strengthening the National Security Interagency Process." In *Keeping the Edge*, edited by Ashton Carter, 276-284. Harvard: Kennedy School, 2000.

Dickinson, Elizabeth, "The First Wikileaks Revolution?", Foreign Policy http://foreignpolicy.com/2011/01/13/the-first-wikileaks-revolution/ (accessed October 27 2014).

Dickinson, Matthew. "The Institutionalization of the National Security Staff, 1949-1991." In *2003 Meeting of the American Political Science Association*, 38, 2003.

DiPrizio, Robert C. *Armed Humanitarians: U.S. Interventions from Northern Iraq to Kosovo*. Baltimore: Johns Hopkins University Press, 2002.

Doyle, Richard B. "The U.S. National Security Strategy: Policy, Process, Problems." *Public Administration Review*, (2007): 624-629.

Drechsler, Donald R. "Reconstructing the Interagency Process after Iraq." *Journal of Strategic Studies*, (2007): 3-30.

Dreyfuss, Robert, "Obama's Women Advisors Pushed War against Libya", The Nation http://www.thenation.com/blog/159346/obamas-women-advisers-pushed-war-against-libya (accessed March 15 2013).

Dugan, Andrew, "Support for Syria Action Lower Than Past Conflicts", The Gallup Poll http://www.gallup.com/poll/164282/support-syria-action-lower-past-conflicts.aspx (accessed September 25 2013).

Economist, "It Takes a Village to Support a Military Intervention" http://www.economist.com/blogs/democracyinamerica/2011/03/libya_0.

Economist, "Responsibility to Protect: The Lessons of Libya" www.economist.com/node/18709571.

Economist, "Germany and Kosovo: The War Divides." *The Economist*, (1999).

Eder, Mari K. *Leading the Narrative, the Case for Strategic Communication*. Annapolis: Naval Institute Press, 2011.

Ellis, John, "Why Are We in Libya? Obama Administration Releases Strategic Framework 2.0. April 4, 2011" http://articles.businessinsider.com/2011-04-04/politics/29999468_1_libya-iran-nuclear-weapon

Entman, Robert M. *Projections of Power: Framing News, Public Opinion, and U.S. Foreign Policy*. Chicago: University of Chicago Press, 2004.

Fearon, James D. "Domestic Political Audiences and the Escalation of International Disputes." *The American Political Science Review* 88, no. 3 (1994): 577-592.

Ferroggiaro, William, "The U.S. And Rwanda, 1994, Evidence of Inaction", George Washington University http://www2.gwu.edu/~nsarchiv/NSAEBB/NSAEBB53 (accessed October 14 2014).

Finnemore, Martha. "Constructing Norms of Humanitarian Intervention." In *The Culture of National Security*, edited by Peter J. Katzenstein, 153-185. New York: Columbia University Press, 1996.

Fitzgerald, David and Ryan, David. *Obama, U.S. Foreign Policy and the Dilemmas of Intervention*. New York: Palgrave Macmillan, 2014.

Fitzwater, Marlon. "Statement by Press Secretary Fitzwater on Additional Humanitarian Aid for Somalia." Washington, D.C.: White House, Office of the Press Secretary, 1992.

Flournoy, Michelle. "Strategic Planning for National Security: A New Project Solarium." *Joint Force Quarterly*, (2006): 80-86.

Forte, Maximillian. *Slouching Towards Sirte: Nato's War on Libya and Africa*. Montreal: Baraka Books, 2012.

Fox News, "Polling Mixed on Intervention in Libya" http://www.foxnews.com/politics/2011/03/28/polling-mixed-intervention-libya (accessed October 27, 2014 2014).

Gerhard Schroeder Foundation. http://gerhard-schroeder.de/en/war-peace (accessed 20 November 2014).

Freedman, Lawrence. "On War and Choice." *The National Interest* May/June, 2010, (2010).

Friedman, Benjamin, "Intervention in Libya and Syria Isn't Humanitarian or Liberal" http://nationalinterest.org/blog/the-skeptics/intervention-libya-syria-isn%E2%80%99t-humanitarian-or-liberal-6739.

Friedman, Thomas L. "Obama on the World: President Obama Talks About Iraq, Putin, and Israel." *The New York Times*, 8 August 2014 2014.

Gaddis, John Lewis. *Surprise, Security, and the American Experience*. Cambridge, MA: Harvard University Press, 2004.

The Gallup Poll, "Americans Approve Military Action against Libya" http://www.gallup.com/poll/146738/Americans-Approve-Military-Action-Against-Libya.aspx (accessed October 27, 2014 2014).

The Gallup Poll, "Americans Hesitant, as Usual, About U.S. Military Action in Balkans" http://www.gallup.com/poll/3994/americans-hesitant-usual-about-us-military-action-balkans.aspx (accessed November 10 2014).

The Gallup Center for Muslim Studies, "Snapshot: Nato Intervention in Libya Unpopular in Arab World" http://www.gallup.com/poll/154997/Snapshot-NATO-Intervention-Libya-Unpopular-Arab-World.aspx (May 31, 2012).

Gamson, W.A. and Modigliani, A. "The Changing Culture of Affirmative Action." In *Research in Political Sociology* edited by R.G. Braungart & M.M. Braungart. Greenwich, CT: JAI Press, 1987.

Garwood-Gowers, Andrew. "The Responsibility to Protect and the Arab Spring: Libya as the Exception, Syria as the Norm?" *University of New South Wales Law Journal* 36, no. 2 (2013): 594-618.

Gates, Robert M., "Statement on Libya by Robert Gates (House Armed Services Committee)", www.voltairenet.org http://www.voltairenet.org/article169227.html (accessed October 27 2014).

Gates, Robert M. *Duty, Memoires of a Secretary at War* Borzoi. New York: Alfred A. Knopf, 2014.

Gellman, Barton. "Allies Facing the Limits of Air Power." *The Washington Post*, March 28, 1999 1999.

Gellman, Barton. "The Path to Crisis: How the United States and Its Allies Went to War." *The Washington Post*, April 18, 1999 1999, A1.

George, Alexander. *Presidential Decision Making in Foreign Policy: The Effective Use of Information and Advice*. Boulder, Colorado: Westview Press, 1980.

Gibbs, David N. *First, Do No Harm: Humanitarian Intervention and the Destruction of Yugoslavia*. Nashville: Vanderbuilt University Press, 2009.

Glazier, Rebecca A., and Boydstun, Amber E. "The President, the Press, and the War: A Tale of Two Framing Agendas." *Political Communication*, no. 29 (2012): 428-446.

Goldstein, Jon. "Humanitarian Intervention Comes of Age." *Foreign Affairs*, no. Nov/Dec (2011): 48-59.

Goldstone, Jack. "Understanding the Revolutions of 2011." *Foreign Affairs*, no. May/June (2011): 8-16.

Goodenough, Patrick, "Kerry - 2011 Military Intervention in Libya Not Vital to U.S. Security", CNSNews.com http://www.theguardian.com/world/2011/mar/17/libya-air-strikes-urged-us-un (accessed October 1, 2014 2014).

Gordon, Michael. "U.S. And Russia Reach Deal to Destroy Syria's Chemical Arms." *The New York Times*2013.

Greenstein, Fred I. *The Presidential Difference: Leadership Style from Fdr to Barack Obama*. 3 ed. Princeton: Princeton University Press, 2009.

The Guardian, "Libya Air Strikes Urged by U.S. At UN" http://www.theguardian.com/world/2011/mar/17/libya-air-strikes-urged-us-un (accessed October 27 2014).

Gvosdev, Nikolas. "Decline of Western Realism." *The National Interest*, (2012): 8-19.

Haass, Richard N. *War of Necessity, War of Choice: A Memoir of Two Iraq Wars*. New York: Simon and Schuster, 2009.

Hady, Amer, and Singer, P.W. *Restoring America's Good Name: Improving Strategic Communications with the Islamic World*: National Defense University, 2006.

Halberstam, David. *War in a Time of Peace*. New York: Scribner, 2001.

Harris, John F. "Advice Did Not Sway Clinton on Airstrikes." *The Washington Post*, April 1, 1999 1999, A1.

Hehir, Aidan. *The Responsibility to Protect: Rhetoric, Reality, and the Future of Humanitarian Intervention*. New York: Palgrave Macmillan, 2012.

Hempstone, Smith. "Dispatch from a Place near Hell." *The Washington Post*, August 23, 1992 1992.

Hempstone, Smith. *Rogue Ambassador: An African Memoir*. Sewanee, TN: University of the South Press, 1997.

Hill, Christopher R. *Outpost: Life on the Frontline of American Diplomacy – a Memoir*. New York: Simon and Schuster, 2014.

Hirsh, Michael. "How Social Media Could Help Obama Make His Case on Syria." *The Atlantic Monthly*, no. August 30 (2013): 1-2.

Holbrooke, Richard. *To End a War* The Modern Library. New York: Random House, 1999.

Holzgrefe, J. L. and Keohane, Robert O. *Humanitarian Intervention: Ethical, Legal and Political Dilemmas*. Cambridge: Cambridge University Press 2003.

Houghton, David Patri. *The Decision Point: Six Cases in U.S. Foreign Policy Decision Making*. Oxford: Oxford University Press, 2013.

http://www.mcclatchydc.com, "Http://Www.Mcclatchydc.Com/2011/03/25/111084/Human-Rights-Advocate-Samantha.Html", McClatchy http://www.mcclatchydc.com/2011/03/25/111084/human-rights-advocate-samantha.html (accessed October 27, 2014 2014).

Huntington, Samuel. *The Soldier and the State: The Theory and Politics of Civil-Military Relations*. Cambridge, Massachusetts: Belknap Press of Harvard University Press, 1957.

Hyland, William. *Clinton's World: Remaking American Foreign Policy*. West Port, CT: Praeger, 1999.

Ignatieff, Michael. "The Challenges of American Imperial Power." *Naval War College Review* 56, No. 2., no. Spring (2003): 9-18.

International Communications Association. "The Framing of the U.S. Intervention in Somalia 1992-1994: Convergence and Divergence of Official Frames and Media Frames, International Communications Association." *International Communications Association*, (1995).O'Hanlon, Michael. "Winning Ugly in Libya." *Foreign Affairs*, no. March/April (2011): 1-3.

International Convention on Intervention and State Sovereignty. *The Responsibility to Protect, Final Report*, 2001.

Jeffrey, Terrence P., "Obama's Libyan Intervention Has Lowest Approval of Any Military Op Polled by Gallup in 4 Decades", cnsnews.com http://cnsnews.com/news/article/obama-s-libyan-intervention-has-lowest-approval-any-military-op-polled-gallup-4-decades (accessed November 15, 2013 2013).

Johnson, Dominic D.P. . "The Rubicon Theory of War: How the Path to Conflict Reaches the Point of No Return." *International Security*, (2011): 7-40.

Johnston, Phillip. *Somalia Diary: The President of Care Tells One Country's Story of Hope*. Atlanta, GA: Longstreet Press, 1994.

Jones, Bruce. "Libya and the Responsibilities of Power." *Survival*, no. May (2011).

Jones, Jeffrey, "Americans Shift to More Negative View of Libya Military Action", Gallup http://www.gallup.com/poll/148196/Americans-Shift-Negative-View-Libya-Military-Action.aspx (accessed October 10, 2014 2014).

Journalism.org, "Libya Search" http://www.journalism.org/search/Libya/ (accessed October 27 2014).

Journalism.org, "News Coverage Index, February 29-March 6, 2011" http://www.journalism.org/2011/03/06/pej-news-coverage-index-february-28-march-6-2011/ (accessed October 27 2014).

Katzenstein, Peter J. *The Culture of National Security* New Directions in World Politics, Edited by John Gerard Ruggie. New York: Columbia University Press, 1996.

Keiswetter, Allen. "An Arab Spring Primer." *Foreign Service Journal*, (2012): 15-18.

Kelley, Michael. "Surrender and Blame." *The New Yorker*, (1994).

Kern, Soeren, "Why France Was So Keen to Attack Libya", Gatestone Institute http://www.gatestoneinstitute.org/1983/france-libya-attack (accessed 26 November 2014).

Kim, Victoria. "Japan Damage Could Reach $235 Billion, World Bank Estimates." *The Los Angeles Times*, March 21, 2011 2011.

Kissinger, Henry. *Diplomacy*. New York: Touchstone Books, 1994.

Klarevas, Louis J. "The Polls-Trends: The United States Peace Operation in Somalia." *Public Opinion Quarterly* 64, (2000): 523-540.

Klein, Edward. *The Amateur: Barack Obama in the White House*. Washington, D.C.: Regnery Publishing, 2013.

Krauthammer, Charles. "The Unipolar Moment." *Foreign Affairs* 70, no. 1 (1991): 23-33.

Krieg, Andreas. "Motivations for Humanitarian Intervention: Theoretical and Empirical Consid." *Springer Science and Business Media*, (2012).

Langlois, Catherine C and Langlois, Jean Pierre. "Behavioral Issues of Rationality in International Interaction." *Journal of Conflict Resolution*, (1999).

Lewis, Michael. "Npr Interview with Michael Lewis, Presidential Biographer. "Inside Obama's Decisions, from Libya to Lunch.", edited by NPR Staff: National Public Radio, 2012.

Lindgren, Simon. "The Potential and Limitations of Twitter Activism: Mapping the 2011 Libyan Uprising." *Triple C*, (2013): 207-220.

Lindsay, James "The New Apathy." *Foreign Affairs* 79, no. 5 (2000).

Linsky, Martin. *Impact: How the Press Affects Federal Policy Making*. New York: W.W. Norton and Company, 1986.

Lippman, Thomas W. *Madeleine Albright and the New American Diplomacy*. Boulder, CO: Westview Press, 2000.

Livingston, Stephen and Eachus, Todd. "Humanitarian Crisis and U.S. Foreign Policy: Somalia and the Cnn Effect Reconsidered." *Political Communication* 12, (1995): 413-429.

Lizza, Ryan. "The Consequentialist: How the Arab Spring Remade Barack Obama's Foreign Policy." *The New Yorker*, (2011).

Lofland, Valerie J. . *Somalia: U.S. Intervention and Operation Restore Hope*. Newport, Rhode Island: The United States Naval War College, 2012.

Ludowese, Jeryl. "Strategic Communication: Who Should Lead the Long War of Ideas?" U.S. Army War College, 2006.

Madigan, Charles M. "Polls: Public Support for War Slipping." *The Chicago Tribune*, May 28, 1999 1999.

Marcella, Gabriel. "National Security and the Interagency Process." In *U.S. Army War College Guide to National Security Policy and Strategy*, 239-260. Carlisle, PA: U.S. Army War College, 2004.

Marcella, Gabriel. *Affairs of State: The Interagency and National Security*. Carlisle, PA: Security Studies Institute, 2008.

McDermott, Rose. *Political Psychology in International Relations*. Ann Arbor: University of Michigan Press, 2006.

McGreal, Chris. "Libyan Rebels Urge West to Asassinate Gaddafi as His Forces near Benghazi." *The Guardian*March 14, 2011.

Mearsheimer, John. *The Tragedy of Great Power Politics*. New York: W.W. Norton and Company, 2000.

Mediaite.com, "Admiral Mike Mullen – One of the Outcomes of the Operation Could Leave Gadaffi in Power" http://www.mediaite.com/tv/adm-mike-mullen-one-of-the-outcomes-of-the-operation-could-leave-gaddafi-in-power/ (accessed October 27 2014).

Mintz, Alex. *Understanding Foreign Policy Decision Making*. Cambridge: Cambridge University Press, 2010.

Mintz, Alex, and Redd, Steven B. "Policy Perspectives on National Security and Foreign Policy Decision Making." *Policy Studies Journal* 41, no. S1 (2013): S11-S37.

Motter, Jeff. "American Exceptionalism and the Rhetoric of Humanitarian Militarism: The Case of the 2004 Indian Ocean Tsunami Relief Effort." *Communication Studies* 61, no. 5 (2010): 507-525.

Mullenbach, M. J. and Matthews, G. P. . "Deciding to Intervene: An Analysis of International and Domestic Inuences on United States Interventions in Intrastate Disputes." *International Interactions* 34, no. 1 (2008): 25-52.

Murdock, Clark A. *Beyond Goldwater Nichols: Defense Reform for a New Strategic Era Phase 1 Report*. Washington, DC: Center for Strategic and International Studies, 2004.

Nanabhey, Mohammed. "From Spectacle to Spectacular: How Physical Space, Social Media and Mainstream Broadcast Amplified the Public Sphere in Egypt's 'Revolution'." *The Journal of North African Studies*, (2011): 573-603.

Natsios, Andrew. *U.S. Foreign Policy and the Four Horsemen of the Apocalypse: Humanitarian Relief in Complex Emergencies* The Washington Papers. Washington, D.C.: Center for Strategic and International Studies, 1997.

Newman, Edward. "Failed States and International Order: Constructing a Post-Westphalian World." *Contemporary Security Policy* 30, no. 3 (2009): 421-443.

Niekerk, Brett Van. "Social Media and Information Conflict." *International Journal of Communication*, (2013): 1162-1184.

Nye, Joseph. *Soft Power*. New York: Public Affairs, 2004.

Nye, Joseph. *Presidential Leadership and the Creation of the American Era*. Princeton: Princeton University Press, 2013.

Oakley, John L. Hirsch and Robert B. *Somalia and Operation Restore Hope: Reflections on Peacemaking and Peacekeeping*. Washington DC United States Institute of Peace Press, 1995.

Obama, Barack Hussein. "ABC, CBS, NBC Break in with Pres. Obama Comments on Syria." August 30, 2013.

Obama, Barack Hussein, "Remarks by the President in Address to the Nation on Libya" www.whitehouse.gov (accessed March 24th, 2013).

Office of U.S. Foreign Disaster Assistance. *Situation Report No. 10, "Somalia-Civil Strife"*. Washington, D.C.: Office of U.S. Foreign Disaster Assistance, 1992.

Okechukwu, Groupson-Paul. "Politics and Failures of Ethics of Humanitarian Intervention in African Conflicts." *Journal of Alternative Perspectives in the Social Sciences, University of Abidjan, Nigeria* 3, no. 3 (2011): 581-606.

O'Meara, Andrew. "Civil Military Conflict within the Defense Structure." *Parameters, Journal of the Army War College*, (1978): 85-92.

Ose, Erik. "War Weary Public Rejects Attacking Syria." *The Huffington Post*, September 12, 2013 2013.

Oxford University Press. *Independent International Commission on Kosovo Report*. Oxford: Oxford University Press, 2000.

Padgett, Deborah. K. . *Qualitative Methods in Social Work Research: Challenges and Rewards*. Thousand Oaks, CA: Strauss and Corbin, 1998.

Panetta, Leon. *Worthy Fights*. New York: Penguin Press, 2014.

Pape, Robert A. "When Duty Calls: A Pragmatic Standard of Humanitarian Intervention." *International Security* 37, no. 1 (2012): 41-80.

Parker, Emily, "Why Don't We Care About Syria" http://www.slate.com/articles/technology/future_tense/2012/02/syria_uprising_twitter_and_social_media_revolution_fatigue_.html (accessed February 14).

Parker, Peter, "Obama Seeks Approval by Congress for Strike in Syria", The New York Times http://www.nytimes.com/2013/09/01/world/middleeast/syria.html?_r=0 (accessed November 1 2014).

Parrish, Karen. "Shift in Middle East Requires U.S. Engagement." *Armed Forces New Service* March 2, 2011, (2011).

Paul, Christopher. *Strategic Communication: Origins, Concepts, and Current Debates*. Santa Barbara, CA: Praeger, 2011.

Pendleton, John H. *National Security: Key Challenges and Solutions to Strengthen Interagency Cooperation*, 2010.

People-press.org, "Public Opinion Runs against Syrian Air Strikes" People-press.org (accessed November 20 2014).

Pew Research Center for the People and the Press, "Question Search ", Pew Research Center for the People and the Press http://www.people-press.org/question-search/?qid=461620&pid=51&ccid=51#top. (accessed June 27, 2014 2014).

Pew Research Journalism Project, "Libya Drives the News as Concerns Grow", Pew Research Journalism Project http://www.journalism.org/2011/04/03/libyan-diplomacy-events-remain-atop-news-agenda/ (accessed May 20, 2014 2014).

Pew Research Journalism Project, "A Shifting Libya Narrative Is No. 1", Pew Research Journalism Project http://www.journalism.org/2011/03/06/pej-news-coverage-index-february-28-march-6-2011/ (accessed October 19, 2014 2014).

Pfiffner, James P. "Decision Making in the Obama White House." *Presidential Studies Quarterly* 41, no. 2 (2011): 244-262.

Phillips, David L. *Liberating Kosovo*. Cambridge, MA: Belfer Center, 2012.

Pinto, Maria Do Ceu De Pinho Ferreira. "Mapping the Obama Administration's Response to the Arab Spring." *Review of Brasilian International Politics*, (2012): 109-130.

Pious, Richard M. *Why Presidents Fail: White House Decision Making from Eisenhower to Bush Ii.* New York: Rowman and Littlefield Publishers, Inc., 2008.

Pollack, Joel B., "Hagel 2011: Obama Wrong on Gadhafi, Libya Was a Mistake" http://www.breitbart.com/Big-Peace/2013/02/22/Hagel-2011-Obama-Wrong-on-Gadhafi-Libya-Was-a-Mistake (accessed November 28 2014).

Pollack, Kenneth. "Let Us Now Praise Great Men: Bringing the Statesman Back In." *International Security*, (2001): 107-146.

Pollingreport.com, "Serbia/Yugoslavia", Pollingreport.com http://www.pollingreport.com/serb9904.htm (accessed October 3, 2014 2014).

Pollingreport.com, "Polling Report on Libya", Pollingreport.com http://www.pollingreport.com/libya.htm (accessed October 27, 2014 2014).

Poole, Walter S. *The Effort to Save Somalia.* Washington, D.C.: Joint History Office, Office of the Chairman of the Joint Chiefs of Staff, 2005.

Porter, Roger B. *Presidential Decision Making: The Economic Policy Board.* New York: Cambridge University Press, 1980.

Powell, Colin L. *My American Journey*. New York: Balentine Books, 1996.

Power, Samantha "Bystanders to Genocide" www.theatlantic.com/.../2001/9/bystanders-to-genocide/4571 (accessed September 2001).

Power, Samantha. *A Problem from Hell: America and the Age of Genocide.* New York: Harper Collins, 2002.

Putnam, Robert D. "Diplomacy and domestic politics: the logic of two-level games." *International Organization*, Volume 42, Issue 3, Summer 1998: 427-460.

Prashad, Vijay. *Arab Spring, Libyan Winter*. Baltimore: AK Press, 2012.

Pugh, Michael. "Peace Operations." In *Security Studies, an Introduction*, edited by Paul D. Williams, 407-419. New York: Routledge, 2008.

Quackenbush, Stephen. "The Rationality of Rational Choice Theory." *International Interactions*, no. 30 (2004): 87-107.

Rasmussen, Anders Fogh. "NATO after Libya." *Foreign Affairs*, no. July/August (2011): 2-6.

Redd, Stephen B. "The Influence of Advisors and Decision Strategies on Foreign Policy Choices: President Clinton's Decision to Use Force in Kosovo." *International Studies Perspectives* 6, (2005).

Reisner, Hiram. ""Brzezinski - Libya Action Isn't War, but Necessary Intervention."." *Newsmax*, no. March 24, 2011 (2011).

Renshon, Jonathan, and Renshon, Stanley. "The Theory and Practice of Foreign Policy." *Poltiical Psychology*, (2008): 509-536.

ResponsibilitytoProtect.org, "The Crisis in Libya" http://www.responsibilitytoprotect.org/index.php/crises/crisis-in-libya.

Polling Report.com, "Polling Report on Serbia and Yugoslavia, 1999" http://www.pollingreport.com/serb9905.htm (accessed September 20, 2014 2014).

Reuters, "Timeline of U.S. Syrian Crisis", Reuters http://www.reuters.com/article/2013/08/31/us-syria-crisis-timeline-idUSBRE97U0D820130831 (accessed November 14 2013).

Rieff, David. "R2P, Rip." *The New York Times*, November 7, 2011.

Riley, Mollie. "Hillary Clinton: 'My Biggest Regret Is What Happened in Benghazi'." *The Huffington Post*, January 27, 2014 2014.

Rodman, Peter. *Presidential Command: Power, Leadership, and the Making of Foreign Policy from Nixon to George W. Bush*. New York: Alfred A Knopf, 2009.

Rogin, Josh. "How Obama Turned on a Dime toward War." *Foreign Policy*, (2011).

Ross, Dennis. *Statecraft: And How to Restore America's Standing in the World.* New York: Farrar, Straus and Giraux, 2007.

Rothkopf, David. *Running the World: The inside Story of the National Security Council and the Architects of American Power* Public Affairs. New York: Perseus Group, 2005.

Rutherford, Kenneth R. *Humanitarianism under Fire: The U.S. And Un Intervention in Somalia*. Sterling, Virginia: Kumarian Press, 2008.

Sadat, Mir H. and Daniel B. Jones. "U.S. Foreign Policy Towards Syria: Balancing Ideology and National Interests." *Middle East Policy Council*, (2013): 12.

Sahnoun, Mohamed. *Somalia: The Missed Opportunities*. Washington, D.C.: U.S. Institute for Peace, 1994.

Schnabel, Albrecht and Thakur, Ramesh. *Kosovo and the Challenge of Humanitarian Intervention: Selective Indignation, Collective Action, and International Citizenship*. New York: United Nations University Press, 2000.

Schneider, Matt, "Admiral Mike Mullen-One of the Outcomes of the Operation Could Leave Gaddafi in Power" http://www.mediaite.com/tv/adm-mike-mullen-one-of-the-outcomes-of-the-operation-could-leave-gaddafi-in-power/ (accessed October 27 2014).

Schröder, Gerhard, "War and Peace" http://gerhard-schroeder.de/en/war-peace/ (accessed November 20 2014).

Schröder, Gerhard. *Deutsche Sicherheitspolitik an Der Schwelle Des 21. Jahrhunderts', Rede Von Bundeskanzler Schröder Vor Der*

35. Münchener Konferenz Zur Sicherheitspolitik. München: Stichworte zur Sicherheitspolitik, 1999.

Schröder, Gerhard. "Erklärung Von Bundeskanzler Gerhard Schröder Zur Lage Im Kosovo." *Stichworte zur Sicherheitspolitik*, (1999): 41.

Schroeder, Gerhard. *Entscheidungen: Mein Leben in Der Politik*. Hamburg: Ullstein, 2006.

Schuessler, John. "Necessity or Choice? Securing Public Support for War." In *Midwest Political Science Association*, 2004.

Schuessler, John. "When Wars of Necessity Become Contested as Wars of Choice." In *2004 Annual Meeting of the American Political Science Association*, 2004.

Sciolino, Elaine. "Mission to Somalia: The Big Job Ahead." *The New York Times*, December 4, 1992 1992.

Scolino, E., and Bronner, E. "How a President, Distracted by Scandal, Entered the Balkan War." *The New York Times*, April 18, 1999 1999.

Sheffer, David. "Lessons from the Rwandan Genocide." *Georgetown Journal of International Relations* 5, no. Summer/Fall (2004).

Solana, Javier. "Statement to the Press by NATO Secretary General Javier Solana." North Atlantic Treaty Organization, 1998.

Sommer, John G., and Collins, Carole C. "Humanitarian Aid in Somalia: The Role of the Office of U.S. Foreign Disaster Assistance (Ofda) 1990-1994." *Refugee Policy Study Group*, no. November, 1994 (1994).

Stalder, Felix. *Manuel Castells: The Theory of the Network Society* Key Contemporary Thinkers. Boston: Polity Press, 2006.

Stavridis, James, and Daalder. "NATO's Victory in Libya." *Foreign Affairs*, (2012).

Stavridis, James G. "Strategic Communication and National Security." *Joint Force Quarterly*, (2007): 4-7.

Steinberg, James. "Preventive Force in U.S. National Security Strategy." *Survival*, (2006): 55-72.

Stewart, Patrick. "A New Lease on Life for Humanitarianism." *Foreign Affairs*, no. March/April (2011): 1.

Stolberg, Sheryl Gay. "Still Crusading, but Now on the Inside." *The New York Times*, March 29, 2011 2011.

Stratfor.com, "France and the UK Have Different Motives for Intervening in Libya" http://www.forbes.com/sites/energysource/2011/03/29/france-u-k-have-differing-motives-for-intervening-in-libya/ (accessed 18 November 2014).

Strauss, Anselm and Corbin, Juliet. *Basics of Qualitative Research Techniques and Procedures for Developing Grounded Theory*. 2 ed. London: Sage Publications, 1990.

Strobel, Warren P. *Late Breaking Foreign Policy: The News Media's Influence on Peace Operations*. Washington, D.C.: U.S. Institute of Peace, 1997.

Taffel, Sy. "Manuel Castells – Communication Power." In *Media Ecologies and Digital Activism: thoughts about change for a changing world*, 2010, 2010.

Talbot, Strobe. *The Russia Hand: A Memoir of Presidential Diplomacy*. New York: Random House, 2003.

Talentino, Andrea Kathryn. *Military Intervention after the Cold War: The Evolution of Theory and Practice* Global and Comparative Studies Series 4. Athens, Ohio: Ohio University Press, 2005.

Talev, Margaret. "Samantha Power: The Voice Behind Obama's Libya Action." *McClatchy Newspapers*2011.

Terbush, John, "Poll: Plurality Oppose Libyan Intervention, but Support Protecting Civilians", Talking Points Memo http://talkingpointsmemo.com/dc/poll-plurality-oppose-libyan-intervention-but-support-protecting-civilians (accessed October 17, 2014 2014).

Tisdal, Simon, "Sudan Fears Us Military Intervention over Darfur" http://www.theguardian.com/world/2009/jan/15/sudan-unamid-obama (accessed November 20, 2014 2014).

U.S. Department of State Office of the Historian, "Intervention in Haiti" http://history.state.gov/milestones/1993-2000/haiti (accessed July 29, 2014 2014).

U.S. House of Representatives Select Committee on Hunger. *Humanitarian Tragedy in Somalia: Hearing before the Select Committee in Hunger, 102nd Cong., 2d Sess, Report Serial No. 102-120, January 30, 1992. Testimony by Andrew Natsios*. Washington, D.C.: U.S. House of Representatives Select Committee on Hunger, 1992.

U.S. Marine Corps, "About the 26th Marine Expeditionary Unit" http://www.26thmeu.marines.mil/About/MEU.aspx (2014).

U.S. Senate Committee on Foreign Relations. "Testimony of James Kunder before the U.S. Senate Committee on Foreign Relations Subcommittee on African Affairs." (1992).

United Nations General Assembly. *Session 57 Verbatim Report 2. A/57/Pv.2 - President Bush United States*. New York: United Nations 2002.

United Nations. *UN Secretary General's Report S/24343*. 1992.

United Nations, "Security Council Resolution 1199", The United Nations http://unscr.com/en/resolutions/1199 (accessed October 16 2014).

United Nations Security Council. *United Nations Security Council Resolution 1160*. United Nations, 1998.

United Nations. *Report of the Independent Inquiry into the Actions of the United Nations During the 1994 Genocide in Rwanda*. New York: United Nations, 1999.

University of the West of England, "Kosovo Documents" www.ess.uwe.ac.uk/kosovo/kosovo-documents7.htm (accessed October 16 2014).

University of the West of England, "Intervention in Kosovo", University of the West of England www.ess.uwe.ac.uk/kosovo/kosovo-documents7.htm (accessed October 16, 2014 2014).

Van Evera, Stephen. *Guide to Methods for Students of Political Science*. Ithaca, NY: Cornell University Press, 1997.

Vira, Varun, and Cordesman, Anthony. *The Libyan Uprising: An Uncertain Trajectory*. Washington, DC: Center for Strategic and International Studies, 2011.

Walt, Stehpen. "Top Five Reasons Obama Should Pick Chuck Hagel for Secdef." *Foreign Policy*, (2012).

Waltz, Kenneth. *Theory of International Politics*. Long Grove, IL: Columbia University Press, 1979.

The Washington Post Editorial Board. "One, Two, Many Rwandas." *The Washington Post*, no. April 17, 1994 (1994): A 15.

The Washington Post Editorial Board. "What Obama Botched in Libya." *The Washington Post* May 5, 2014 2014.

The Washington Post Editorial Board. "One, Two, Many Rwandas." *The Washington Post*, April 17, 1994 1994, A15.

Webster, Frank. *The Information Society Reader*. New York: Routledge, 2003.

Weiss, Thomas G. *Humanitarian Intervention*. 2 ed. War and Conlict in the Modern World. Cambridge: Polity Press, 2012.

Wendt, Alexander. "Constructing International Politics." *International Security*, no. Summer (1995): 71-81.

Wendt, Alexander. *Social Theory of International Politics*. Cambridge: Cambridge University Press, 1999.

Werth, Matthias. "Es Begann Mit Einer Lüge (Teil 1) - Deutschland Im Kosovo 99." 10 mins: WDR Fernsehen, 2001.

Wertheim, Stephen. "A Solution from Hell: The United States and the Rise of Humanitarian Intervention 1991-2003." *Journal of Genocide Research*, (2010): 149-172.

Western, Jon. "Sources of Humanitarian Intervention: Beliefs, Information, and Advocacy in the U.S. Decisions on Somalia and Bosnia." *International Security* 26, no. 4 (2002): 112-142.

Wheeler, Nicholas J. *Saving Strangers: Humanitarian Intervention in International Society*. New York: Oxford University Press, 2003.

Whittaker, Alan G. *The National Security Policy Process: The National Security Council and Interagency System* Vol. Annual Update. Washington, DC: Industrial College of the Armed Forces, National Defense University, 2011.

Williams, Paul D. and Bellamy, Alex J. "Principles, Politics, and Prudence: Libya, the Responsibility to Protect, and the Use of Military Force." *Global Governance* 18, (2012): 273-297.

Wilson, Scott. "On Libya, Obama Willing to Let Allies Take the Lead." *The Washington Post*, March 9, 2011 2011.

withheld. "Social Media: A Double Edged Sword in Syria." *Reuters,* 2011, 1-5.

Wittkopf, Eugene. *The Domestic Sources of U.S. Foreign Policy*. Lanham, MD: Rowman and Littlefield Publishers, 2004.

Wolfers, Arnold. *Discord and Collaboration*. Baltimore: Johns Hopkins University Press, 1962.

Woll, Peter. *American Bureacracy*. New York: Norton, 1977.

World Balkans Special Report, July 1999. "Kosovo: The Jerusalem of Serbia." *The Washington Post*1999.

Yetiv, Steve. *Explaining Foreign Policy: U.S. Decision Making and the Gulf War*. 1 ed. Baltimore: Johns Hopkins University Press, 2004.

Zambelis, Chris, "Information Wars: Assessing the Social Media Battlefield in Syria", U.S. Army https://www.ctc.usma.edu/posts/information-wars-assessing-the-social-media-battlefield-in-syria (accessed June 10 2013).

Zenko, Micah. *Coercive Diplomacy before the War in Kosovo, Case 252*. Georgetown: Walsh School of the Foreign Service, 2001.

Zenko, Micah. *Between Threats and War: U.S. Discrete Military Operations in the Post Cold War World* Stanford Security Studies. Stanford, California: Council on Foreign Relations, 2010.

Zennie, Michael. "Obama Campaign Website Taken Down by Syrian Electronic Army - the Latest Target of Pro-Assad Hackers." *Mail Online*, no. October 27 (2012).

Zunes, Stephen. "Bahrain's Arrested Revolution." *Arab Studies Quarterly*, (2011): 145-164.

APPENDIX I: Additional Polling Data

Polling Data on U.S. Intervention in Libya, March 10-May 24, 2011			
	Poll/Yes	No	Unsure
March 10-13	Pew Research Center		
U.S. Responsible to act?	27	63	10
Sanctions?	51	40	9
No Fly Zone?	44	45	11
Bombing Libyan defenses	16	77	7
Troops to Libya	13	82	5
March 10-13	ABC/Washington Post Poll		
U.S. force to create no fly zone?	49	45	6
March 11-13	CNN/Opinion Research Corp. Poll		
No Fly Zone?	32	62	4
Should U.S. lead a response?	23	74	4
March 14-16	Fox News Poll		
President Handling Situation Well?	43	35	21

U.S. military involvement?	25	65	9
March 18-20	CNN/Opinion Research Corp. Poll		
No Fly Zone?	70	27	3
Ground Forces?	28	70	1
Protecting Civilians an important policy goal?	83	10	7
March 18-21	CBS Poll		
President's Handling of the Situation?	50	29	21
Libya important to U.S.?	38	88	6
Approve Military Action?	68	26	6
Airstrikes Begin on March 19			
March 21	Gallup Poll[1]		
Intervention in Libya?	47	37	16
March 24-27	Pew Research Center		
Remove Gaddafi Primary Aim?	46	43	11
March 25-27	USA Today/Gallup		
President Handling Situation Well?	44	44	12
Should U.S. be in the lead?	10	87	4
March 24-28	AP Poll		
President Handling Situation Well?	54	43	3
Approve of U.S. Involvement in Libya?	48	50	2
POTUS Address on intervention			

[1] http://www.gallup.com/poll/146738/Americans-Approve-Military-Action-Against-Libya.aspx. Accessed on 27 October 2014.

March 30-April 3	Pew Research Center		
Intervention Right Decision?	50	37	13
Clear Goals?	30	57	12
March 31-April 4	NBC/Wall Street Journal		
No Fly Zone	66	23	4
Intervention Right Decision?	52	41	7
April 15-20	CBS/New York Times Poll		
President's Actions	39	45	16
May 24-26	CNN Poll		
President's Actions	45	48	7
Removal of Gaddafi	68	26	1

Full key polling data on intervention in Libya, March-May 2011. Information taken from Polling Report, available at http://www.pollingreport.com/libya.htm. Accessed on 27 October 2014.

APPENDIX II: LITERATURE REVIEW

The purpose of this review is to provide a comprehensive overview of the relevant literature to the topics of U.S foreign policy decision making, armed humanitarian interventions and the media and issue framing processes utilizing the intellectual frameworks developed by Graham Allison, Steve Yetiv, Robert Entman, and Manuel Castells to illuminate the reviewed literature and identify the gaps in research that the book will fill. Ultimately, the review both suggests and validates research questions for the book, including the hypothesis and thesis statement.

The methodological approach of the book this review is intended to underpin is: A definition of armed humanitarian intervention for the discussion, derived from an examination of the key sources in the field, including Nicholas Wheeler's *Saving Strangers*. This is followed by an examination of U.S. government foreign policy decision making processes, with examples provided by Steven Redd's "Policy Perspectives on National Security and Foreign Policy Decision Making" and Robert Putnam's "Diplomacy and the Diplomatic Process: The Logic of Two-Level Games" as well as others. This continues into an examination of bureaucratic decision making theories, particularly those proposed by Graham Allison in *Essence of Decision,* Jonathan Bendor and Thomas Hammond's, "Rethinking Allison's Models*,"* Steve Yetiv's *Explaining Foreign Policy*, and others; as well as the strategic communication development process with Robert Entman's *Projections of Power* and Manuel Castell's *Communication*

Power and continues into three case studies which will bring both the decision process and messaging cycle into focus. The case studies selected reflect humanitarian crises which ultimately led to military intervention by the U.S., including Somalia in 1992, Kosovo (former Yugoslavia) in 1999, and Libya in 2011, in each case showing the development and implementation of the decision making and communication processes, including the statements and memoires of key involved persons and theoretical as well as historical records of the relevant events. Two mini-cases of non-intervention, in Rwanda in 1995, and Syria in 2013, are also examined to the same criteria in order to show processes that did not lead to armed humanitarian intervention.

Theme One: Armed Humanitarian Interventions

The purpose of this portion of the review is to determine a definition for armed humanitarian intervention in order to provide a baseline to the discussion of the decision making and framing processes as well as the case studies. By their nature, such interventions seem to be what Richard Haass would call "Wars of Choice" rather than of necessity, so establishing that definition will also feed into the discussion of how wars of "Choice" can be framed to build public support for them.[1]

Nicholas Wheeler's *Saving Strangers* is a central work on the subject of humanitarian intervention, and with Andrea Talentino's *Military Intervention after the Cold War* describes the major military and non military interventions of the first decade of the post Cold War era, with a strong focus on the decisions to military interventions with an increasingly humanitarian focus; Somalia, Yugoslavia, and Kosovo.[2] Both also discuss various reasons why the great powers failed to intervene in other humanitarian disasters, such as Rwanda, and the impact

---

[1] Haass, Richard N. *War of Necessity, War of Choice: A Memoir of Two Iraq Wars*. New York: Simon and Schuster, 2009. 3.

[2] Talentino, Andrea. 2005. *Military Intervention after the Cold War*. Ohio University Press: Athens, Ohio. 1-4.

that has had on the development of humanitarianism as a cause for international action. Wheeler posited four circumstances in which humanitarian based violations of sovereignty could successfully occur. First, grievous humanitarian harm must be evident without intervention. Second, armed force must be used as a last resort. Third, proportional force to objectvies must be used. Finally, there must be a reasonable and high chance that force will actually solve the problem.[3] Each of these factors is assumed in the broader definition of armed humanitarian intervention for this study. Taken together, these two works provided a general background on the reasons for the various interventions, as well as the political debates which surrounded each individual intervention and the political idea of armed and unarmed humanitarian interventions.

Taking a theoretical approach, Martha Finnemore utilized the then newly developed theories of constructivism to analyze the issue of humanitarian interventions in a U.S. foreign policy context. Finnemore's point is that a definition and justification for humanitarian intervention cannot be found in traditional liberal and realist visions of the world, but that the context under which the interventions occur. Her basic definition of armed humanitarian intervention is use of the armed forces to intervene in the territory of a sovereign state for purposes which are related to the human security of the inhabitants of the area but not directly to the security of the intervening power. These types of intervention are not new, and she traces the history of such interventions through the 19th and 20th centuries, noting that before the end of the Second World War, most humanitarian interventions had to do with protecting Christian minorities from some act or another by the Ottoman Turks. This frames a discussion as to the definition of what human and therefore human security means. To westerners, she argues, the definition of human is one that has expanded considerably over the last century, to the point that the definition of humanitarian is not debated to the extent that the concepts of legitimacy is in

---

[3] Wheeler, Nicholas J. *Saving Strangers: Humanitarian Intervention in International Society.* New York: Oxford University Press, 2003. 488.

terms of interventions.[4] Finally, she notes that the armed humanitarian intervention in Somalia was a watershed in this wider understanding of the definition of interventions and sovereignty, as seen when Secretary General Boutros-Gali critiqued the United States for intervening in Bosnia but not Somalia, a statement which helped push the Bush administration to its decision to intervene militarily there later in 1992.[5]

Finnemore's work helped to establish the definition for armed humanitarian interventions, as did "When Duty Calls: A Pragmatic Standard of Humanitarian Intervention," in which Robert Pape focused on a revision of the basic tenets of humanitarian intervention following the Libyan intervention as well as the wars in Iraq and Afghanistan, each of which had an element of humanitarian assistance/disaster relief/reconstruction in spite of the fact that neither was couched in humanitarian terms.[6] Most useful to the research is Pape's specific definition for armed humanitarian interventions, which he describes as "an extraordinary military remedy that temporarily sets aside norms of state sovereignty to prevent the imminent death and permanent impairment of people resulting from deliberate actions by their government."[7] This is supported, though stated as a negative by Micah Zenko, whose work on discrete military operations specifically excludes humanitarian affairs missions, since they were not undertaken "to create casualties or cause damage."[8]

Pape notes that humanitarian intervention has been most closely associated with acts of genocide, which in itself became a critical issue in the aftermath of the Second World War. Genocide, as defined by the 1948 convention for its prevention

---

[4] Finnemore, Martha. "Constructing Norms of Humanitarian Intervention," from *The Culture of National Security*, Peter Katzenstein, ed. Columbia University Press: New York 1996, 153-185. 175.
[5] Ibid. 184.
[6] Pape, Robert. "When Duty Calls: A Pragmatic Standard of Humanitarian Intervention." *International Security*, Summer, 2012: 41-80. 43.
[7] Ibid. 44. Holzgrefe , J. L. and Keohane, Robert O. *Humanitarian Intervention: Ethical, Legal and Political Dilemmas*. Cambridge: Cambridge University Press 2003. 1 and 18.
[8] Zenko, Micah. *Between Threats and War: U.S. Discrete Military Operations in the Post-Cold War World.* Stanford Security Studies. Stanford, California: Council on Foreign Relations, 2010. 6.

and punishment, set out its definition as acts "committed with the intent to destroy… a national ethnic, racial, or religious group."[9] He notes that this set too high a bar, causing the Rwanda and Darfur genocides to go unchallenged. On the other hand, he decries the current trend toward Responsibility to Protect (R2P), as setting the bar too low. While Pape's proposed solution is beyond the scope of this book, his work also provides all of the case studies with a wealth of supporting data. Pape's definition offered the most succinct, but broadly based definition for humanitarian interventions, and forms the core of the definition which will be used in this study.

Stephen Wertheim offered a critique of Ambassador Samantha Power's post Kosovo work *A Problem from Hell*, a work with which Wertheim has significant difficulties. In this work, Wertheim looks at the history of U.S. humanitarian interventions, with a particular focus on the post-cold war era, from 1991-2003. Key interventions discussed are Somalia and Kosovo, however Wertheim also delivers a useful counterfactual case study of how an intervention in Rwanda might have played out had the U.S. and international community felt the need to do so.[10] Tellingly, Wertheim in no way assumes that such an intervention would have been timely or successful, and, of greater use to the overall argument of the book, spends some effort to show that there was no interest on behalf of either senior leaders, the media, or the public for such an intervention.

Wertheim notes that humanitarian type interventions were already part of the rhetoric of U.S. foreign policy before the end of the Cold War, but that their implementation afterward, with an emphasis on armed military action, became a sign both of American triumphalism and a measure of its great power status, particularly with the rise of the neo-conservatives in the late 1990s.[11] Unsurprisingly, he notes the negative impact that the perceived failure in the Somalia intervention had on future efforts and the dampening effect it had on them

---

[9] Pape. 41.
[10] Wertheim, Stephen. "A solution from hell: the United States and the rise of humanitarian intervention 1991-2003." *Journal of Genocide Research*, 2010: 149-172. 154-155.
[11] Ibid. 150-151.

for some time after, the 1994 Haiti intervention notwithstanding. Power became a key player in the Libya intervention, and her work and Wertheim's response were necessary to build an understanding of the Obama administrations attitude toward armed humanitarian intervention.

In *Humanitarian Intervention*, from 2012, Thomas Weiss also offers a definition coined from Adam Roberts: "A coercive action by one or more states involving the use of armed force in another state without the consent of its authorities, and with the purpose of preventing widespread suffering or death among the inhabitants."[12] Further, Weiss offers insights into the constraints imposed on framing efforts for Somalia, Kosovo, and Libya, particularly when the stakes in those operations rose, for example, with the infamous death of eighteen American soldiers in Mogadishu which brought the Somalia intervention to a close, and created what Weiss called a drought of U.S. armed humanitarian interventions in its wake (with significant impact for Rwanda in 1994).[13]

Turning to international organizations and their impact on humanitarian intervention, Aidan Hehir discusses the history and progress of humanitarian interventions, with some emphasis on how the U.S. became involved in each of them, with a discussion of the major U.S. post-Cold War interventions, such as Kosovo, with a particular emphasis on the Libya intervention. Hehir describes the role of key individuals in pushing for intervention and helping to frame it, in the case of Libya, this includes Susan Rice, U.S. Ambassador to the UN at the time.[14] Furthermore, Hehir argues that the issue of humanitarian intervention calls for a "fundamental restructuring" of the UN in order to take into account such operations and their impact on sovereignty.[15]

Hehir's work dovetails into a specific discussion of armed humanitarian intervention and R2P by Alex Bellamy, who argues that peace operations, in other

---

[12] Weiss, Thomas. *Humanitarian Intervention.* Cambridge, MA: Polity Press, 2012. 6.
[13] Ibid. 8.
[14] Hehir, Aidan. The *Responsibility to Protect: Rhetoric, Reality, and the Future of Humanitarian Intervention*. London: Palgrave MacMillan, 2012. 13.
[15] Ibid. 11.

words, the efforts by UN and other forces to maintain and enforce peace in war ravaged areas, began in the Cold War area as a “vision-less” reaction to international crises.[16] As the author notes, however, in the Post-Cold War era, thinking at the UN and in the humanitarian aid community has added peace operations to those activities which proponents argue would ultimately lead to a so called liberal peace. A key part of this is a significant change in the interpretation of sovereignty. In contrast to the Westphalian state system, a liberal peace would, according to the author, put the international community in charge of the sovereignty of those states it deemed to be weak or failing. R2P, which posits that the International Community has the right to intervene when states fail to protect the human security of their people, is included in this expanded assumption of power. R2P was part of the foundation for, but not specifically cited as, a justification for the Libya intervention.

Reforms to peace operations were suggested by then Secretary General Kofi Annan and Special Representative Lakhdar Brahimi of the United Nations. Brahimi suggested that peacekeeping needed to become more robust and flexible, that more input from troop contributing countries was needed to ensure commonality, and that mandates should reflect existing capabilities, requiring, if necessary, that the same forces which performed peace keeping would also stay for peace enforcement operations.[17] One product of these suggestions was the formalization of the idea of R2P, which calls for UN members to intervene either to prevent serious suffering, stop genocide, war crimes, or crimes against humanity, or to rebuild societies which have been devastated as a result of such actions or failures.[18] This went so far as to place the concept of human security higher than

---

[16] Bellamy, Alex J. "The Responsibility to Protect." In *Security Studies: An Introduction, 1st Edition*, Paul D. Williams, editor. New York: Routledge, 2008. 422-437. 422.

[17] Pugh, Michael. 2008. "Peace Operations." In *Security Studies: An Introduction*, by Paul D. Williams, editor. New York: Routledge, 2008. 407-419. 413.

[18] Pape. 51. Further tenets were that the mission must be achievable, and be as small (tailored) as possible in its execution.

that of the nation state.[19] This utopian desire, however, was not specifically endorsed by the UN Security Council, in part because of its implied "Responsibility to Prevent," abridgements of human security rather than simply reacting to their occurrence.[20]

Criticisms of peace operations and R2P include sensitizing peace operators to gender roles and human rights issues, particularly in light of widespread abuses during the Yugoslav Civil War and related conflicts of the 1990s, in which aggressors and peace-warriors alike were accused of violations. As noted by Pugh, in the decades since Somalia the UN is leaving such operations to groups of like-minded states, and staying clear of combat operations.[21] Finally a proposal to use paramilitary and police forces (the example given is the Italian Carabinieri) into a peace operation in order to lessen the "war" image and militancy of the peacekeepers is under consideration. What is unstated in the writings is a way to ensure that such operations neither are nor are perceived as simply a new way for imperial powers to get away with interventions and violations of the sovereignty of small states.

Definition: Based on this review of the literature and the numerous definitions provided by the authors, the definition for armed humanitarian interventions for this study is: "A Coercive action by one or more states, in the legitimate context of an international organization, involving the use of armed force in another state without the consent of its authorities, and with the purpose of preventing widespread suffering or death among the inhabitants."[22] Furthermore, "It is an extraordinary military remedy that temporarily sets aside norms of state sovereignty to prevent the imminent death and permanent impairment of people resulting from deliberate actions by their government."[23] This section set out to determine a

[19] The ICISS states that, after the host country, the Security Council has the primary responsibility to act.
[20] Bellamy, 2008. 426-427.
[21] Pugh. 417.
[22] Pape. 44.
[23] Wertheim. 140-141.

definition for humanitarian interventions as a framework for case study selection and analysis. Each of the following sections will look at gaps, where they exist, in the literature in order to provide focus for the study.

Theme Two: The National Security Decision Making Process

This theme examines the specific processes used by the National Security Council, the wider foreign affairs, humanitarian assistance, and disaster relief communities, the intelligence community, the military, and the White House to drive foreign affairs decision making.[24] Specific themes focus on the disparate powers of several key organizations; the National Security Council (NSC), the Department of State (DOS), the U.S. Agency for International Development (USAID), the Department of Defense (DOD), and the Intelligence Community, to advise the president on decisions.

A valuable resource for understanding the U.S. national security interagency process and the NSC is provided by Whittaker, Brown, et al., in an annual report on the subject for the National Defense University based on interviews with relevant leaders and other extant scholarly work on the presidency and leadership. This document describes the interagency process from top to bottom, noting the various committees that comprise both the NSC and Homeland Security Council (HSC) from their inception to the present day. The authors note the composition of the NSC and its staff, in which the leads are generally political appointees, but the subject matter experts are provided by the cabinet agencies. Based on the author's personal experience, this system of permanent and temporary staff does little to enhance interagency cooperation. A key point is the discussion of presidential preference in decision-making style. Presidents Eisenhower, Clinton, and others wished for their staffs to present them reasoned courses of

[24] The military terms the wider government community, except for the Department of State and the intelligence community, the interagency.

action based on consensus among themselves.[25] Others, such as Presidents Kennedy and Obama, preferred to hear the direct opinions of interagency leaders, which Whittaker referred to as a "gladiatorial arena," to hear the why and wherefore of disagreements, and then make their decisions.[26] This work was useful because, while not primary source material, it showed the history and framework of the national security decision making apparatus and how it grew up to serve the needs of the various presidents.

In their 2000 contribution to *Keeping the Edge* regarding strengthening the national security process, former senior leaders John Deutsch, Arnold Kanter, and Brent Scowcroft discuss the current state of the process as well as then current issues, and the potential for reform of the interagency decision making process. In their view, an ongoing process of "information gathering, decision making, and implementation" underlies government operations, positing that the right organization is central for setting the appropriate information requirements on which to base decisions.[27] A key point for them is the ongoing gap in training, outlook, and expectations between the two most significant stakeholders in the interagency process, the DOS and DOD. Further, the two departments (as well as the other members of the interagency process) are highly dissimilarly funded, particularly in terms of short term crisis management (the three to five year budget cycle for most agencies precludes this), so that interagency processes can be difficult to implement.[28] This concurs with Whitaker's assessment of the DOD as a greater than equal partner, with some missions that usurp the DOS' traditional primacy in diplomatic affairs.[29] It further reflects the seminal findings of Samuel

---

[25] Daalder. Ivo, and Destler, I.M. *In the Shadow of the Oval Office: Profiles of the National Security Advisors and the Presidents They Served - from JFK to George W. Bush*. New York: Simon and Schuster, 2009. 250.
[26] Whittaker, Alan G. "The National Security Policy Process: The National Security Council and Interagency System Annual Update." Washington, DC: Industrial College of the Armed Forces, National Defense University, 2011. 10.
[27] Deutsch, John. "Strengthening the National Security Interagency Process," in *Keeping the Edge*, edited by Ashton Carter. Harvard: Kennedy School, 2000, 276-84. 269.
[28] Ibid. 270.
[29] Whittaker. 52.

Huntington in *The Soldier and the State*, in which he explains in great detail the factors which make the military officer (and the departmental ethos) stand out from other government servants and leaders.[30] Further, none of the authors discuss the framing and support building processes for the decisions they make.

As noted in Donald Drechsler's "Reconstructing the Security Process after Iraq," the most famous example of the breakdown of interagency cooperation in recent years was the by-design failure of the DOS and DOD to work together on post-kinetic operations planning for Operation Iraqi Freedom, which had far reaching consequences since key measures in the rebuilding effort that should have been identified in planning were missed and had to be dealt with on the fly.[31] Drechsler advocates reforms to the process to force the two agencies to work together more consistently as a preventative measure for the recurrence of such failures.

Deutsch et. al. offered three models for NSC reform to remedy these weaknesses, including greater centralization of control of the security apparatus in the NSC, a regionally focused system, and the creation of a separate homeland security structure. They also advocated for a strengthening of the position of CIA Director, a step which was, to an extent, taken with the establishment of the Office of the Director of National Intelligence in 2005. What is interesting about this is that many of these options were adopted by the Bush Administration to create the HSC and the Office of the Director of National Intelligence. This article and the Drechsler work serve as a background for understanding the decision making body, and process, of today.

---

[30] Huntington, Samuel. *The Soldier and the State: The Theory and Politics of Civil-Military Relations*. Cambridge, Massachussetts: Belknap Press of Harvard University Press, 1957. Deutsch, Whittaker, and the others cited posit key differences between DOD and DOS including things like time views (DOS takes a long view, DOD a short term view), scope (broad for DOS, Narrow for DOD) and workload (wealth and manpower strength means that a DOD desk officer can often focus on problems that the cash and personnel strapped DoS can not.) Marcella (2004) adds differences in mindset on training (needed by DOD, not by DOS) and ambiguity (welcomed by DOS, disdained by DOD).

[31] Drechsler, Donald R. "Reconstructing the Interagency Process After Iraq." *Journal of Strategic Studies*, 2007: 3-30. 6.

One of the problems in implementing the type of interagency reform is that noted by Richard Doyle for Public Administration Review in 2007. Namely, there are no hard and fast rules for how the interagency process is to work.[32] The NSC of course has principles and deputies committees, but it relies on individual relationships and personalities to get the work done and for decisions to be reached, which brings the all of the differences in culture and funding back into focus. The congressional requirement for the executive branch to create a periodic National Security Strategy (NSS) is also inadequate as a function for forcing cooperation in planning issues and crisis management.[33]

Michele Flournoy, who would later become Director of Defense Policy Planning under President Obama, echoed these sentiments in, *Strategic Planning for National Security: A New Project Solarium* in 2006, decrying the fact that there was no formalized process for national security planning, even a decade and a half after the end of the Cold War.[34] Her solutions include a requirement for a Quadrennial National Security Review much like those performed by the Departments of State and Defense, a pan-government, inter-agency process including the intelligence community to handle issues from the information state to plan implementation, and a reformed budget process capable of allocating funds according to the policy guidance of the president rather than the competing department needs.[35] This is reinforced by Marcella's 2004 contribution to the Army War College's *Guide to National Security Policy and Strategy* and its call for a dedicated National Security staff with its own incentives, professional standards, and rewards, as is the case in the DOD Joint Community.[36] Flournoy's call for a specified budget is echoed in Brook's 2012 "Budgeting for National Security, a

---

[32] Doyle, Richard B. "The U.S. National Security Strategy: Policy, Process, Problems," *Public Administration Review*, 2007: 624-9. 626.
[33] Ibid. 626.
[34] Flournoy, Michelle. "Strategic Planning for National Security: A New Project Solarium," *Joint Force Quarterly*, 2006: 80-6. 80.
[35] Ibid. 81.
[36] Marcella, Gabriel "Chapter 17, National Security and the Interagency Process," in *U.S. Army War College Guide to National Security Policy and Strategy*. Carlisle, Pennsylvania: U.S. Army War College, 2004, 239-60. 254.

Whole of Government Approach," in which the author argues that the whole of the non-DOD portion of the security apparatus is underfunded, even under normal conditions, and that a redesign or re-imagining of interagency roles and responsibilities would have to be accompanied by a rethinking of the budgets allocated for those activities.[37]

Flournoy's recommendations were echoed in the early days of the Obama Presidency by a General Accounting Office (GAO) report on the specific subject of interagency cooperation. They add the need for the creation of specifically collaborative organizations, and a workforce trained to support those organizations, to the basic recommendations made by other contributors to this review. A key example of the failure of agencies to align on each other is the unresolved example of the misalignment of areas of responsibility between the DOD's regional combatant commands and the DOS's regional bureaus.[38] The Fiscal Year 10 National Defense Authorization Act went some way toward fixing this issue, as it required the president to designate a commission to develop such a system.[39] In the 2010 Government Accounting Office report, John Pendleton noted a lack of clarity on which agency might lead what type of effort as a key failure of the current system, which ties into the overall criticisms raised by Flournoy, Deutsch, and others in this study.[40]

Writing after the Vietnam War, Lieutenant Colonel Andrew O'Meara's *Civil Military Conflict* builds on Huntington's analysis from *The Soldier and the State*, noting a series of divisions between military and civilian leaders which bleeds over from a purely defense perspective into the national security realm. He emphasizes the very different training and skill sets of the military officers, as well as a different set of role expectations, claiming that the senior military leader

---

[37] Brook, Douglas A. "Budgeting for National Security: A Whole of Government Perspective," *Journal of Public Budgeting, Accounting, and Financial Management*, 2012: 32-57. 37.
[38] Pendleton, John H. "National Security: Key Challenges and Solutions to Strengthen Interagency Cooperation" Washington D.C.: General Accounting Office, 2010. 7.
[39] Ibid. 1.
[40] Ibid. 5.

expects, and is dismayed, when he finds himself out of control, while the civilian leader is inculcated with the principle of tightly controlling the military.[41] Further, differences in governance style between liberal and conservative administration can also cause significant consternation among military leaders, who find themselves alternately empowered or undercut depending on which party is in power.[42] Further, modern communications allow all senior leaders, including civilians, unprecedented levels of access and control over the slightest minutia of operations, to include combat, a trend which is most famously seen in Vietnam, but has increased in pervasiveness in the decades since.[43]

A countervailing opinion, and one which may well reflect the realities of the post-cold war paradigm, is provided by Deborah Avant, who noted in "Conflicting Indicators of "Crisis" in American Civil-Military Relations" that the 1990's saw a swing in the opposite direction, toward an expansion of military roles and influence, to the point where military leaders are said to have negatively influenced policy. One example provided is that of Colin Powell's interference in policies on the Yugoslav Civil War, which saw the military focusing on its desired tasks rather than the goals proposed by civilian leadership, and Powell actively influencing outcomes beyond the expected role of trusted advisor.[44] Indeed, as will be seen in the case studies, the military stood, in the main, against each of the interventions undertaken. Avant proposes several fixes for this separation of goals, primarily focused on reversing the military's separation from civil society both in physical proximity and in mindset, possibly through a reinstitution of the draft,

In *National Security and the Interagency Process*, Gabriel Marcella discusses the development of the interagency national security decision making since the Second World War, noting its beginnings as a means to achieve total

---

[41] O'Meara, Andrew. "Civil Military Conflict within the Defense Structure." *Parameters, Journal of the Army War College*, 1978. 85-92. 87.
[42] Ibid. 88.
[43] Ibid. 89.
[44] Avant, Deborah. "Conflicting Indicators of "Crisis" in American Civil-Military Relations. *Armed Forces and Society*, Vol. 24, No. 3, Spring 1998, 375-388. 376.

wartime mobilization.[45] According to Marcella, the NSC serves to provide information and policy advice to the president, manage the policy coordination process, monitor policy implementation, manage crises, articulate the president's policies, perform long term strategic planning, liaison with the U.S. Congress and foreign governments, and coordinate summits and international visits.[46] With this in mind, Marcella notes that the interagency environment is a process, rather than a place, and embodies more than the narrowly defined mission of the NSC. Further, such a process, to perform optimally, must have such factors as perfect goal setting, complete intelligence, flawless articulation, etc., in other words, a utopian perfection which is impossible to achieve in the real world.[47] Finally, he notes that a central problem with the whole process is its lack of centrality or central control. This means that things work when personalities mesh, and they don't when they don't.[48] Marcella's findings are mirrored in those of "Institutionalization of the National Security Staff, 1949-2001," by Matthew Dickinson, who noted that the national security staff assists the president with mitigating uncertainty both in in foreign policy planning but also in mitigating what he calls "bargaining outcomes" including domestic politics. Dickinson reviewed the roles of powerful advisors in the 1970's, but also how the embarrassment of the Iran Contra Affair led to a more curtailed role for the Council under President George H.W. Bush, and how President Clinton expanded the NSC's role to address international economic issues, but largely kept the Bush model in place.[49]

John Burke's work is in agreement with the general responsibilities of the NSC and interagency leaders as articulated by Marcella in his concept of the need for a Neutral broker in the decision making process. He focuses on the necessity for the national security advisor to act as an "honest broker" to make the system

---

[45] Marcella, 2004. 239.
[46] Ibid, 2004. 243-244.
[47] Ibid. 245.
[48] Ibid. 253.
[49] Dickinson, Matthew. "Institutionalization of the National Security Staff, 1949-2001." *2003 Meeting of the American Political Science Association*, 38, 2003. 12.

function effectively. This "managerial custodianship" requires balancing actor resources, bringing in new advisors to advocate for unpopular decisions, making sure that there are always multiple channels of information to assist presidential decision making, and monitoring the system as needed.[50] The article discusses the development of the national security advisor in this role, starting with President Truman and Eisenhower's national security advisors, who focused narrowly on their duties as described above. This of course changed with the appointment of Henry Kissinger, who set the bar for activist advisors. The broker, versus activist role has been seen with Brent Scowcroft, and to a lesser extent Sandy Berger among recent presidencies, and this fact bears significantly on the quality of the decision making process and the outcomes of that process, something that is borne out in the case studies.[51]

Concluding the look at the NSC structure and interagency issues is the CSIS report "Beyond Goldwater Nichols" Clark Murdock notes successive failures to achieve whole of government solutions, a problem which has hindered success in intervention missions.[52] He makes a series of recommendations for improvement of the decision making process, including the creation of an assistant on the NSC staff with the specific job of integrating agency plans and strategies, mirrored by similar bodies in the relevant cabinet agencies.[53] Deeper presidential review of complex operation planning procedures, and designation of on the ground interagency leads for complex operations are also mandated, and this stands in agreement with Ross's support of Richard Holbrooke's role in Yugoslavia discussed below.[54] The general agreement among writers on the NSC and the interagency is that the DOD is not structured or intended to go it alone in foreign policy planning and implementation, just as DOS and the other key members of the

[50] Burke, John P. "The Neutral/Honest Broker in Role in Foreign-Policy Decision Making: A Reassessment." *Presidential Studies Quarterly*, 2005: 229-258. 230.
[51] Ibid. 236.
[52] Murdock, Clark A. *Beyond Goldwater Nichols: Defense Reform for a New Strategic Era Phase 1 Report*. Wahsington: Center for Strategic and International Studies, 2004. 60.
[53] Ibid. 63.
[54] Ibid. 64.

interagency, such as the FBI, the Department of Commerce, USAID, and others cannot achieve their maximum capability without working in concert.

Peter Rodman, focusing directly on the office of the presidency, generates a series of insights on what makes a successful presidency in terms of foreign policy development. His work, based on his personal experience and interviews, is one of the primary foundations for the development of the case studies because of its broad scope and specific detail on relevant decision making and decision makers. Rodman's chief observation is that a president must know when and where to apply his personal will to issues, while successfully managing his staff such that that will gets applied even when the president himself cannot do so.[55] While Rodman casts a wide net, the most useful sections of his work deal with the presidencies of George H.W. Bush and Bill Clinton. Rodman details the workings of each presidency, from the unified team of Bush to a Clinton team that was chosen in some ways to reflect the new president's lack of interest in foreign affairs, evidenced by Warren Christopher, or to prevent threats from the Defense Department, which lead to Les Aspin's appointment there, since he was perceived to be weak.[56] The work does not specifically address the Bush decision to enter Somalia, however, significant time is spent discussing the Clinton decision making process and how it bore on the decision not to intervene in Rwanda, but to do so in Kosovo.

In his 2009 work on presidential leadership, Joseph Nye examines how a series of U.S. presidents contributed to what he calls the U.S. primacy of the 20th and 21st Centuries. Nye characterizes leaders as transactional or transformational, depending on their motives and personal styles. Of greatest interest to this book is Nye's description of President George H. W. Bush as a transactional leader, so called because his motives were good, and he did not seek fundamental change to the world system.[57] Of value to the overall theme of the book is Nye's assessment

---

[55] Rodman, Peter. *Presidential Command: Power, Leadership, and the Making of Foreign Policy from Richard Nixon to George W. Bush*. New York: Alfred A. Knopf, 2009. 140.
[56] Ibid. 205, 207.
[57] Nye, Joseph. *Presidential Leadership and the Creation of the American Era*. Princeton: Princeton University Press, 2013. 6.

that presidential leadership was, indeed, pivotal to the development of foreign policy and the framing of strategic communication messages.

Based on the personality of a given president, and the constitutional seniority of the various cabinet members, the interagency process can be dominated by a powerful cabinet member. The most recent example of this is the role that Vice President Cheney and Defense Secretary Rumsfeld played in the Bush administration. These types of relations can limit the effectiveness of the NSC and the interagency community to get their plans cleared through the president.[58] In *Statecraft: How to Restore America's Standing in the World*, Dennis Ross engages in a discussion of interventions in the post-Cold War Era, and notes the success in Bosnia when a single trusted agent (in this case, Richard Holbrooke) took the lead in formulating and implementing policy.[59]

Supporting the "One Man" argument, Gordon Craig focuses on Kissinger's role as a "great man", moving the focus of power and decision making down one level from the president to a trusted advisor. This was a unique situation, since Kissinger often operated independently from his presidential masters, but always had to reason with their personalities.[60] Kissinger centralized the foreign policy apparatus, juggling, and, when necessary deceiving, both his international and domestic interlocutors, including, on occasion, his bosses.[61] Zbigniew Brzezinski, who served Carter as Kissinger had served Ford and Nixon, adds weight to the discussion of foreign policy decision making. He emphasizes his personal relationship with President Carter, and how others, who did not share the same level of personal connection, were increasingly less able to get their opinions heard and policies implemented. This was most clearly exhibited with Secretary of State

---

[58] Nye. 29.
[59] Ross, Dennis. *Statecraft: And How to Restore America's Standing in the World.* New York: Farrar, Straus and Giraux, 2007. 135.
[60] Craig, Gordon. *The Diplomats, 1939-1979.* Princeton: Princeton University Press, 1994., 571. "...his mercurial yet morbidly suspicious chief. This meant accommodating himself to Nixon's distinctly odd working habits; it also required unquestioning support for questionable policies."
[61] Ibid. 580.

Cyrus Vance, and the series of conflicts he and Brzezinski had with each other.[62] Moreover, a system of decision making that was highly centralized in the White House under a dominant president created a situation in which the National Security Advisor was increasingly the bureaucratic beneficiary of active presidential predominance. In their history of the NSC and the National Security Advisors, Ivo Daalder and I.M. Dester also note the unique role that one man, such as Kissinger, could play, recognizing that specific steps would be taken by subsequent chief executives to limit the power of the National Security Advisor, or any other single person, to control events.[63] They concur with assessments of other relevant players such as Brent Scowcroft as completely loyal to George H.W. Bush,[64] and Anthony Lake's Council, per Bill Clinton's design, as focused, at least in the beginning of the administration, on de-prioritizing foreign policy,[65] but steadily forming a decisive, problem solving partnership, especially after transitioning to the leadership of Lake's former deputy, Sandy Berger.[66] In the same vein, Burke advocated for a return to the honest broker role for the National Security Advisor, noting that this choice is ultimately up to the president who makes the choice of advisors and roles.[67]

Eugene Wittkopf and James McCormick turn our attention to the role of domestic factors on foreign policy decision making. In their compilation of articles, the author/editors examine the sub-unit level actors who impact U.S. foreign policy, namely, the media, the Congress, the public, and others. The authors spend significant time discussing the armed humanitarian interventions in Somalia and Kosovo, reaching similar conclusions to the other authors cited in this review. The authors emphasize the self-view of the U.S. as an idealistic power, how this plays

---

[62] Brzezinski, Zbigniew. *Power and Principle: Memoirs of the National Security Adviser 1977-1981*. New York: Farrar, Strauss, and Giroux. 524.
[63] Daalder. Ivo, and Destler, I.M. *In the Shadow of the Oval Office: Profiles of the National Security Advisors and the Presidents They Served - from JFK to George W. Bush*. New York: Simon and Schuster, 2009. 305.
[64] Ibid. 168.
[65] Ibid. 215.
[66] Ibid. 207.
[67] Burke, 2005. 250.

out domestically, and how left over pressures and predilections from the Cold War era impacted U.S. interventions.[68] They also note the growing education, motivation, and understanding gap between the U.S. defense establishment and the civilian national security apparatus, a factor which has contributed to misunderstandings as borne out in the case studies. Emphasis is also placed, as in other cited works, on what personality traits the president brings to decision-making, how he chooses to staff his national security apparatus, and who he chooses to lead it in terms of their impact on the decision making process. This work specifically reinforces Robert Putnam's view of foreign policy development as a "two-level" game in which the role of different domestic political groupings exerts direct influence on, and is directly influenced by, foreign policy decisions.[69]

Literature Gaps Revealed: The most significant gap that has been revealed in the works reviewed is a lack of connection between the national security decision making process and the process of framing the decisions resulting from it to stakeholder audiences, in other words, through the media and other communications tools to the American people. While the media are mentioned as an influencer on policy, policy as an influence on the media is not covered. It is this gap which the book proposes to fill. While there are a variety of structures in place to facilitate decision making, there appears to be no set mechanism or process to achieve a similarly strong level of information dissemination to relevant stakeholder audiences. This can result in a lack of support or even resistance to decisions of if and at what level to launch armed humanitarian interventions.

Theme Three: Decision Making Theories and the "Powerful Leader"

The purpose of this section is to review extant debate on rationality and the decision making process and drawing relevant conclusions on that process and how

---

[68] Wittkopf, Eugene and McCormick, James. *The Domestic Sources of U.S. Foreign Policy: Insights and Evidence.* Lanham, MD: Rowman and Littlefield, 2004. 15.

[69] Putnam, Robert D. "Diplomacy and domestic politics: the logic of two-level games." *International Organization*, Volume 42, Issue 3, Summer 1998: 427-460. 434.

it fits in with the larger discussion on humanitarian affairs and framing. Furthermore, the definition of "powerful leader" in foreign policy decision making is discussed.

The foundational work on crisis decision making is Graham Allison's *Essence of Decision*, as updated in 1999 with Phillip Zelikow. *Essence of Decision* uses a discussion of the Cuban Missile Crisis as the background for a deeper analysis of the methods used by leaders to reach decisions in times of peace and crisis, although notably without significant attention to the issue of how the decision making and framing processes interact. One of the main contributions of Allison's work is the Rational Actor Model (RAM) of government politics, decision making, and group dynamics. The RAM posits that actors "consider problems of policy in terms of largely implicit conceptual models that have significant consequences for the context of the thought."[70] The first section of the work considers the definition of rationality, as well as a discussion of the first, implicit conceptual model (Called the Classical Model). Its core concepts are: A ranking of objectives, discussion of alternatives, attachment of consequences to the alternatives, and a rational selection of the alternatives to act upon based on required goal completion. This model's assumptions are: Unitary states are the key actors, states act rationally, calculating costs and benefits for actions, and that the world is a "Hobbesean Jungle," or anarchic in the neorealist sense in which there is no higher authority to moderate state action. In such an environment, it is assumed that states will seek to increase their security and power.[71]

Further expanding on the concept of rationality is "The Rationality of Rational Choice Theory." In this article, Stephen Quackenbusch defends rationality by noting that it is not a unified theory, and that a lack of understanding of rationality has created confusion as to its ultimate value, since it is actually a

---

[70] Allison, Graham, and Zelikow, Philip. *Essence of Decision: Explaining the Cuban Missile Crisis, Second Edition*. Longman: New York, 1999. 18.
[71] Ibid. 37.

cover term for a series of different theoretical arguments.[72] In order to rectify this, the author seeks to clarify instrumental rationality, focusing on the role of assumptions (both provable and unprovable) in rational decision making.[73] He claims that assumptions should be judged by their usefulness rather than their veracity, and that conflating rational decision making with economic choices, as early analysts did, is fraught with danger, since rationality must encompass more than economic awards and outcomes.[74] This argument on assumptions and rationality supports the implementation of a rational actor model, in that key assumptions must be made and the resultant conclusions acted upon in the decision making process, without normative judgment on the good or bad nature of decisions.[75] In other words, a decision need not be perceived to be good in order to be perceived as rational.

Furthering the discussion of rational decision making, Catherine C. Langlois and Jean-Pierre P. Langlois discuss the issues that rationality causes in behavior. The authors present behavior and rationality from a game theoretical standpoint, providing a series of examples, concluding that neither evolutionary nor classical game theoretical arguments are adequate to explain changes in strategic behavior.[76] Their vision of a "rational" strategy would utilize a combination of strategies designed to hold opponents to a single pattern of behavior while deterring them from harmful moves.[77] They claim that their process roughly mirrors diplomatic and political discourse, because decisions can be made without plans being fully revealed to the other player.[78] This seems to be relevant to the issue of

---

[72] Quackenbush, Stephen. "The Rationality of Rational Choice Theory." *International Interactions*, no.30, 2004. 87.
[73] Ibid. 89.
[74] Ibid. 91.
[75] Ibid. 95. This instrumental rationality, or the rationality of rational theory as alluded to in the title.
[76] Langlois, Catherine C. and Jean-Pierre. "Behavioral Issues of Rationality in International Interaction." *Journal of Conflict Resolution*, 1999. 627.
[77] Ibid. 628.
[78] Ibid. 640.

foreign policy decision making in that each party to the decision must engage in these thought processes in order to negotiate bases for action.

Returning to a discussion of Allison's models, the second model developed is the Organizational Process Model (OPM), in which leaders tend to break down problems along organizational lines, and are therefore often limited to reacting to crises with pre-existing plans because of the time required to develop new plans. This conforms to Peter Woll's work on the American bureaucracy, which posits that role of the any federal bureaucracy, regardless of its location in the hierarchy is significant in the barriers that can be erected to discussion, and implementation, of any agenda, even that of the president. This is well represented by the change of focus which fundamentally altered the calculus in the Somalia intervention.[79]

The third model, and the one most applicable to the interagency process as it applies to the Libyan intervention, is the Governmental Politics Model (GPM). In this model, these decisions are viewed as "outputs of large organizations functioning according to standards of behavior."[80] Key here is that organizational, not individual, dynamics and cultures influence outcomes. Bureaucracies serve themselves first, then their higher authorities. Large gaps form between the choices of leaders and the implementation capabilities and priorities of subordinate organizations. Organizations do not easily or efficiently share information, resulting in potentially incomplete information for decision makers. The OPM and GPM provide a basis for enhanced explanation and predictions. The authors argue that their expanded models can also be used to analyze decision making processes in extra-governmental fields such as law, economics, or business.[81] In these models even a shared goal can cause conflict because of the differing views of leaders based on the points of view of their parent organizations, personal interests, and backgrounds. In such an environment, even a paramount leader, such as the

[79] Woll, Peter. *American Bureacracy.* New York: Norton, 1977. 206-207.
[80] Allison and Zelikow. 143.
[81] Ibid. 7.

president, must seek consensus with his subordinates, if for no other reason than to prevent misunderstandings.[82]

Because of these limitations, the personalities of key leaders and their propensity to fight for their views or acquiesce, even to the paramount leader, are central. This is witnessed in the case study discussion of the Somalia and Libya interventions, when key senior leaders such as the U.S. Ambassador to the UN and the Secretary of State appear to have been pivotal in swaying President Obama both to intervene, and to do so under humanitarian auspices. The Governmental Politics Model takes the perspective that government behavior is not unitary at all, but made up of a wide array of actors, each pulled by numerous priorities which may not be central to the issue at hand. Crucial to the model is the idea that "the leader's initial preferences are rarely a sufficient guide for explanation or prediction."[83] Bargaining takes place amongst agencies of varying relative power and interests, sometimes crippling the ability to make rational choices.

Jonathan Bendor and Thomas Hammond take a critical look at the three major models postulated by Graham Allison in the first edition of *Essence of Decision*.[84] They recognize the importance of Allison's work and its centrality to the study of the impact of bureaucracy on decision making. However, it is that centrality of importance which causes their concern, as they describe the models as largely descriptive rather than prescriptive or theoretical. Part of their critique lies in the fact that they are writing nearly two decades after the release of *Essence of Decision*, with much history, including new perspectives on the Cuban Missile Crisis, between them. It was this type of criticism as well as a desire to update the model that led Graham Allison to team up with Philip Zelikow to rewrite *Essence of Decision* in 1999.

Four typologies are developed by the authors for use in examining Allison's three models. The first focuses on the number of actors. Unlike states, which are

---

[82] Allison and Zelikow. 7.
[83] Ibid. 259.
[84] Bendor, Jonathan, and Hammond, Thomas. "Rethinking Allison's Models." *The American Political Science Review*, Vol. 86, No. 2 (Jun., 1992), 301-322. 301.

viewed as unitary actors, decision making groups are broken down into constituent groups.[85] This leads to questions of similarity of goals, which is not guaranteed with large groups.[86] Third is the assumption that all players are rational.[87] Fourth, rationality notwithstanding, is how informed or uninformed the actors are. The authors find the RAM to be too simple in its examination of rationality. In part this is because of uncertainty on whether rational actors have just one goal or many.[88] Another potential flaw is Allison's seeming presumption that decisions taken at key points in time draw their decision cycles to an end. This does not pay adequate note to the ongoing impacts of decisions, changes in circumstances, as seen in Somalia, and the possible need for revisits of the same topics. In part, this weakness is attributed to a lack of adequate progress in game theory as a tool when Allison first wrote the book.

The second model, the OPM, is described by the authors as Allison's strongest work. They criticize it, however, for its core assumption that the actors making decisions will follow simple organizational rules or standard operating procedures.[89] These rules include: Straight lines of organization, programmed character, and the constraints placed on the number and types of choice by these rules. The authors posit that the rationality of behavior is based on various inputs, including information. Limits on information can impact the quality of the rules and the decisions made. Other limitations of the model include the lack of acknowledgement of the possible non-linear nature of crises as well as the combined, complex interplay of multiple actors and choices. In other words, events will be far more complex and far less linear that acknowledged by Allison.[90] Further, operating rules and may be more numerous and complex than individual actors can process. Additionally, hierarchy, or how smaller decisions/influencers

---

[85] Bendor and Hammond. 304.
[86] Ibid. 305.
[87] Ibid.
[88] Ibid.
[89] Ibid. 309.
[90] Ibid.

fit into a larger picture, is not recognized in Allison's work. Furthermore, modern bureaucracies are not always as sluggish or staid as Allison proposed. Indeed, organizations can potentially bring more cognitive power to bear on issues than individuals.[91] Finally, modern decision makers are not as uninformed as assumed (and may be quite specialized, although sometimes in different ways).

Critiques of the GPM focus on whether the highest levels of the government actually work in the manner supposed by Allison. The authors question if goals of leaders at the cabinet level are actually so disparate, and both whether and why a president would have to bargain with his own appointees.[92] The authors posit that a president would try to avoid bargaining if possible, and that he would be in a paramount position unless his subordinates possessed sources of information and or power/support outside of the executive branch.[93] It could be suggested this could be seen in action during the Somalia intervention decisions of the Bush administrations, and far less so in the Clinton and Obama interventions, with the differences explained by the unique personalities in play.

Concerning Allison's use of the Cuban Missile Crisis as the empirical backdrop to his analytical models, the authors posit that, in spite of Allison's analysis, the key decisions in the crisis were taken by the president and a very small inner group, and were not the result of bargaining or political compromise.[94] The author's claim that the GPM is both too complex and inadequately cognizant of the importance of hierarchy in the decision making process. In conclusion, the authors conclude with a final warning against the kind of devotion to Allison's model that sprung up after its promulgation.

Stephen Redd and Alex Mintz expound upon the decision making models, introducing Applied Decision Analysis (ADA) method and bias in decision

---

[91] Bendor and Hammond. 311-312.
[92] Ibid. 314.
[93] Ibid.
[94] Ibid.

making.[95] The ADA creates a decision matrix for the user, which focuses on available alternatives, decision dimensions, and rates each decision dimension in terms of the implications of that decision. Examination of decisions according to this rule can help do determine which of the processes was used, and therefore how the leader thinks or is influenced. This model would be very useful if applied through systematic interviews with key leaders on specific decision making cycles, such as those surrounding the selected case studies.[96]

In *Explaining Foreign Policy*, Steve Yetiv attempts to broaden the tools developed by Allison by use of a new case study, that of the decision making process which surrounded the U.S. led coalition's armed rejection of Iraq from Kuwait in 1991. One of his refinements of the Allison models was a Theory of Government Politics, by which key leaders acted as "pied pipers" and brought others along with them through persuasive power, particularly if the outlook of and relationships among the group members were similar and strong.[97] Yetiv's model appears particularly persuasive for explaining the interventions in Kosovo and Libya, in which powerful actors, not always at the cabinet level, formulated their positions and dragged other key leaders along, ultimately also participating in the public framing of the issues, although this is not discussed explicitly. The idea of "pied pipers" provides part of the basis for the "powerful leaders" referenced in this study.

It must be noted, of course, that both Allison and Yetiv wrote about unique events which are unlikely to recur. This does not render their work merely historical, but implies that other theories and narratives can augment their explanatory power. One of these narratives is provided by Richard Haass, who, writing about his experience as a cabinet official in both Bush administrations, noted that there seemed to be little if any discussion around the decision to begin

---

[95] Redd, Stephen B., and Mintz, Alex. "Policy Perspectives on National Security and Foreign Policy Decision Making." *Policy Studies Journal*, 2013: 11-37. 11.
[96] Ibid. 26.
[97] Yetiv, Steve A. *Explaining Foreign Policy: U.S. Decision Making and the Gulf War.* Baltimore: Johns Hopkins University Press, 2004. 120.

the second Iraq War in 2002-2003. Rather, it appeared that the decision was made nearly unilaterally by President Bush and then pushed to the cabinet for planning.[98] This is in contrast to environment under which the decisions of the first Gulf War were undertaken.[99]

Moving from group dynamics to the role of the individual, Byman and Pollack begin their engagement of theory by discussing why other researchers have dismissed or under-studied the role of the individual in international politics. The reasons given focus on the difficulty of crafting theories which can explain individual actions and their importance, something that the authors look to rectify with their own work. The authors significantly engage other theories, particularly realism. Given their aim, this is primarily done through an exposition of Ken Waltz's seminal work *Man, the State and War,* and the three images of analysis, man, society, and the international system as well as his *Theory of International Politics*.[100] They acknowledge Waltz's inclusion and explanation of the role of man, even if they note that Waltz's dismissal of the role of the individual leaves a gap in the overall analysis. Case studies utilized to emphasize the role of the individual include leaders such as Hitler, Napoleon, Saddam Hussein, and Hafez al Assad, and the authors take pains to demonstrate that it was their personal actions which were the primary drivers for decisions and events. In terms of the selected case studies, less malevolent examples of seminal leaders are the Presidents, Bush and Clinton, and other key leaders, such as Secretaries of State Albright and Clinton. This emphasis on the role of the individual combines with that of Yetiv's "pied piper" to identify the "powerful individual" who can sway opinion in decision making.

Dominic Johnson and Dominic Tierney posit that wars can begin because of a transfer from a deliberate planning mode to an execution mode amongst

---

[98] Haass, Richard N. *War of Necessity, War of Choice: A Memoir of Two Iraq Wars.* New York: Simon and Schuster, 2009. 6.
[99] Ibid. 82-83.
[100] Byman, Daniel L. and Pollack, Kenneth M. "Let Us Now Praise Great Men: Bringing the Statesman Back In." *International Security* 25, No. 4 (2001): 107-146. 111.

civilian and military leaders.[101] Once this transition takes place, it becomes significantly more difficult to defuse a situation, or to steer leaders to choose non-combative courses of action. Thus, even when peaceful options may be available, leaders stick to their chosen path, often toward war.[102] This construct seems particularly useful for a discussion of the road to intervention in Somalia.

Through this theory, the authors hope to resolve several key issues. One is apparent fear of war in times of peace and limited tension contrasted with overconfidence in the crisis phase leading to conflict.[103] A second is that leaders are the primary actors in international relations, and that their actions may lose rationality once an implemental mindset has taken hold.[104] Although not the only example given, the events of the summer of 1914 and the outbreak of the First World War in Europe form a centerpiece for explanation and support for the theory.

Overconfidence is the first component of the argument to be analyzed. A series of historical examples are given to demonstrate that the road to war (in this case the Second World War and the 1991 Gulf War) moved from the theoretical to the inevitable, feelings of fear and uncertainty gave way to overconfidence and overestimation of capabilities. In the case of the Second World War, the foreign policy establishment in Great Britain collectively could be described as having went through a series of four psychological phases, ending in confidence that the war could be won. Similarly, confidence in the U.S. of a successful outcome to the Gulf War increased as war became more likely through the winter of 1990-1991. The authors hypothesize that overconfidence can be traced back to the closed nature of the implemental mindset, since, in both cases, the only variable which changed was that of time, here described as nearness to likely conflict. No important change in military capability took place in either case. This methodology can be seen in action in all three of the case study interventions.

---

101 Johnson, Dominic, and Tierney, Dominic. "The Rubicon Theory of War: How the Path to Conflict Reaches the Point of No Return" *International Security* 36, No. 1 (2011): 7-40. 7.
102 Ibid.
103 Ibid.
104 Ibid. 8.

The implemental mindset is described as unreceptive to issues or questions which challenge the chosen course of action.[105] Information that is received tends to be processed in a way that it supports pre-existing plans, while an "illusion of control" over events can set in.[106] Of particular interest is evidence that leaders in the implementation mindset even dismiss personal danger and everyday risks such as illness or accidents.[107] Overconfidence and the implemental mindset are brought together as influencers on war perceptions. The authors posit that perceptions of war can be traced to three event types: Leaders can choose conflict, have it chosen for them (entrapment) or slide into war as a result of uncontrollable turmoil. The "slide" to war can be furthered by the implemental mindset and overconfidence posited by the Rubicon Theory of War.

In conclusion, the authors note that an implementation mindset need not be completely negative, and state that it can endow leaders with the discipline and will to see operations through to completion. However, they caution against allowing such endowments to drift into excessive risk taking and refusal to accept information inputs which could defuse crises. They posit that leaders, expecting this behavior, should plan to both harness and mitigate its effects.[108] Notably, the article does not enter into a discussion of the processes leaders take to frame and justify their positions during the crisis planning events discussed.

Rose McDermott's *Political Psychology in International Relations* serves as a strong analytical accompaniment to Allison's work. This book examines the various strains of thought and analysis surrounding political psychology, including recommendations on how future research can move the field forward and make it more useful to political science researchers.[109] One key point of this work is that

---

[105] Johnson and Tierney. 15.
[106] Ibid. 17.
[107] Ibid. 11.
[108] Ibid.
[109] McDermott, Rose. *Political Psychology in International Relations*. Ann Arbor, MI: University of Michigan Press, 2004. 17-20.

context and history are crucial in understanding psychology and its impact on the decision making process.

McDermott focuses on theories of politics and International Relations and their impacts on the study of political psychology. Realism, Liberalism, Marxism, the domestic policy model, the RAM, Constructivism, and the role of individuals are discussed, leading into a discussion of developmental psychology. In fact, the role of upbringing on individual leaders is referred to several times through the course of the book, with attention to specific reference to Hitler, Woodrow Wilson, Nixon, and Ghandi among others. Further, discussion of choice and chance, and the impact of one on the other, is discussed.[110] As the author notes, chance does not self-correct, in spite of the commonly-held belief that it does. For example, rolling the dice repeatedly still gives the same chance for a given outcome as existed in the first roll, in spite of the human mis-perception that odds change.[111]

Chapter four discusses cognition and attitudes and the interaction between them. Attitude change, predicted in part by the number of interlocutors around the person making decisions, is discussed as a key part of this process. Similarly, social rules, hierarchy/authority, and norms can influence attitudes, while cognitive dissonance, or the ability to hold one set of views for a considerable period while acting in a way which may contradict that belief. The power of context is explained as forcing attitudes and drives to change, thus changing perceptions and cognition. This leads into a discussion of behavior, which begins with the role of crises and how the resultant sub-optimal or bad decision making. Crises can cause leaders to omit key data and objectives, fail to examine costs and risks, fail to find adequate information, process information selectively, fail to reconsider previously rejected alternatives, and failure to consider issues of implementation and monitoring.[112] International terror networks and the methods of recruitment, training, and operation of terrorists, the military, and other groups are examined in this light,

---

[110] McDermott. 271-273.
[111] Ibid. 61.
[112] Ibid. 124.

focusing on emotion and its role in the decision making process. Jealousy, reciprocity, and other traits are derived from this, and can heavily impact decision making.

Chapters eight and nine of the study focus on the role of the leader and the impact of group think, respectively. Chapter eight emphasizes the need to understand a leader's history and emotional underpinnings in order to understand that leader's motivations and choices.[113] Chapter nine focuses on Irving Janis' groupthink theory, and the ways in which a group can shape individual choices and learning.[114] Graham Allison's three models from Essence of Decision are specifically analyzed, with the author claiming that the organizational process and bureaucratic politics models are not mutually exclusive of one another. Weaknesses of groupthink, which align closely to the earlier discussion of the impact of stress on the decision making process, include an illusion of invulnerability and a feeling of overconfidence as crucial factors, along with the power of the group to coerce.[115] This is borne out in the case studies, particularly with the Somalia and Kosovo interventions.

In "The Theory and Practice of Foreign Policy Decision Making," Jonathan and Stanley Renshon discuss the development of decision making processes, noting that the beliefs and psychological lenses with which leaders view the world will necessarily impact their decisions.[116] The Renshons base their work on earlier studies by Alexander George utilizing psychoanalytic theory, noting the impact of entry biases, time pressure, stress, and threat/security levels can distort or lessen the quality of decision making. This is in line with other cited works, most notably the Rubicon Theory of War. For purposes of this book, threat will be interpreted as political, rather than military threat, given the nature of the interventions to be discussed.

---

[113] McDermott. 216.
[114] Ibid. 249.
[115] Ibid. 253.
[116] Renshon, Jonathan and Stanley A. The Theory and Practice of Foreign Policy Decision Making. *Political Psychology*, Vol 29, No. 4, 2008. 509.

Literature Gaps Identified: The definition of the powerful leader was discussed, with a focus on how informed and motivated leaders who can sway opinion in decision making and framing dominate decision making processes. The major literature gap revealed by this research concerns the selling of decisions to the stakeholder audience. This audience could include foreign countries, partisan political leadership, other key groups, but is primarily meant as the public. Little note is given in most of the works examined to the process by which the president, a key leader, or the government convinces these audiences, and most particularly the public, of the need to implement the decisions made in the processes discussed. This leads to the question of how intervention decisions are justified to stakeholders. Is there a connection between the process of decision making and the framing of that decision? Is framing simultaneous with decision making, or does it follow the decision? Is the planning for both concurrent? This is a question which will be addressed in the case studies, but the evidence examined in them seems to indicate that all of the aforementioned times for a discussion of framing occur depending on the nature of the decision and situation.

A further potential gap, as mentioned in the reviews, is very specific nature of the examples selected by Allison and Yetiv for their reviews. First, the Cuban Missile crisis took place in an era of bi-polarity and with a level of threat (nuclear war) that does not currently exist, and is unlikely to return in exactly the same fashion. Yetiv's example of the first Gulf War was shaped by a massive U.S. predominance in the immediate aftermath of the Cold War, as well as a level of unity and professionalism in the national security team. Both of these factors are also highly time and personality dependent, and may be difficult to replicate. This is an important issue which must be borne in mind when developing the methodology of the paper and applying it to the case studies.

Theme Four: Framing Policy and Strategic Communication

Given the demonstrated nature of armed humanitarian operations as non-threatening to the intervening state, the "War of Choice" embarked upon must then be communicated to the public in such a way as to build and maintain support.[117] This theme focuses on the methods the interagency community and the government used to frame and communicate their themes and messages concerning their opponents and world events in connection with their decisions to intervene. It is not specifically tied to the national security decision making process, and this fact allows for questions to be asked linking the two issues.

Robert Entman provides the primary source for the issue of framing, focusing attention on the efforts of the government to frame key events, and the media's countervailing efforts to "counter-frame" them.[118] The theory he develops, the Cascading Network Activation Model, describes the process by which frames are used "to generate support or opposition to a political actor or policy," as well as how the stakeholders can shape the process.[119] Entman uses a series of historical examples to show that the government is generally successful in framing when it can call on shared themes and ideals and get its themes in "early and often." Yetiv also adds to this discussion by describing the methodology used by Bush in constructing an image of Hussein as a new Hitler, and the overwhelming need to confront him rather than face a "New Munich."[120]

Manuel Castells' work focuses on a variety of communications issues, noting that power is based on the ability to form, shape and adjust networks and messages.[121] In chapter three, Networks of Mind and Power, the author focuses on the development and implementation of frames as devices for control of

---

[117] Haass, 2009. 10.
[118] Entman, Robert. *Projections of Power: Framing News, Public Opinion, and U.S. Foreign Policy.* Chicago: University of Chicago Press, 2004. 1-3.
[119] Ibid. 47.
[120] Yetiv. 94-95.
[121] Castells, Manuel. *Communication Power.* New York: Oxford University Press. 2009. 3.

communication of messaging, including examples on the government media framing of the U.S. invasion of Iraq in 2003.[122] This section provides a central foundation for arguments on the U.S. framing of interventions connected with the Arab Spring. Conflicting framing agendas, as Castells describes, are also referenced by Glazier and Boydstun in their 2012 discussion in *Political Communication* of the conflicting frames generated by the Bush Administration and the media regarding the War in Iraq, in which the White House, after initial success, was increasingly unable to dominate the framing effort to the public.[123]

James Fearon, in contrast, focuses on the perceptions of the domestic political audience and how they can shape national security decsions. According to Fearon, leaders will view decisions as having varying "audience costs," and decisions on when, if, and how to pay those costs will impact decsion making.[124] This helps Fearon to deal with the question of how states choose to engage in conflict when there may appear to be other solutions available. The perception of the leader making the choice, according to Fearon, might be that all options have been exhausted.[125] Hindrances to the decision making process can include perception of the time and political and economic price of mobilization. Questions of national honor and political price can also come into play, and this is borne out in the Kosovo case study, in which it can be argued that the U.S. was shamed into its reaction to Serbian attrocities by a failure to act in the case of the Rwandan massacres of 1994-1995 as well as the previous events of the Yugoslav Civil War.

Lawrence Freedman provides background for a discussion on how to frame conflicts with "On War and Choice." The author expands the concept of wars being of choice and of necessity, reaching back to medieval philosophers such as Maimonides, who predated the discussion with his concepts of obligatory and

---

[122] Castells. 165-189.
[123] Glazier, Rebecca A., and Boydstun, Amber E. "The President, the Press, and the War: A Tale of Two Framing Agendas." *Political Communication*, 29:428-446, 2012. 428.
[124] Fearon, James D. "Domestic Political Audiences and the Escalation of International Disputes." *The American Political Science Review*. Vol. 88, No 3., September 1994, 577-592. 577.
[125] Fearon. 577.

discretionary Wars.[126] Freedman takes the view that a humanitarian style intervention would contradict the rabbinical concept that wars of discretion, or choice, would be inherently offensive.[127] The case studies will demonstrate, however, that the rabbis were most likely correct in their assumption, since each of the examined studies involved offensive action for humanitarian goals. This argument is continued in two presentations for the American Political Science Association, in which John Schuessler noted that a war can be justified when it can be shown to be defensive in nature (or of such impact to national security that an offensive is required), cheap, and easy to win, and that decision makers create such perceptions successfully in cases where interventions take place.[128] This type of salesmanship, according to the author, is particularly difficult for the U.S., which is an insular power which faces few threats of direct attack.[129]

In *Selling a "Just" War: Framing, Legitimacy, and U.S. Military Intervention*, Michael Butler uses a series of case studies to examine how U.S. national authorities built support for both kinetic and humanitarian interventions from the end of the Cold War to the invasion of Iraq in 2003. While it most closely supports the Kosovo case study, the book provides useful insights to the concept of framing and how it is tied into the decision making process. This book is the only work identified in this literature review which implicitly ties national security decision making on the decision to intervene with the requirement to explain the decision to a wide variety of audiences, in other words, to frame policies.

For Butler, the crux of the argument reaches back to just war theories, and the ways in which interventions can be framed to play to the core liberal underpinnings of U.S. philosophy and foreign policy. Framing an action as just, righting a wrong, or protecting the innocent are all tactics that were used in framing

---

[126] Freedman, Lawrence "On War and Choice." *The National Interest*, May/June 2010. 9.
[127] Ibid. 10.
[128] Schuessler, John. "When Wars of Necessity Become Contested as Wars of Choice." Presentation for the American Political Science Association, September 2-5 2004. 2.
[129] Schuessler, John. "Necessity or Choice? Securing Public Consent For War." Presentation for the Midwest Political Science Association, April 15, 2004. 9.

the Kosovo crisis as well as the other interventions in the case studies. For frames to work, they must be credible, salient, and dynamic, and the Kosovo intervention is examined as a series of presidential speech actions emphasizing all of these points.[130]

Admiral James Stavridis, a noted military advocate of and expert on Strategic Communication (SC), adopts a military approach, noting its power as an enabler for operational forces.[131] He acknowledged the role of the national security apparatus and entreated leaders to "take an early and persistent role in deciding how ideas and decisions are shaped and delivered.[132] For Stavridis this need required a shared understanding of what SC is and is not, particularly in an international context.[133] This is re-enforced by Joseph Nye, who in *Soft Power*, warned that "A communications strategy cannot work if it cuts against the grain of policy," reiterating the need for coordination of messaging at the highest levels.[134] Further discussion is provided by Christopher Paul's *Strategic Communication: Origins, Concepts, and Current Debates* from 2011 in which he notes that a successful framing or communication strategy calls for synchronizing messages with deeds.[135] Mari Eder also echoes this entreaty in *Leading the Narrative, the Case for Strategic Communication.*[136]

In a Strategy Research Project for the Army War College, Colonel Jeryl Ludowese examined the interagency process, specifically as it related to SC, and offered several relevant recommendations and solutions. He notes that the U.S. Department of State sits at the pinnacle of the SC Project, but echoed the opinions of other contributors to this review, namely that a common understanding of the

---

[130] Butler, Michael J. *Selling a "Just" War: Framing, Legitimacy, and U.S. Military Intervention.* New York: Palgrave Macmillan, 2012. 156.
[131] Stavridis, James G. "Strategic Communication and National Security." *Joint Force Quarterly*, 2007: 4-7. 4.
[132] Ibid. 4, 7.
[133] Ibid. 7.
[134] Nye, Joseph. *Soft Power.* New York: Public Affairs, 2004. 110.
[135] Paul, Christopher. *Strategic Communication: Origins, Concepts, and Current Debates*. Santa Barbara, CA: Praeger, 2011. 8-9.
[136] Eder, Mari. *Leading the Narrative, the Case for Strategic Communication*. Annapolis: Naval Institute Press. 2011. 29-31.

term must come before meaningful collaboration is possible.[137] His recommendation is for some form of return to something like the U.S. Information Agency to sit at the pinnacle of the Interagency SC process for all government communications efforts outside the U.S., and be led by a government wide "Director of Strategic Communications."[138]

Jeff Motter describes the framing of the U.S. relief effort which followed the 2004 tsunami in Indonesia, noting the samaritan, exceptionalist identity attributed to the effort by the White House.[139] For Motter, the case exhibits a wider U.S. effort to identify with Muslim populations both in Indonesia and elsewhere, such as President Clinton's comments on U.S. actions in Kosovo and Bosnia as primarily protective of Muslims. Continuing the discussion of the tsunami relief effort, Jaime Alvarado's "New Multilateralism in Action for Peace: A Case Study of the US - led Operation Unified Assistance in the Asian Tsunami Disaster," describes the functioning of the U.S. led international relief effort for Indonesia in light of U.S. efforts to foster security cooperation in Asia following the September 11 terrorist attacks on US soil.[140] The relief effort is described as an overtly hegemonic act aimed at demonstrating that that the U.S. was benevolent and could be a valued long term partner for countries in the region.[141]

Returning to the impact of the media, Babak Bahador examines two factors in relations to the U.S. Intervention in Kosovo. The first is the occurrence of five event spikes which inspired significant upticks in media coverage of the crisis. The second are five political events, and Bahador demonstrates the connections between the two sets of events, noting that in four out of five cases, it was the media which

---

137 Ludowese, Jeryl C. "Strategic Communication: Who Should Lead the Long War of Ideas?" Carlisle, PA, U.S. Army War College, 2006. 3.
138 Ibid. 22.
139 Motter, Jeff. "American Exceptionalism and the Rhetoric of Humanitarian Militarism: The Case of the 2004 Indian Ocean Tsunami Relief Effort." *Communication Studies*, 2010: 507–525. 509.
140 Alvarado, Jaime. "New Multilateralism in Action for Peace: A Case Study of the US-led Operation Unified Assistance in the Asian Tsunami Disaster." *Global Economic Review*, 2007: 183-192. 184-186.
141 Ibid. 184.

built the frame for intervention. In only one case did the government appear to build such a frame. Bahador's purpose is to discuss the "CNN effect," an argument that the media can successfully own the debate on issues through the display of unexpected, shocking images which were used by the media to show shortcomings in administration policy toward the Kosovo issue and the government of Serbia.[142] Interestingly, the one obvious instance of government framing dominance over the mainstream media networks was during Operation "Determined Falcon," a series of exercises involving NATO air assets in June 1998. This overt act successfully led the debate on the Kosovo issue while it was underway.[143]

Continuing the media discussion, Adam Berinsky and Donald Kinder focused on the Kosovo crisis and framing article addressing framing and the American public's perception of government policies and foreign policy. [144] The authors quote Gamson and Modigliani, who describe a frame as "A central organizing idea or story line that provides meaning to an unfolding strip of events, weaving a connection among them. The frame suggests what the controversy is about, the essence of the issue.[145] They also note Entman's theory the media have taken on an increasingly independent framing role since the end of the Cold War bi-polar situation.[146] These conclusions are based on an experiment performed by the authors in which audiences were exposed to a series of controlled news articles on Kosovo, with the end result that readers took on the point of view that was fed to them in purposefully tailored news stories.

Literature Gaps Revealed: One gap is an explanation for the frequent disconnect between U.S. public opinion and that of policy makers and framers. The

---

[142] Bahador, Babak. "The CNN Effect on Western Policy Before the Kosovo Intervention: A Book." London School of Economics and Political Science, International Relations Department, 2004, Presented at the 2004 ISA Conference, Montreal, Canada. 17, 44-45.
[143] Ibid. 26.
[144] Berinsky, Adam J. and Kinder, Donald R. "Making Sense of the Issues Through Media Frames: Understanding the Kosovo Crisis." *The Journal of Politics* Vol. 68, No. 3, August 2006, 640-656. 640-641.
[145] Gamson, William A. and Modigliani, Andre. "The changing culture of affirmative action." In R.G. Braungart & M.M. Braungart (Eds.), *Research in political sociology* (Vol. 3, pp. 137-177). Greenwich, CT. JAI Press, 1987. 143.
[146] Berinsky and Kinder. 641.

communication process at the national level is also little discussed, as most of the literature is focused on the media as a receiver rather than how the government and elites act as providers of information. This study bridges this gap by providing a theory of the government communication process and how the foreign policy community interacts with its stakeholder audiences. Butler is the only identified source who implicitly ties in the decision making process to the framing or explanation process to try to build a coherent picture of the whole of the process.

While downward information flow is a gap, upward pressure also requires further explanation. While the role of media as receiver is heavily covered in the literature, its own role in driving foreign policy action is not a focus of the sources reviewed. That role fits into the decision making process as a whole, not the communication process, and will be discussed in that light in the methodology and case studies.

Theme Five: The Case Studies – Somalia, Kosovo, Libya – and the Non-Interventions in Rwanda and Syria

The purpose of this section of the literature review is to examine key works on each of the case studies to determine what gaps may exist in the writing, and how each can shed light on the question of if and how the strategic decision making process is linked to the framing process for armed humanitarian interventions. The case studies are based on primary source documents, including media articles and programs, polls, memoirs, and testimony. The sources examined in the study include some of those materials as well as analytic works which bring focus to the events examined.

David Halberstam examines the George H.W. Bush and Clinton administrations with a focus on how each reacted to foreign policy issues. He discusses the Bush decision to intervene in Somalia and the resultant debacle which followed. He traced the development of humanitarian interventions which began shortly thereafter with Haiti and culminated with the Kosovo intervention of 1999.

The author detailed the development of the Clinton foreign policy, which was primarily an adjunct to domestic political concerns and an effort to capitalize on the so called "peace dividend" following the end of the Cold War.[147] Halberstam's analysis is augmented by that of William Hyland, who focused on Clinton's political personality, which was primarily domestic focused, and how that focus played out in foreign policy.[148] Conflicts with senior military leadership as discussed in theme two, and a relatively hands off Secretary of State (Warren Christopher) plus a prediliction to take events personally and apply an often innapropriate domestic political frame were hallmarks of the administration.

David Phillips provides a useful overview both of the U.S. decision to intervene in Kosovo and the interventions which both preceeded and followed it, namely Somalia, Rwanda, and Libya. Primarily focused on Kosovo, the book discusses the lead up to the Yugoslav Civil War as well as the role of key personalities in pushing for the intervention, most notably Madelaine Albright, General Wesley Clark, and Richard Holbrooke. This fits with an overall discussion of the key role of individuals in forcing key decisions to be made. Further, Phillips disucces the impact of the Somalia intervention and the failure to intervene in Rwanda in terms of the increased pressure that placed on the Clinton administration to act in Kosovo.[149] Finally, the author establishes a rubric for armed humanitarian intervention, positing that there are only a set of definable circumstances under which such interventions should occur. He then applies that criteria to the Libya intervention to describe how and why the Obama adminstration intervened there.

In *Waging Modern War,* Wesley Clark discusses the development of the humanitarian crisis in the former Yugoslavia, tracing the change in the crisis as time went on. While the conflict in Bosnia and Herzegovina was portrayed primarily in security terms this changed when Serbia cracked down on the province of

---

[147] Halberstam, David. *War in a Time of Peace.* New York: Scribner, 2001. 231.
[148] Hyland, William. *Clinton's World: Remaking American Foreign Policy.* London: Praeger Books, 1999. 8.
[149] Phillips, David L. *Liberating Kosovo.* Cambridge, MA: Belfer Center, 2012. 90.

Albania.[150] Clark led the NATO response which resulted from the successful framing of the operation in humanitarian terms. Madelaine Albright's *Madame Secretary* and Richard Holbrooke's *To End A War* detail their own personal roles in the Somalia and Kosovo humanitarian crises, supporting the argument that powerful spokespersons and strong individual leaders can both sway the foreign policy process but can also impact the implementation and positive framing of armed humanitarian interventions.

In his second autobiography, Secretary of Defense Robert Gates discusses his career, with a focus on his tenure as Secretary of Defense during the administrations of George W. Bush and Barack Obama. He provides significant insight into the National Security decision making process which is in line with other authors in this review. He notes, however, that the Obama White House had a very strong tendency to concentrate power at its center rather than distributing decision making and authority outwards.[151] He goes on to note that this is a trend with antecedents to the Truman administration, although that in the Obama White House it reached its peak to-date both in terms of power concentration and in military micro management.[152] While his autobiography focuses on decisions regarding the Iraq and Afghanistan wars, he also notes his strong resistance to the intervention in Libya due to a combination of his perceptions that the American people were war-weary and that Libya posed no significant security threat to the United States.[153] While Secretary Gates did spend significant time on his dealings with Congress, and discusses war weariness as a problem, there is little mention made of the process of explaining his department's decisions to the American people, particularly with decisions such as the Libyan intervention, and this leaves room for the proposed research contribution of this book.

---

[150] Clark, Wesley. *Waging Modern War*. New York: Public Affairs, 2012. 108-109.
[151] Gates, Robert. *Duty: Memoires of a Secretary at War*. New York: Alfred A. Knopf, 2014. 288.
[152] Ibid. 585-586.
[153] Ibid. 182.

Nikolas Gvosdev directly examines the use of humanitarian themes in the Libyan intervention as well as the decision making process which led to the decision. He argues that there was "little effort to portray twenty-first century Libya as a looming security threat to the United States."[154] For them, the administration's embracing of humanitarian issues as the primary cause for intervention is a significant turn away from traditional national security motives.[155] In fact, significant administration leaders loudly noted the lack of security interest even while the intervention was taking place. This implies a serious disconnect amongst the key interagency foreign policy decision makers. However, in citing the U.S. reaction to humanitarian crackdowns in Bahrain and elsewhere, he does acknowledge that neorealist themes (especially oil resources) still resonate,[156] a point which would become more apparent when the Obama administration attempted to justify an intervention in Syria in 2013. Gvosdev notes that the administration elected to portray the threat Gaddafi posed to his own citizens as the primary justification for intervention.[157] The Kosovo intervention, in particular, was, by contrast, framed both in security and humanitarian terms. In fact, for Gvosdev, it is the Kosovo intervention which marked the watershed between security focused framing and humanitarian focused efforts.[158] Gvosdev considers this fundamental switch to be a move toward increased Wilsonianism and away from realism in U.S. foreign policy.[159]

Taking a different tack, Pierre Atlas contributed "U.S. Foreign Policy and the Arab Spring: Balancing Values and Interests" for the *Digest of Middle East Studies*. This 2012 work claims that the contraction of decision cycles caused by the rapid press of events in the spring of 2011 was impossible for policy makers to

---

[154] Gvosdev, Nikolas. "Decline of Western Realism." *The National Interest*, 2012: 8-19. 8.
[155] Ibid. 8.
[156] Ibid. 16.
[157] Ibid. 8.
[158] Ibid. 12.
[159] Ibid. 9.

adapt to.[160] The result was significant discord between the common threads of U.S. policy, idealism and realism, and a series of decisions made with short term goals in mind[161] Ironically, according to Atlas, it is the move toward an idealistic approach to Egypt and Syria, rather than the realist approach to Syria and Bahrain, which is in discord with traditional U.S. approaches in the region.[162] Atlas uses three key speeches by President Obama on the Middle East and the Arab Spring to show how far along the idealist path the administration has become. The vacillation between realism and idealism is also noted in Pinto's *Mapping the Obama Administration's response to the Arab Spring*, which notes that the administration eventually came around to the idea that a different policy would be needed for each Arab country, and that a one size fits all approach would not work.[163]

Atlas noted a continuing struggle within U.S. foreign policy between the realists and the idealists. This theme recurs throughout the literature, and is most clearly revealed by two separate cases, the Libyan armed humanitarian intervention, and the hard handed approach the administration took to the spread of the Arab Spring to Bahrain.[164] In that case the administration gave Saudi Arabia the green light to intervene and crackdown on dissent. The authors point out that the inclusion of an idealistic strain into U.S. dealings with the Middle East is the incongruity, and represents an ideational change in U.S. policy toward the region.

In *Exit Gaddafi,* Ethan Chorin describes the message development process for the U.S. and its foundational claim that Gaddafi was a bloody tyrant who was about to launch a massacre on a dissenting part of his population. The discussion drew heavily on the overall UN opinion that Libya's failure to protect its people was a failure of its sovereignty that could only be rectified by the international community. Chorin describes the divergence in U.S. leadership statements as

---

160 Atlas, Pierre M. "U.S. Foreign policy and the Arab Spring: Balancing Values and Interests." *Digest of Middle East Studies*, 2012: 353-85. 354.
161 Ibid.
162 Ibid. 359.
163 Pinto, Maria. D. "Mapping the Obama administration's response to the Arab Spring." *Review of Brasilian International Politics*, 2012. 125.
164 Ibid. 354.

shown by the gulf between the statements of the White House and the Department of Defense as well as a bipartisan group in the NSC, the Senate and the House of Representatives who spoke out against the intervention, with oil being a key issue on both sides of the debate. Pro-interventionists noted the threat to Europe's oil resources and the loss of investment opportunities.[165] Chorin noted that the interagency conflict between the Departments of State and Defense was a deadlock, as a result of which the will and the plan for Libyan intervention would have to be constructed by powerful spokespersons who could trump the bureaucracies, specifically discussing how Secretary of State Clinton became that person.[166] The president was convinced over a three day period to switch his personal effort toward intervention. This hastened the passing of United Nations Security Council Resolution 1973 within weeks and facilitated the U.S. intervention, in contrast with similar efforts which took months to construct, such as the Kosovo intervention of the 1990s.[167]

Chorin and Bruce Jones, who provided "Libya and the Responsibilities of Power" for *Survival* in 2011, note how the concept of R2P was invoked in Libya by Washington insiders who believed that "The will to humanitarian intervention, destroyed by Bush administration actions in Afghanistan and Iraq, must be rebuilt." Secretary of State Clinton and Ambassador to the UN Susan Rice bore the burden of selling R2P to the rest of the world as a justification for intervention.[168] The two were joined, significantly, by NSC Directors Samantha Power and Gayle Smith. Their collaboration seems to be a successful example of interagency cooperation, as they joined Rice and Clinton as the leading government hawks on intervention, convincing others to fall into line both by appealing to humanitarianism and by

---

[165] Dreyfuss, Robert, "Obama's Women Advisors Pushed War against Libya", The Nation http://www.thenation.com/blog/159346/obamas-women-advisers-pushed-war-against-libya. Accessed March 15 2013. 215.
[166] Of note is the contrast between those in diplomatic roles urging force, while the military urged diplomacy. Chorin, Ethan. *Exit Gaddafi: The Hidden History of the Libyan Revolution.* London: Saqi Books. 230-231.
[167] Jones, Bruce. "Libya and the Responsibilities of Power." *Survival*, May: 2011. 53.
[168] Prashad, Vijay. *Arab Spring, Libyan Winter.* Baltimore: AK Press, 2012. 176.

noting the benefits that intervention would provide to U.S. standing in the Arab world, according to Chorin.[169]

Mir Sadat examines the U.S. approach toward Syria, but with a direct focus on the situation there and developing U.S. responses to it. The article points out the different operational, strategic, and diplomatic environment in Syria as compared with Libya and Egypt, which had completely different historical relations with the U.S., and did not have great power support (in the form of Russia) in the sense that Syria does.[170] The authors concur with other contributors in that the U.S. has been forced to modify its approach toward each of the different countries impacted by the Arab Spring.

Maria Pinto echoes others in discussing the U.S. response to the Arab Spring, with a focus on Syria.[171] The U.S. is described as ambivalent and reflective of an overall decline in U.S. power and status in the Middle East, and by inference, worldwide. Comparisons and criticisms are made of the ambivalent policies of the U.S. in Egypt and Syria versus the forceful and violent stance taken in Libya. According to the author, the U.S. was forced to realize that a regional, or general solution would not work, and that responses to the Arab Spring events would have to be done on a country by country basis. This article will be useful in helping to explain the variance in U.S. responses to the Arab Spring events. Finally, Emily Parker addresses one of the fundamental issues of this study, namely, why was the administration unable to secure an intervention for Syria when it had previously in Libya? [172] Several reasons are given, including the different strategic situation as well as the simple fact of "war fatigue" in a country which is still bogged down in several wars at the time of writing.

---

[169] Chorin. 215 and 231. As a result of this they became known as the "Warrior Women."

[170] Sadat, Mir H. "U.S. Foreign Policy Interests Toward Syria: Balancing Ideology and National Interests." Middle East Policy Council, 2013. 1. The direct quote is: "America has been unable to develop and maintain a consistent position toward Syria. Instead, divergent impulses have guided American policy with regard to that state."

[171] Pinto. 109-130.

[172] Parker, Emily. "Why Don't We Care About Syria?" *Slate* Online, 2012. 2. http://www.slate.com/articles/technology/future_tense/2012/02/syria_uprising_twitter_and_social_media_revolution_fatigue_.html. Accessed on September 30, 2013.

Appendix II

The Review in Review

This literature review brought together a disparate set of criteria and arguments about the decision making process, framing, strategic communication, and the definition of humanitarian intervention. The works have been linked to each other by theme, and organized in support of an interagency examination using the Allison/Yetiv/Brendon models to determine when, if, and how the interagency decision making process was effective, and, if not, why. This was combined with an effort to understand issue framing and how armed humanitarian interventions were sold to critical stakeholders, such as the U.S. public. Extant literature on the interagency strategic communications process was examined, with particular emphasis on the efforts of very senior leaders to sway the process. This research also explained the interagency strategic communications process and how interagency discussions are used to frame issues for public and international consumption.

INDEX